Security Unbound

Security concerns have mushroomed. Increasingly numerous areas of life are governed by security policies and technologies. *Security Unbound* argues that when insecurities pervade how we relate to our neighbours, how we perceive international politics, how governments formulate policies, at stake is not our security but our democracy. Security is not in the first instance a right or value but a practice that challenges democratic institutions and actions.

We are familiar with emergency policies in the name of national security challenging parliamentary processes, the space for political dissent and fundamental rights. Yet, security practice and technology pervade society heavily in very mundane ways without raising national security crises, in particular through surveillance technology and the management of risks and uncertainties in many areas of life. These more diffuse security practices create societies in which suspicion becomes a default way of relating and governing relations, ranging from neighbourhood relations over financial transactions to cross-border mobility. *Security Unbound* demonstrates that governing through suspicion poses serious challenges to democratic practice. Some of these challenges are familiar, such as the erosion of the right to privacy; others are less so, such as the post-human challenge to citizenship.

Security Unbound provokes us to see that the democratic political stake today is not our security but preventing insecurity from becoming the organising principle of political and social life.

Jef Huysmans is Professor of Security Studies, The Open University, UK.

WITHDRAWN
FROM STOCK
QMUL LIBRARY

Critical Issues in Global Politics

This series engages with the most significant issues in contemporary global politics. Each text is written by a leading scholar and provides a short, accessible and stimulating overview of the issue for advanced undergraduates and graduate students of international relations and global politics. As well as providing a survey of the field, the books also contain original and groundbreaking thinking, which will drive forward debates on these key issues.

Security Unbound

Enacting democratic limits

Jef Huysmans

Routledge
Taylor & Francis Group

LONDON AND NEW YORK

First published 2014
by Routledge
2 Park Square, Milton Park, Abingdon, Oxon OX14 4RN

and by Routledge
711 Third Avenue, New York, NY 10017

Routledge is an imprint of the Taylor & Francis Group, an informa business

© 2014 Jef Huysmans

The right of Jef Huysmans to be identified as author of this work has been asserted by him in accordance with the Copyright, Designs and Patent Act 1988.

All rights reserved. No part of this book may be reprinted or reproduced or utilised in any form or by any electronic, mechanical, or other means, now known or hereafter invented, including photocopying and recording, or in any information storage or retrieval system, without permission in writing from the publishers.

Trademark notice: Product or corporate names may be trademarks or registered trademarks, and are used only for identification and explanation without intent to infringe.

British Library Cataloguing in Publication Data
A catalogue record for this book is available from the British Library

Library of Congress Cataloging in Publication Data
Huysmans, Jef, author.
Security unbound : enacting democratic limits / Jef Huysmans.
    pages cm. -- (Critical issues in global politics)
    Includes bibliographical references and index.
1. Privacy, Right of. 2. Democracy. 3. Electronic surveillance--Social aspects. 4. Electronic surveillance--Political aspects. 5. Information technology--Social aspects. 6. Information technology--Political aspects. 7. Social psychology. 8. Social control. I. Title.
    JC596.H88 2014
    323.4'3--dc23
                    2013031455

ISBN: 978-0-415-44020-2 (hbk)
ISBN: 978-0-415-44021-9 (pbk)
ISBN: 978-1-315-81724-8 (ebk)

Typeset in Bembo
by Taylor & Francis Books

Contents

Acknowledgments

This book is concerned with the political effects of diffusing insecurities. Like much of my work on security, it has its roots in the understanding that when security issues, institutions and practices take a prominent role in the organisation of social, political, cultural and economic issues, inequalities, exclusions, violence and other limits to democratic politics become more pronounced. In this book, I look in particular at how both exceptionalist modes of securitising and more diffusing processes of assembling suspicion enact limits to democratic practice. It draws at times extensively and at others more indirectly on insights developed in the context of various projects and collaborations that I have been involved in during the last seven years. They include the work on exceptionalism that I did in discussion with researchers of the European Commission-funded FP7 project CHALLENGE (the Changing Landscape of Liberty and Security in Europe); discussions on the evolving social construction of threats in many workshops that were part of European funded COST Action A24, including the c.a.s.e. collective; research on mobility and the enactment of European citizenship that I did with Claudia Aradau, Vicki Squire and Rutvica Andrijasevic in workpackage 3 'Enacting Mobility: Making a More Democratic European Citizenship' in the FP7-funded project ENACT (Enacting European Citizenship); the work on citizenship and security that I developed with Xavier Guillaume and in the continuing exchange of ideas on acts of citizenship with my colleague Engin Isin; some of the work done for the ESRC-funded International Collaboratory on Critical Methods in Security Studies; and discussions in the Centre for Citizenship, Identities and Governance, in particular in its Research Programme Securities and, when that programme was concluded, in the Research Programme Enactments. I am indebted to far too many people in the context of these projects and collaborations to mention them all here but without them my understanding of security and politics would not be where it is now.

In addition I would like to thank Victoria Basham for research assistance at the very early stages of this book, and the students and colleagues at the University of Namur where I taught earlier drafts of the book as Franqui Chair in 2010–2011. A special thanks also to my doctoral students Helen Arfvidsson, P.G. Maciotti, Bruno Magalhaes and Stephan Scheel, and to Anne-Marie D'Aoust for discussions in several seminars, one of which coined the final title of the book. I benefited from many comments on several other occasions where I presented ideas and draft chapters of the book. In particular I would like to thank for comments and questions participants at the keynote address 'The Politics of Insecurity: Threats, Speech Acts and Beyond' at the workshop 'Critical Voices in IR', the University of Geneva and Graduate Institute Geneva (IHEID), Geneva (10 April 2008); the seminar 'What is in an Act? Diffusing Politics of Insecurity' at the Central European University, Budapest (3 November 2010); the CAST Research Seminar at the University of Copenhagen of 14 December 2011; the keynote 'Security Unbound: Insecurity, Democracy, Political' at the conference International (Dis)order: Disruptions, Exclusions and Alternatives' at the Institute of International Relations, PUC-Rio, Rio de Janeiro (29 October–1 November 2012); the seminar 'Security Unbound: Enacting Limits of Democracy' at the Free University of Brussels (ULB), Brussels (12 March 2013); and the panel on International Political Sociology at the AFSP (Association française de science politique) 12th conference in Paris, 9–11 July 2013. I also want to thank Craig Fowlie from Routledge for first inviting me to write for the Critical Issues in Global Politics series and then for bearing with me when I kept on moving the deadlines because of other commitments that continued to interfere with finishing the book. And as usual, Leen, Lucas and Hannah deserve big hugs for the many distractions that make life so interesting.

1 Security unbound and democracy

Security is unbound. Language and images of insecurity are everywhere. Migration, global warming, bugs in the house, paedophiles, civil wars, crime statistics, collapsing economies, weapon proliferation, Mexican flu, genocide, terrorism, riots, salmonella, water pollution, energy insecurity; and, the list can go on and on. Our lives and times seem to be defined by multiplications of dangers, threats, risks, uncertainties, anxieties. To account for this some speak of the rise of cultures of fear; others of the dominance of risk management and pre-emptive government; some focus on widening conceptions of insecurity, others on the making of neurotic citizens; some highlight the commodification of security, others the mobilisation of existential threats for political and professional legitimacy. If the multiple languages, images, technologies and institutions of insecurity are indeed defining of our times, what does that mean? What is at stake when security unbinds?

The many insecurities are not equivalent, do not co-exist in one site, and do not systematically reinforce one another. Neither do they come together in a global threat or a more loosely defined global assemblage of dangers. They are dispersed, different, and sometimes connected, sometimes not. Constructing a theory that synthesises them around a global threat, a grand cultural or civilisational change, or a hegemonic order will give the impression of a homogeneity that does not really exist. It will misrecognise the contemporary liquidity of security as solidifying (Bauman, 2000), as if there is a fixed landscape in which dangers are organised in hierarchies ranking them in terms of importance and in light of global developments such as a changing geopolitical order with rising and falling great powers or an expanding socioeconomic and governmental order, often named 'neoliberal'.

This book starts from the understanding that security is unbound, that insecurities are rendered as multiple and, through often banal, non-intense dispersing. Its defining question is: what is politically at stake in the scattering of insecurity and how can security studies contribute to understanding the political significance of the multiple circulations of multiple insecurities?

Insecurity and democracy

Although I seek to open a political stake in the contemporary world, I will not start in today's world. I want to return to two essays written by Franz Leopold Neumann, within about a year before he died in a car crash in 1954: 'The concept of political freedom' (Neumann, 1996 [1953]) and *'Angst und Politik'* (Neumann, 1954). Franz Neumann was a member of the early Frankfurt School—a strand in critical theory developed at the Institute for Social Research in Frankfurt am Main (founded in 1923). As so many of its members, he was intellectually and politically engaged with the crisis politics of the Weimar Republic, the rise of fascism and the formation of National Socialism in Germany in the 1920s and 30s. After the National Socialists came to power he sought refuge in London and in 1936 moved to New York.

Both essays were written on the back of extensive studies of the rise and politics of National Socialism (Neumann, 1967 [1944]). Yet they also reflect a context of increased politics of fear in the US after the Soviet Union tested its first nuclear weapon in 1949, Mao gained control over China and the US got involved in the war in Korea. During that period the repression of communist sympathisers, and anyone thought to be one, seriously intensified in the US.

In 1953 he concluded his essay 'The concept of political freedom' with the following observation:

> [Democracy's] essence consists in the execution of large-scale social change maximizing the freedom of man. Only in this way can democracy be integrated; its integrating element is a moral one, whether it be freedom or justice. ... But there is opposed to this a second integrating principle of a political system: fear of an enemy. ... If the concept 'enemy' and 'fear' do constitute the 'energetic principle' of politics, a democratic political system is impossible, whether the fear is produced from within or without.
>
> (Neumann, 1996: 222–23)

Neumann's conclusion invites us to answer the question 'What is politically at stake in security practice?' with 'democracy'. This is very familiar ground for those who have now been exposed for over a decade to debates on the violation of fundamental rights and democratic processes in the wake of the terrorist violence in the US on 11 September 2001 and the pervasion of counter-terrorist policies in everyday life. As it has been familiar for those who experienced emergency powers instituted to deal with economic crises and violent repression of political opposition, or who lived through various other moments where the politics of fear and foregrounding enemies suppressed democratic principles and processes.

Yet Neumann does a little more than simply saying that democracy and politics of fear do not go well together because the latter invites secrecy or emergency laws while democracy demands transparency and due process. He invites us to read security as a practice of making 'enemy' and 'fear' the integrative, energetic principle of politics displacing the democratic principles of freedom and justice. In this interpretation, security practice does not simply nibble at the edges of democracy but is inherently anti-democratic because of the conception of politics and society that it inscribes in the world through its actions. Enacting relations to others and one's environment as always dangerous, fearful and inimical translates into a politics that limits and hollows out democratic organisations based on principles of freedom and justice. Later in this book I will expand the concept of security from its focus on fear and enemies to issues of risk and uncertainty, but for now let us stay with Neumann.

Taking up Neumann's invitation, security can thus be understood as a political force. It is not simply a policy responding to threats and dangers. Neither is it a public good or value. It is a practice with a political content. Security is a practice not of responding to enemies and fear but of creating them. It enacts our world as if it is a dangerous world, a world saturated by insecurities. It invests fear and enmity in relations between humans and polities rather than simply defending or protecting political units and people from enemies and fears. For Neumann the reference to enemy and fear had quite specific resonances with National Socialist mobilisations of fear as a political instrument to further destabilise the political system in interwar Germany and to demonise and persecute communist movements, progressive political parties and racially identified groups. It also resonated with the mobilisation of fear under McCarthyism and more generally US Cold War politics. In evoking enemies and instituting the defence of society as political priority, security practice sustains fearful and vulnerable self-identification and organises relations to others not in terms of justice or reciprocity, for example, but in terms of an existential struggle for survival in which enemies and friends need to be clearly separated.

The idea that security practice organises relations in terms of insecurity is not linked to a particular historical context only. It is somehow immanent to what security practice is: security is about securing against insecurities. There is no way of doing security without foregrounding insecurities. No enemy, no need to have an army. Remember the debates about the peace dividend in the 1990s. With the Soviet Union disintegrated and the bipolar power struggle between communism and capitalism, East and West, gone, defence budgets were cut, many countries abolished compulsory military service, etc. Remember also the speedy change from celebrating people breaking down the Iron Curtain, to warnings about the dangers of too many people crossing the now more open border. Claims of the possibility that people would massively migrate from east to west as a danger for Western European societal stability sustained calls for limiting and managing the potential free movement of people by configuring freedom into danger. A similar securitising took place in the midst of the Arab Spring in 2011. Support for challenges to autocratic and dictatorial regimes went hand in hand with, at some point, quite dramatic warnings about the negative consequences of too many people seeking refuge in Western Europe. When security policy and institutions enact a situation, they change the framing and legitimate repertoires of action by reiterating the existence of insecurities and by seeking to govern political and social relations as potentially inimical, dangerous or risky. In that sense, security practice always securitises; it necessarily inscribes insecurities in the world.

Neumann's analysis of fear also introduces an understanding of security as a practice with a political content. Neumann does not simply speak about spreading fear and enmity as such but rather about how it risks to shift the 'integrating' or 'energetic' principle of politics and the political system to one that makes democracy impossible; one that displaces justice, freedom, equality, fraternity with enemy and fear; fear and enemies are politically mobilised to play a key role in political contests and processes of legitimisation. Again one of his specific historical references was the Nazi deployment of violent militia, political iterations of external threats, and demonising political opposition as internal enemies as a strategy to eliminate political opposition and institute an authoritarian state.

What I want to take from this is that security is a political practice that is defined through its tensions with the democratic organisation of political life. Democracy is a political stake in security practice, not simply because of fundamental rights being violated in the name of security but because security practice inherently organises social and political relations around enemies, risks, fear, anxiety. When insecurities pervade how we relate to our neighbours, how we perceive international politics, how governments formulate policies, at stake is not our security but our democracy. For Neumann, this means in particular that foregrounding enemies and fear displaces practices of mediating differences and conflicts through principles of justice and freedom. Neumann's political lesson is that when we observe a pervasiveness of insecurity in people's lives and of politics governing and mobilising these insecurities, we should ask if insecurity is becoming the energetic principle of politics. If so, for anyone invested in democratic politics alarm bells should go off. Analytically Neumann's insights invite us to organise security studies around a double sensitivity: one to moments of insecurities pervading social and political life, and the other to security being a practice that inherently enacts the limits of democracy. Translating this double sensitivity into a study of insecurity is what I call developing 'a political reading of security practice' and is the main purpose of this book.

This book is thus an introduction to security that foregrounds political dimensions of security practice. Instead of mapping new security problems or presenting different approaches or theories of security, the book introduces security as a practice that interferes in politics. More specifically, the book starts from the observation that, as an immanent part of seeking to secure something, security practice enacts limits of democratic politics. This inherent tension between democratic politics and security practice defines the political content of security. It invites a political reading of security rather than a security reading of politics. I will develop this idea of a political reading of security more extensively in the next chapter. But first let us fast forward from the 1930s and 50s to 2002.

Unbinding security

In the heat of debates following the (12 October 2002) bombing in Bali, Indonesia, and the political reactions to it, British historian and commentator Timothy Garton Ash wrote:

> There is an atmosphere emerging here, an atmosphere of menace which the media help to transport and magnify. And don't we know it already from a hundred bad movies? The hard question now is whether the conduct of the 'war against terrorism', in this atmosphere of menace, might not end up being as much a threat to our own freedoms as terrorism itself.
>
> (Ash, 2002)

Ash's is one of many warnings about negative consequences of political and security reactions to what is now known as 9/11 and the subsequent bombings in Bali, Madrid, London and other global cities. Warnings about democracy being threatened by the political and security policies that claim to protect democracy against its enemies have been central to the political and judicial contestation of counter-terrorism policies. For example, the Center for Constitutional Rights in the US contested the moves towards a stronger executive-centred government in US responses to 9/11:

> Since that time [11 September 2001], the Bush administration, the United States Justice Department and the United States Congress have enacted a series of Executive Orders, regulations, and laws that have seriously undermined civil liberties, the check and balances that are essential to the structure of our democratic government, and indeed, democracy itself.
>
> (Center for Constitutional Rights, 2002)

Hearing democratic alarm bells is not unusual in contestations of intense moments of insecurity. Yet Ash's way of phrasing echoes Neumann's in a different way. Instead of focusing on civil liberties and checks and balances being undermined in counter-terrorism regulations and legislations, he refers to an atmosphere. An atmosphere is something much vaguer, more diffuse, but also socially and culturally more pervasive than specific legislations. Referring to the media and popular culture as vehicles of the emerging 'atmosphere of menace' expresses a worry about this atmosphere being breathed across society. It also situates reactions to terrorism in longer term cultural accustoming of people to catastrophic scenarios, and stark distinctions between good and evil.

In his analysis of fear and politics, Neumann argued that fear becoming an integrating political principle was not simply the result of strategic political use of violence, intimidation and unifying people around fear of the enemy. It hooked into wider societal pervasions of anxiety. He did not point towards popular culture and the media in the first instance but to the economic depression and, more generally, the inherent insecurity that organising economic life through free market competition in which fortunes can be created but also quickly lost inscribes into society and individuals (Neumann, 1954: 34–37). For both Neumann and Ash, the alarm bell is indeed about democracy but they also draw attention to how social, economic and cultural processes, rather than strictly legislative and political decisions, work insecurities into an energising force that challenges freedom.

Especially after having read Neumann's work on the politics of fear and the rise of National Socialism, I feel strongly that this is a warning we should take seriously. Yet hooking the diffusion of insecurities into 'the war against terrorism', although understandable, relevant and done by many, has serious limits. In the wake of several waves of politicising terrorism, it is tempting to make the war against terrorism the key process, the central change that caused the wider societal dispersal of insecurity and the intensified presence of a politics of fear. Focusing on terrorism one easily misses that 'the atmosphere of menace', or what I prefer to call 'the unbinding of security', does not depend on a wave of terrorist actions and their politicisation. It involves a much wider and diversified set of processes that work the limits of democracy in various ways.

To name a few that spring immediately to mind: global warming and images of environmental catastrophes, transversal flows of deadly viruses, popular cultures diffusing intense violence, human trafficking, the rise of vigilante, the dispersal of CCTV, the commodification of security, the politicisation of migration as endangering legal order, educating children of the dangers of meeting strangers. Securitising is multiple, fragmented, often disconnected, but it spreads insecurity into a wide range of social relations, and organises in its various modulations policies and practices of governance. In this book, I will look in particular at surveillance combined with risk governance as a technological mode of connecting insecurities and governing social and political relations by means of suspicion.

Not all these processes coalesce around an enemy, fear of a particular event, or an objectified menace, and they certainly do not come together around one particular inimical development—like a particular catastrophe or an army ready to invade. Environmental change is security-wise linked to overpopulation, rising sea levels and unruly migration. These links are mostly not treated as building up to one massive threat but are enacted in a more fragmented way.

Individually, as well as taken together, the dispersing of insecurities steadily eats away at the limits of security practice; it stretches the boundaries of what can be called insecurity, including when, where and how security institutions are mobilised. One of the key characteristics of contemporary profuse securitising is that it sustains a governmental process of making security limitless. I use the concept 'security unbound' to express this development. What I mean by it is thus not simply that many insecurities circulate through our lives simultaneously and in succession. The more important issue is that the principles, cultures, practices and categorical distinctions that limit where and when security practices, perceptions and affects 'operate' are challenged too. These challenges can take many forms. They include, among others: violating fundamental rights and due process in criminal justice practice; indiscriminate security controls at borders; gating neighbourhoods; blurring distinctions between economic migration, refuge and crime; rendering the line between humanitarian aid and military intervention increasingly ambivalent; counter-insurgency watering down the prohibition of torture; sending drones to kill suspected terrorists in other sovereign countries.

The limits of security are important for the democratic control of security practice. They define key sites where democratic politics define the role of security, and set limits to where, when and how security practice can govern subjects, social relations, economics and politics. Among the key limits here are: the limits of legitimate use of violence; the limits of criminal practice and the differentiation between crime, deviancy, abnormality and normality; the limits to the societal and political role of the military and the police; and the limits to private practices of self-securing. Changing, diluting or deleting these limits challenge the democratic control over security; it makes security more pervasive, and renders the tensions between security and democracy more prominent.

Security practice also enacts limits of democracy. It brings limits of democratic practice into political play. For example, in the name of threats to societal stability and political independence, claims can gain traction that democratic practice has reached its limits as a mode of governing effectively. In moments, situations and processes like these, security practice makes democracy and its limits a stake of the political game. Dispersing insecurities connects to this development by multiplying and intensifying the sites and moments when security practice challenges and raises questions about limits of democratic practice. Security practice is then political because it combines the profusion of insecurity with both the unbinding of customary, constitutional and political limits to security practice, and challenges to democratic practice that raise limits to democracy as a key political issue. Security unbound thus takes Neumann's warning about the devastating effects of making fear of the enemy a central energetic force of society and politics as the basis for a political analytics of the contemporary profusions of insecurity. This analytics is defined by a double democratic concern: a concern with unbinding the democratic limits to security practice and a concern with the expansion and intensification of security practice limiting democratic practice (i.e. a concern with how security practice brings into play limits of democratic practice). As will be set out later in this book, security unbound limits democracy in challenging ways. The political stake of security unbound is therefore not simply democratically reinstating limits to security practice but also reinventing what a democratic politics can be that can bear upon profuse security practice.

Overview

The idea that an 'atmosphere of insecurity' pervades societies asks for an understanding of how this 'atmosphere' is created, through which processes and actors, and what insecurity means in fractured and dispersed modes of operation. Does insecurity refer to the rendition of a terrorist enemy or does it work precisely by defining insecurities in ways that disconnect it from engaging an enemy? What is the difference between security working through enemy constructions and other forms of securitising? Do the different techniques enact the limits of democracy partly differently? In other words, do different techniques of securitising pose different challenges to the democratic organisation of political life and invite different modes of political contestation and resistance? In this book I will argue that the unbinding of security today implies that security analysis cannot be limited to existential and geopolitical international relations between enemies or to state-organised social control involving the military and police. The latter remain important but the dispersing of insecurities, and its political and social consequences, often work in more fragmented and transversal ways that challenge the central role of the state. Dispersing is also less exclusively tied into renditions of existential threats and exceptional crises that dominate national security traditions; it operates more through governing uncertainties, surveillance, and political economies of data transfers and risk knowledge.

The political reading of security unbound that I propose therefore conceptualises simultaneously differences in techniques through which insecurities are rendered—the security thickness of security practice— and in the modes of bringing limits of democratic practice into political play—the political thickness of security practice. Although both security and political thickness are closely connected, I will initially focus on the security qualities and then on the political dimensions for each of the techniques of securitising that I introduce in this book. For heuristic and political reasons this book contrasts in particular two techniques of securitising: exceptionalist securitising and diffuse securitising through assembling suspicion. Exceptionalist securitising works through the creation of existential threats and emergencies. It has been central to international security studies. The diffuse assembling of suspicion, in particular in its modality of surveillance and governing uncertainty and risks, has rapidly gained significance in the international security studies literature in the last decade and a half, however. Heuristically, the contrast between the two is important in order to draw attention to the central role that moments, sites, and processes of surveillance, and risk management and governing through uncertainty play in the contemporary profusion of insecurities. In addition, the contrast is a method of drawing out that the diffusions of insecurities that are taking place cannot be embedded unproblematically into a world of bureaucratised modern states and their exceptionalist renditions of insecurities. They work transversally and mostly in unspectacular ways. Politically, the contrast is used to show that diffuse securitising, because it fractures moments and sites of decisions, poses quite specific and highly challenging questions for democratic modes of limiting technocratic, autocratic and transgressive security governance—challenges that exceptionalist politicisations do not so easily bring into view. Although elements of diffuse assembling suspicion are increasingly researched in international security studies, they remain less familiar. I therefore spend more time on conceptualising diffuse securitising and assembling suspicion. Yet both exceptionalist securitising and diffuse assembling suspicion are important for understanding the characteristics and political implications of the contemporary unbinding of security.

This book is organised as follows. In the next chapter, I develop the idea of a political reading of security and its difference from security readings of politics. After explaining how the book positions itself within developments in security studies, the chapter discusses the relation between democracy and security. In the last two decades, the relation has been largely conceptualised in positive terms in international studies. Security is the practice of protecting democracy, or democratisation is interpreted as a key security strategy. Instead, I foreground the immanent tension between democracy and security as the conceptual device through which to read security politically. To that purpose, security is defined as the enactment of democratic limits.

Chapter 3 introduces an exceptionalist understanding of security. Here I unpack the security and political thickness that is invested in the traditional conception of security in international studies. Insecurity implies an existential situation in which the survival of a unit is at stake. Politically, it raises the question of exceptionalism as a form of governing the limits of democratic politics. The chapter discusses how exceptionalist security practice challenges two limits of democratic politics: the constitutional limits of executive government and the limits of the political role of the military and militarisation. In addition, I ask how exceptionalist security policies, which tend to separate the high politics of security from the low politics of everyday practice, pervade everyday life. In doing so, they create intimate sites in which rights and moral principles are asserted, contested and violated.

Chapters 4, 5, 6 and 7 conceptualise diffuse securitising and how it works differently from exceptionalist processes of securitising. Chapter 4 explains the concept of diffuse securitising and its relevance today. In Chapter 5, I introduce a technique of diffuse securitising that I refer to as 'assembling suspicion', and how it works differently from exceptionalist modes of security practice. In particular, I highlight how assembling suspicion does not work on the basis of aggregating various insecurities into an existential threat that intensifies political relations. Instead it works through circulations and juxtapositions of risks, uncertainties, dangers. It keeps relations horizontal and flexible rather than hierarchical and centring. Politically, it challenges bureaucratic and statist organisations of social control and, by implication, the democratic institutions and processes through which democratic states limit security practice. In Chapters 6 and 7, I explore two issues that play a key role in how assembling suspicion works the limits of democracy. After a brief overview of the relation between surveillance and democracy, Chapter 6 examines democratic issues that arise when surveillance interferes excessively in privacy. The chapter also evaluates the limits of interrogating the political significance of surveillance through the issue of privacy. Chapter 7 deals with the question of how the technological nature of assembling suspicion limits the possibilities for democratic politics. Technology and the prioritising of technical and professional expertise are often perceived as de-democratising. In both Chapters 5 and 6, I highlight that diffuse securitising pushes the challenges to democracy quite a bit further than is often assumed, challenging the familiar use, and maybe even the very relevance, of key categories through which democratic politics is mostly conceived, such as the need for public deliberation of values, the relative autonomy of citizens and rights of privacy.

In the concluding chapter of this book, I return to the heuristic and political relevance of contrasting exceptionalist securitising and diffuse assembling of suspicion today.

Before moving to the next chapter, it is probably worth noting that in this book I do not measure limits of democracy against a systematically set-out conception of democracy. In other words, I do not propose a particular definition of democracy. Instead, I loosely introduce how, within the very practices of security, certain aspects that we associate with democratic politics are at stake. In that sense, this book is not a political sociology of democracy or a contribution to democratic political theory. This book is primarily about the politicality of security practice, interpreted through how security practice enacts limits of democratic politics. In particular, it seeks to translate Neumann's concern with the detrimental effects of the political rise of fear and enmity as organising principles of politics into a security studies that focuses on the contemporary challenges that the unbinding of security poses to democratic politics.

2 Political reading of security

How should one introduce knowledge about security as an issue that is clearly critical in contemporary politics but covers multifaceted issues and meanings? This book proposes a political reading of security practice. Claims of insecurity and security mobilise specific modalities of political life. They enact constructions of political agency, authority, political community and sites of political contestation. For example, claiming that nuclear weapons pose a security problem can mean different things. It can refer to the possibility of a nuclear accident as a result of a computer failure. In that case experts of nuclear computer technology hold significant authority and most likely play a significant role in the political contestation of security. The insecurity claims then mobilise technocratic conceptions of politics. If the claim refers to the possibility of nuclear war between superpowers, it draws attention to diplomatic conceptions of international politics and the capacity of state leaders to deter other states from using nuclear weapons.

To take another example: the political significance of immigrants and refugees crossing the Mediterranean in shaky vessels seeking entry into the European Union. Often the political contestation of insecurity takes place in legalistic terms. Claims for the protection of human rights compete with claims of illegality and the need to return illegal immigrants. Courts and the legal profession play a significant role. Equally often the security issue is represented as a matter of numbers. Immigrants are then not rights holders but a physical mass or multitude on the move. Politics turns into a struggle between the European Union—the instituted political community—and a contemporary manifestation of 'the mob'— those claiming wrongs and seeking political voice by moving in numbers against established institutions and boundaries. Rather than the rule of law and human rights, such claims draw in the first instance on a political tradition that is grounded in the rise and mobility of 'the masses' as a political force. Modulating security politics around a calculus of physical force—in this case movement of numbers and physical interception of the movement—structures politics through notions of strategic interaction reminiscent of war rather than through conflicts between rights holders mediated by judicial institutions. Both the legalistic and strategic interpretation illustrate how the rendition of insecurity draws on and circumscribes conceptions of politics. In the former, migration and the insecurities connected to it are caught in a politics that is performed in terms of legal constraints on political authority. In the latter they are framed through a notion of politics that foregrounds a battle between two opposing forces, one that is seeking to enter a polity and the other that is seeking to keep them outside. Migrants enact their political being through legal rights claims in one case and through a historical manifestation of mass movement on the other.

Security is a political practice by virtue of always bringing into play and being connected to certain conceptions of politics. This chapter develops this political interpretation of security and in particular proposes to define security as techniques enacting democratic limits. The first section briefly explores the relation between security and politics, and contrasts a political reading of security with a security reading of politics. It introduces the notion that security is a *technique* that renders insecurities and politics simultaneously. The second section looks at how security and democracy have been related in international studies and proposes a political reading that starts from the inherent tension between security and democracy. The third section proposes to integrate this tension into the study of security by defining security practice as techniques that enact democratic limits by rendering insecurities.

Security and politics

Security practices are often presented as different from political practice. They are an intelligence practice that evaluates which dangers require priority on the basis of the level and acuteness of threat and that does horizon scanning of upcoming dangers. In addition, security is a strategic practice that develops instruments to prevent or mitigate threats and to defend the political community against internal and external violence. Security professionals feed this information into a political process where security budgets and policies are decided in competition with other political priorities by politicians. In this view, the decisions of security actors do not define ways of doing politics. Neither are they seen as defining the political objectives that inform the strategy. Political decisions are taken by others to whom security actors provide information and options.

There is of course a politics of security between the security professionals. Intelligence and strategic work lead to controversies between them about the adequacy of threat evaluation, the relevance of intelligence, and the preferred methods of preventing, mitigating and defending against dangers. These controversies draw security professionals more proactively into the political decision-making process when factions of security professionals lobby political actors to gain support for their point of view or when they take sides in debates between political factions with different security policy preferences (e.g. whether in peace-building operations the military should take on policing roles or not). At this point, one can say that security professionals do perform a politics of security; they are not outside politics. In so far as they struggle between themselves, bring their controversies to define the terms of political debate, and try to influence political decisions they are both embedded in and performing politics without being professionals of politics.

This understanding of the relation between security and politics misses an important political aspect of security practice, however. Security practices are not only embedded in politics by security professionals participating in political contestations; they also enact conceptions of politics. They bring certain understandings of political community, of what constitutes political practice and of the parameters within which politics can be conducted to bear on the situations in which they interfere. By making the state the central referent that needs protecting, national security sustains an international politics of inter-state relation that makes states the central locus of politics, which is a vision of politics that in turn makes the priority of national security—e.g. over individual security—plausible (Walker, 1990; Dillon, 1996; Neocleous, 2008). Here security practice does not simply bring security knowledge, technology and strategies to bear upon politics but embeds conceptions of politics in security practice. When enacting certain conceptions of politics, security practices foreground certain political institutions and predispositions, and challenge others (Walker, 1988, 1990; Der Derian, 1993; Dillon, 1996; Huysmans, 2006; Williams, 2007; Aradau, 2008; Neocleous, 2008). For example, foregrounding an acute and high-level threat often comes with a call for exceptional and emergency decisions that circumvent instituted democratic processes of deliberation and decision making.[1]

To capture the difference between this understanding of the relation between politics and security, and approaches that start from a separation between security and politics, I propose to differentiate security readings of global politics from political readings of security. Security readings of politics focus on the nature of insecurities, the measures to respond to them, and possibly the political and social processes sustaining the insecurities. For example, security knowledge analyses how distrust between great powers makes it difficult to agree far-reaching and binding arms control agreements. When military capacity can be used for both offensive and defensive purposes, expressions of peaceful intentions are not sufficient to counter vulnerabilities created by arms reductions. Instituting detailed verification procedures as well as confidence-building measures, like exchange of military personnel and proposals for a non-offensive defence (i.e. organising a military capacity that can defend territory but not project power into another country's territory), were among the instruments proposed to tackle the problem of distrust.

Security readings of politics analyse the nature of global insecurities and political responses rather than the visions of political order and conceptions of politics that security knowledge and practice incorporate and bring into play. The starting point of security interpretations of the world is often to define threats to something. For example, environmental security can refer to the danger of environmental degradation for the ecological system, the conflict-inducing potentials of water scarcity between states, the danger of skin cancer for individuals, and so on. What insecurity means depends in the first instance on what the threat is—cancer, water scarcity resulting in inter-state war, ecological instability—and what it is threatening—individuals, states, ecological systems. National security can be organised around the threat of a global nuclear war and the imperative to deter it from ever happening. It can also be organised around the threat of political dissent, such as communist parties in the 1940s and 50s and national liberation movements during the struggles for decolonisation. Again insecurity is analysed in the first instance in terms of the conditions and agencies—e.g. nuclear weapons, other states, political movements—that generate threatening developments to some-thing—e.g. the ideological legitimacy of a political regime, the survival of the state.

These security analyses take on a more explicit political dimension when including how different views of security and different levels of funding are contested within the political field. To understand the political and social stakes in security, they include the strategic interactions between political actors facing a security situation as one of the things that needs analysing. For example, a security analysis of environmental threat and malnutrition can include the strategic interactions between some aid agencies lobbying against biofuels because they assess that a turn to biofuels will create food insecurity and environmental movements supporting biofuels as part of the solution for global warming. Yet such an analysis remains close to security interpretations of the world. The politics is one of competition and contestation over how certain actions affect particular given insecurities, and a struggle over which insecurities demand priority over others. The example above identifies a struggle over whether political priority should lie with food security or environmental security, and over the effectiveness and unintended consequences of investing in the development of biofuel for environmental and possibly also energy security reasons. The political struggle concerns prioritising certain insecurities over others with security analyses being an important source that provides information on, in this case, environmental insecurity and the effects of increasing use of biofuel.

In the last two decades security studies has introduced another, constructionist take on security interpretations of politics; one that makes it possible to not take insecurities as givens (Campbell, 1992; Wæver, 1995; Bigo, 1996). This particular take is of special importance for this book. Insecurities can be approached either as given or as politically constructed. In the former, security analyses study what is threatening about Russia cutting off gas supplies to the Ukraine or the US intending to install anti-missile systems in the Czech Republic. They ask how serious the threat is to whom, and what can be done about it. They provide a reality check of the threat and seek to explain it in terms of political motives, structural givens (e.g. geographical location or the anarchical nature of the international system), technological developments (e.g. nuclear weapons) and strategic interaction (e.g. competition over access to natural resources).

The constructionist approach in contrast treats insecurities as politically constructed rather than given (e.g. Campbell, 1992; Wæver, 1995; Bigo, 1996; Dillon, 1996; Buzan *et al.*, 1998; Fierke, 1998; Huysmans, 1998; Bigo, 2000). Insecurities are made by security policies that reframe political relations and global developments as security threats or risks. The most popular formulation of this approach conceptualises security as a speech act—a linguistic act that brings into being what it speaks (Wæver, 1995; Buzan *et al.*, 1998). Security then is like a promise. Saying 'I promise' constitutes the promise. There is no promise outside it being spoken. In this conception, security discourse transforms particular issues into insecurities. For example, security practice turns AIDS/HIV from a medical health issue into a national security threat by emphasising its devastating impact on the national economy. Another example: a military exercise is approached as a preparation for an invasion rather than a routine exercise. Security politics is thus part and parcel of the constitution of insecurities, not just in an action/reaction loop as expressed by the security dilemma but constitutively in the sense that they structure politics around notions of insecurity. In case of the security dilemma, security practice produces insecurities as an unintended effect. Although I may be arming myself for purely defensive purposes, my neighbours cannot be sure that is the case. Because of this uncertainty, my security measures are making them more insecure, which makes them possibly respond by arming themselves, which in turn enhances my insecurities, and so on. From a constructionist point of view the rendition of insecurities is immanent to security practice rather than an unintended effect. Any security practice makes the world knowledgeable as a world of insecurities; it necessarily enacts events and developments as insecure. Here insecurity is not a side effect but a defining effect, or better, a constitutive element of any security practice. For example, after the end of the Cold War, a security institution like NATO did not abandon or redefine itself as an economic or cultural organisation. NATO remained a security organisation that produced security discourses and instruments that continued to inscribe international relations with (new) emerging insecurities, although sometimes quite differently from the old dangers. As long as security organisations remain security agencies, they will necessarily enact insecurities—both by acting on issues as if they are a security problem and by rendering insecure worlds in this action.

Constructionist approaches study the processes that generate particular, sometimes competing, conceptions of insecurity. For example, how did the support for a human security approach by the United Nations Development Programme (UNDP) and United Nations High Commissioner for Refugees (UNHCR) in the struggle over the peace dividend in the 1990s challenge the dominance of national security and military institutions? How successful was it in redefining insecurity in terms of human needs rather than national interests? In these analyses, the nature of security problems does not define the solution (i.e. the security policy), but the 'solutions' that security agencies have available play a significant role in defining the nature of insecurities. For example, security definitions of migration in the European Union were partly the result of security experts of the internal affairs ministries dominating the negotiations of abolishing internal border controls from the mid-1980s onwards at the cost of the foreign affairs ministries. The specific register of solutions or instruments these professionals have available—e.g. policing and surveillance techniques rather than diplomatic relations—framed what kinds of issue the abolishment of internal borders would generate (Bigo, 1996; Guiraudon, 2000, 2003). In this approach, insecurities are not simply a given but become a political choice or an outcome of the competition between various professionals. This interpretation allows the constructionist approach a different take on the political question. The key question is not how to best deal with a threat but whether to approach a particular phenomenon as a security threat or not; whether to make security policies a main instrument in dealing with a phenomenon and what the consequences of so doing are. It leads to an outspoken sociological security analysis that focuses on questions such as: (a) which actors have what authoritative position to define what counts as insecurity; (b) which discourses and institutional routines frame issues as priority insecurities; (c) how are insecurities outcomes of power struggles between political, security, media and judicial actors; and (d) how do social and technological processes organise life around insecurities.

The political reading of security practice developed in this book shares the constructionist understanding that security is not a given but a practice of constituting insecurities. In line with this approach, security is conceptualised as 'techniques of securitising'—or 'methods of rendering insecurities'. As *technique*, security practice is understood through (a) the rationality that organises its way of doing things and (b) the way it strategically enacts this rationality in practical situations by reacting to other actions.[2] In the book, I analyse simultaneously various aspects of rationalities of security that help us to understand what defines the 'securitiness', as different from, for example, the 'cultureness' or 'economicness' of the practice, and the way this 'rationality' plays out in strategic or contested interactions. In particular, I define two techniques of securitising. One that works through the rendition of existential threats and is embedded in national security practice, and one that renders suspicion into an organising principle of sociality through diffusing uncertainties and risks. The former is referred to as 'exceptionalist securitising', the latter as 'assembling suspicion'. I will also use the language of 'modalities' to identify differences in the manner in which a particular technique of securitising operates. For example, in relation to exceptionalist securitising I will distinguish a constitutional modality from a militarising modality.

The central contribution of the book to this constructionist reading is the understanding that security techniques do not simply render insecurities but also parameters of the political contestation of security; that they render not only ways of doing security but also ways of doing politics (see also Walker, 1990; Aradau, 2008; Pram Gad and Lund Petersen, 2011). I want to foreground a political reading of security that takes as its object of analysis how security techniques action specific imaginations of the political nature of living together and in doing so challenge certain modes of political practice. For example, as I will unpack extensively in the next chapter, securitising through the rendition of existential threats includes an exceptionalist enacting of politics. It defines the parameters of political contestations of security as possibilities of and limits to transgressing constitutionally defined fundamental rights and interdependent but balanced relations between legislative, executive and juridical powers.

In doing so it brings an exceptionalist conception of politics and its limits into political play.

The meanings of security thus differ not just in terms of the nature of threats and of entities that are threatened, as has been foregrounded by the concept and analyses of 'security sectors', including environmental, military, economic, societal and political security sectors (Buzan, 1983, 1991: 118–34). For example, the environmental security sector contains developments like global warming threatening the ecological system. It draws attention to issues other than the economic security sector, which focuses on economic developments like a financial crisis threatening the European economic system. The meanings of security also, and for this book more importantly, differ in the conceptions of politics and the political ordering strategies and technologies that security practice invests in the constitution of insecurities (Dillon, 1996; Walker, 1997; Huysmans, 1998, 2006; Aradau, 2008; Neocleous, 2008; Walker, 2010). What different conceptions of collective stakes, authoritative agencies, political struggle and political living together are implied by security practice and the knowledge they enact? For example, analyses of arms control often build on an understanding of anarchical international politics in which states are the main actors that are caught in a situation where no state or institution can guarantee the security of other states by means of sufficiently sanctioned generalised norms and law. The central political problem of international politics then becomes how to build trust in a world where states in their own interest in survival should fundamentally distrust one another. Such a conception tends to authorise the prudent 'statesman' who can decisively act in the national interest without escalating international competition into a war on ideological grounds.

The political reading of insecurity proposed here thus interprets the contemporary complex, multifaceted landscape of security claims and practice in terms of their security and political rationality and in terms of how they bring into play and challenge conceptions of politics. It builds on a constructionist security approach that looks at how security practice renders events into security problems—or, in other words, how it securitises. It extends that analysis to how securitising practices render conceptions of the political. This reading differs from more traditional political sociological interpretations of the link between security and politics. The analysis proposed here does not take insecurities as given and then focuses on how actors compete over which insecurity deserves priority or which security measures are most effective or in need of funding. Such a political sociology would need to be inflected differently for it to study security practice as being simultaneously a security and political technique.[3] It needs to foreground: (i) how such competitions are not just responding to insecurities but are actively taking part in shaping insecurities and organising the world through the distribution of insecurities; and (ii) how mobilising security discourses, institutions and policy instruments impacts not just on the security framing—i.e. have security thickness—but also on how the conduct of politics is framed—i.e. have political thickness.

Democracy and security policies

Interpreting the political technique of securitising is mostly organised in relation to more specific concepts than 'politics'. Among them have been the conceptions of community and sovereignty that security practice enacts (Walker, 1990; Campbell, 1998); the rendition of order in security practice (Dillon, 1996; Huysmans, 1998); the contrast between instrumental control and tragedy and its impact on authority (Dillon, 1996); challenges to liberal neutrality and deliberations (Aradau, 2008; Neocleous, 2008; Behnke, 2011); questions of emancipation (Booth, 1991; Wyn Jones, 1999; Aradau, 2004; Sheehan, 2005); citizenship (Nyers, 2009; Guillaume and Huysmans, 2013); and democracy (Wæver, 1995; Buzan *et al.*, 1998). As indicated in the introductory chapter, this book uses the question of the relation between security and democratic practice as the vehicle for giving political thickness to analyses of securitising.

In contemporary global politics democracy is a major theme in security policy. Democratisation is claimed to be a condition for regional or global security. Dictatorships are not simply seen as a less legitimate form of politics by democracies but also a danger to regional or global security. Democratisation, in contrast, is assumed to create peace and stability. In addition, security is claimed to be a foundational element in demands for and processes of democratisation. The latter cannot succeed unless some basic physical security of citizens as well as the state is guaranteed. At the same time, however, security policies are challenged as undermining democratic institutions and achievements by limiting fundamental rights and possibilities for political dissent among others. This security–democracy nexus makes a political reading of security in global politics pertinent. It triggers questions about the kinds of democracy security policies assert, the limits of securing democracy and, more generally, the political ordering effects of security practice. For example, by making democratisation part of a security strategy, security policy cannot simply be reduced to the instrumental calculation of how to best protect a democratic polity. It becomes part of a policy of instituting certain conceptions of democratic political order.

International studies literature conceptualises the relation between security and democracy mostly in mutually reinforcing ways. This relation flows in two directions. First, it flows from security to democracy. Here security refers to the governmental function of protecting democracy and its proper exercise. The role of security policy is to defend democratic states against external and internal aggressions that challenge the territorial integrity and functional autonomy of democratic states. This is a variant of the general argument that states primarily seek security in an anarchical international system (Waltz, 1954, 1979). It can be found for example in the opening lines of the North Atlantic Treaty that established NATO: 'They [the parties to the treaty] are determined to safeguard the freedom, common heritage and civilisation of their peoples, founded on the principles of democracy, individual liberty and the rule of law' (NATO, 1949). Another argument is that security is a condition for democracy (Etzioni, 2007). Developing and sustaining democratic institutions requires guaranteeing a certain level of security (e.g. Zakaria, 2004).

Secondly, the relation flows from democracy to security. NATO Secretary General Jaap de Hoop (2004–2009) said at an anti-terror summit in Madrid (10 March 2005) that democracy remains the best answer to terror (NATO, 2005). In some of the global democracy arguments, the construction of a global democratic system of government is expected to reduce the insecurities produced by an anarchical international system— i.e. a political system that lacks an overarching authority (Held, 1995; Dryzek, 2006; Shalom, 2008). In the democratic peace argument, shared democracy between states produces international security because democracies do not go to war with each other (Owen, 1994; Russett, 1994; Doyle, 1997; Owen, 1997; Williams, 2007: 42–61). Also the literature on security community, which witnessed a spectacular revival after the end of the Cold War, makes democracy a key condition for instituting sustainable expectations of peaceful change in world politics (Adler and Barnett, 1998). These arguments emphasise the security function of democracy and the idea that the democratisation of states is an instrument for increasing security (e.g. Ottaway, 2003; Owen, 2005).

In both cases security and democracy have a relatively unproblematic relation. They reinforce rather than undermine one another. From the perspective of Neumann's interpretation of how mobilising fear of the enemy impacts on democracy, and in light of intense political debates on counter-terrorism strategies and legislation since 2001, exclusively focusing on this functional relation between democracy and security skews what is in fact a problematic relation (Waldron, 2003; e.g. Huysmans, 2004; Scheuerman, 2006; Whitaker, 2007). The willingness of some in the political, artistic and business elite to suspend democracy and declare the bankruptcy of certain key democratic institutions in the name of defending the democratic state, place security practice in an ambivalent relation to democracy. They indicate that security practice can shift easily from protecting democracy to challenging the very democracy they claim to protect (Ash, 2002; Ikenberry, 2002; Carothers, 2003; Zizek, 2003). Debates about the acceptable trade-off between security and freedom are one of the most visible political manifestations of this ambiguous relation between security and democracy (Tsoukala, 2004, 2006; Bigo and Tsoukala, 2008; Gearty, 2013). Also arguments that counter-terrorist strategies do the work for the terrorists, i.e. undermining democratic forms of governance, express a similar tension between security and democracy.

The revival of interest in the revaluation of political and legal exceptionalism in democracies and the security/liberty relation at the start of the 21st century has been one of several reasons for bringing out an ambivalent and often tense relation between democracy and security. There are various arguments why democracy is problematic from a security perspective. Owing to demands for transparency, institutional checks and balances, and favourable public opinion, security analysts argue that democracy is particularly vulnerable in conditions of acute threat (e.g. Schmid, 1993; Sandler, 1995; Homer-Dixon, 2002; Bruneau and Matei, 2008). Among the reasons given are: decisions are slow; the necessary secrecy of intelligence is questioned by demands for transparency and political accountability (e.g. Rimington, 1994); the political field is more sensitive to media stories and reactions of the public, which consequently challenges the capacity for rational security decision making; and democratic societies are more vulnerable to infiltration because they are less policed and tend to have market economies that are more reliant on free movement. A different argument is the criticism—or correction— of the democratic peace theory that although democracies might be less likely to go to war against each other, the process of democratisation itself increases the probability and scale of violence and insecurity (e.g. Mansfield and Snyder, 1995).

Security policies and institutions are also seen to be problematic for democracy. The debates about the nature and democratic legitimacy of emergency decision making when facing security crises, and the tension between security and liberty, have already been mentioned. The capacity to inflict violence upon citizens by the military, the police and other security institutions, and the possibility of the military using its capacity for violence for its own political ambitions, have been a long-standing concern for democratic regimes. While democracies require military to defend them and police to maintain public order, there is always a concern about the possibility of a military coup or the temptation for security institutions to use their capacity for violence to wield political influence (e.g. Pion-Berlin and Lopez, 1991; Yaniv, 1993; Dandeker, 1994; Segal, 1994; Nelson, 2002; Cawthra and Luckham, 2003; Demirel, 2005; Dominguez, 2007). Shklar coined the term 'liberalism of fear' to express this democratic fear of security institutions (Shklar, 1989; Robin, 2004). It refers to a form of liberalism that is defined around fear of the institutionalisation of 'arbitrary, unexpected, unnecessary and unlicensed acts of force' by public institutions and 'habitual and pervasive acts of cruelty and torture performed by military, paramilitary and police agents' (Shklar, 1989: 29).

The relation between security and democracy is thus far from unproblematic.[4] While much attention in international studies in the last two decades has gone to democracy and democratisation being conditions for security, and even an explicit instrument of security policy, this book starts from the more tense relation between security practice and democracy. More specifically, it unpacks multiple ways in which security practice becomes political by *enacting limits of democracy*. 'Enacting limits' does not only mean acting out limits to democratic practice, such as postponing constitutional guarantees in emergency situations or acting in response to conditions that threaten democratic practice such as excessive violent political dissent. 'Enacting' also means to bring into being that what one claims, that what one acts 'in response to'. Enacting limits to democratic practice is therefore not simply a reaction to limits that are already given but also proactively renders limits. For example, when intelligence agencies demand that secrecy is retained in parliamentary debates and court hearings, they do not simply act out a limit to democratic transparency but bring secrecy into being as that issue where security practice institutes or makes real what counts for them as a legitimate limit to democratic transparency. Enacting is performative in the sense of bringing into the world what security practice takes as the conditions of its action—such as secrecy being the necessary condition for effective intelligence practice.

Enacting limits of democracy creates a political scene in which democratic practices, institutions and principles are brought into play as simultaneously 'a stake' and 'at stake'—that what is simultaneously defining the contest and legitimacy of security practice and that what is potentially endangered or seriously challenged by security practice. In doing so, it creates situations of contestation and struggle over the legitimate conduct of politics, authoritative positions, rights and conceptions of democratic subjects that are collectively instituted, such as the distinction between military and civilian authority, the protection of the right to privacy, and the possibility for reflective autonomous action. In doing so, security practice takes part in defining the terms of political debate on security matters; it defines parameters of legitimate contest of what matters and of the available choices to deal with the issue. In this contest, security practice sustains and enhances the authority of security discourse, institutions and professionals by placing itself as holding the appropriate response to the situation that it partly renders into being—i.e. the insecurities that limit the possibility for democracy. The conception of security as enacting limits of democracy thus combines the idea that security practice securitises with an understanding that this securitising does not just bring into play insecurities but also creates a political scene.

Enacting limits of democracy

Security works the question of the limit of democracy in various ways. First, security practice enacts situations in which democratic politics endanger their own survival. Demands for economic growth and its importance for political legitimacy can lead to ecologically destructive economic policy. Demands for proper judicial and parliamentary review of decisions on going to war can lead to delays when speedy action is called for. Democratic elections and the right to protest can put non-democratic political forces into power. The security answer often requires changes in existing democratic forms of politics for the sake of security. For example, emergencies are said to demand speedy action that requires postponing parliamentary and judicial overview procedures. Dissent is restricted because of the need to unite uncritically against the enemy. Security institutions use violence against citizens deemed dangerous in the interest of protecting other citizens from violence. Intelligence agencies argue that the sources and specific nature of intelligence justifying intervention in another country need to be kept secret so as not to endanger ongoing and future intelligence operations. Security practice here works a double security limit of democracy: democracies endanger themselves and democratic procedures and rights claims increase vulnerability. These modes of raising limits to democratic politics are not in themselves central to democratic politics but rather are brought to the fore and intensified by security practice. The question is not what democracy is one seeking to secure with what kind of security policies. Neither is it what are the specific characteristics of democracy and democratisation and their impact on global security. The question is rather how does security practice render the moments and sites where democratic practice meets its security limits and where claims emerge for displacing democratic practices with non-democratic ones.

Secondly, security works the limits of democracy by drawing lines between the fully democratic, less democratic and non-democratic. The end of the Cold War reframed the question of democracy in global politics. During the Cold War, democracy was regularly used to distinguish between allies of the Western bloc and its enemies who belonged to the Soviet bloc. Communism was one of its others, and communist movements were at times seen as playing democratic politics for the purpose of destroying it. With the disintegration of the Warsaw Pact in 1989 and the Soviet Union in 1991, democracy functioned more explicitly as a global concept attached to an increasingly wide variety of practices: 'Democracy is today the main legitimating principle of government. Around the world, political leaders and activists everywhere proclaim their belief in democracy' (Dryzek, 1999: 30). In democratic theory and politics, this raised the question of what are democracy's functional, territorial and/or temporal limits that make it possible to judge what counts and does not count as democratic practice. Defining democracy goes hand in hand with defining the less and non-democratic. The democratic peace argument implies that policies can distinguish sharply between democratic and non-democratic states and between states capable of democratising and those lost for the cause, which need to be contained or to whom democracy can only be brought by force. The intervention in Iraq to topple Saddam Hussein in 2003 was an example of the latter.

This democratic differentiation that security enacts does not only play out in inter-state politics but also in relation to groups and individuals. Democratic politics asserts boundaries each time categories of people (e.g. children), attitudes (e.g. racism) or behaviours (e.g. violent protest) are identified as not capable of being democratic or as incompatible with democracy (Connolly, 1995; Hindess, 2001; Derrida, 2003; Vanni, 2004). Security practice is one of the practices that action these limits, distinctions and boundaries between democratic and non-democratic subjects, practices and developments. Most explicitly it does this by identifying the deviant and inimical. For example, several European countries limited the free movement of football hooligans in the 1990s. Their behaviour was seen as incompatible with democratic citizenry; they were often portrayed as irrational, beasts and drunks (Tsoukala, 2008, 2009). 'Terrorism' is another label used to mark groups and individuals whose actions are deemed to be unacceptable in democratic politics or whose group dynamics and individual characters make them unable of democratic practice (Tsoukala, 2008). The idea that security enacts the limit of democracy is thus not that security practice identifies and reacts to that which endangers democracy. 'Enacting limits' means that security politics itself constitutes limits of democracy. It actively draws lines between the democratic, the less democratic and the non-democratic political subjects, whether individuals, groups or polities. Enacting such lines is always a political action; it creates political scenes in contesting who counts as a legitimate and proper political subject. For example, the definition of what counted as democratic politics and what did not, was a stake in the struggle for political legitimacy and the kind of state one wanted to institutionalise in the late 19th and early 20th century. Among others, communist theory and politics claimed being democratic, only in a different, and from their perspective, really democratic way (Lenin, 1946 [1917]; e.g. Balibar, 1976). Liberal and social-democratic parties thought differently, of course.

So far, two ways in which security practice enacts democratic limits have been introduced: (a) security practice bringing into political play limitations of pursuing democratic politics in situations of heightened insecurity; and (b) security practice differentiating democratic, less democratic and non-democratic subjects, practices and developments. Besides these two, there is a third and equally important way in which security enacts democratic limits. Security practices can challenge democratically institutionalised limits to both the issues that can be governed through security techniques and the legitimate methods of security governing. In the previous chapter, I captured this particular enactment of democratic limits under the concept 'security unbound'. The issue here is not first of all how security practice questions the viability of 'normal' democratic politics in the face of dangers and the constitution of democratic and less or non-democratic subjects. Rather, the contest is about security practice breaking down distinctions between areas where it can operate and not. For example, in the 1990s NATO expanded its notion of 'out of area' operations through embracing humanitarian interventions and peace-building agendas. In doing so it moved significantly beyond the limits to deploying military power outside the NATO area as they were instituted under the collective defence mechanisms that governed NATO. This change went hand in hand with a blurring and reorganisation of categorical distinctions between military operations, policing, and civilian aid and disaster relief actions. An increasing focus on risk governance in NATO also played a significant role in creating a language and method that facilitated the involvement of a military institution in a wide range of societal processes, including managing consequences of natural disasters, protecting humanitarian aid delivery, governing transnational population flows, etc. (Coker, 2002; Rasmussen, 2006). Here limits are enacted by blurring, stretching or deleting limits to security governance, rather than by establishing limits to democratic politics, as in the case of differentiating between democratic and other subjects.

Developments in NATO in the 1990s and early 21st century are just one example of security policies trying to get purchase on insecurities that they see emerging from globalising and transversalising activities and structures. The idea of a global Islamic terrorist network, the process of global warming, the discourse on transnationally operating criminal organisations, the securitisation of migration, demands for the increased surveillance of the internet are among the many examples of how security policies are defining global and transversal insecurities. 'Globalising' refers to spatially scaling up from inter-state relations to political and security operations that take the world as a whole as their plane of interference. 'Transversalising' refers to challenges to the spatial logic that organises the world in terms of territorial boundaries between states, and variations of scaling up the management of these boundaries, such as the institutionalisation of collective security mechanisms and the drafting of blueprints for a global polity.

The global and transversal operations of security institutions and professionals create two interrelated questions for conceptions of democracy; conceptions that remain largely formulated and instituted in territorially defined polities despite securitising processes doing so much work in structuring transversal and global power relations (Walker, 1988, 1990; Sheptycki, 2000; Balibar, 2002: 192; Bigo, 2008). The most immediate question concerns how to govern democratically global and transversal security institutions and networks of security actors (Wood and Dupont, 2006; Wood and Shearing, 2007). How can transnational networks of police be governed democratically? How should one make globally operating private security companies democratically accountable? Are democratic state institutions adequate or do we require a broader definition of stakeholder institutions and more experimental ways of bringing democracy to bear upon globally and transversally organised security practices? For example, in case of environmental issues stakeholder groups could include local community representatives of badly affected places, environmental movements, business, etc. (Dupont and Wood, 2006: 246). The main democratic issue here is how to regain democratic purchase on securitising processes and institutions that operate beyond the confines of current democratic institutions that limit and hold to account security practice. It asks for studies of the capacity of existing, alternative and experimental modes of democratic action and governance to effectively bear on changing power structures in security areas.

There is a prior question, however, are the securitising processes that are simultaneously reorganising insecurities that matter, and the techniques of governing through insecurities, as exemplified by the rise of risk governance and resilience in international politics in the last two decades, limiting the very possibility for democratic practices to have any bearing upon them? This second question is central to this book. Although the normative and institution-building question of how security can be democratically governed is clearly very important in this context too, my main focus is on how globalising and transversalising security practice and knowledge challenge the possibilities for democratic practice; how they enact the limits of democracy in multiple ways.

This interest in how the limits of democratic practice are brought into play by security practice in multiple ways has led me to not use an institutional definition of democracy. My method is not to measure a particular security practice against a model or an ideal type of democracy. Instead I work with an understanding that securitising enacts various and often multiple aspects of what can be seen as categories of democratic practices. They are categories that express fractional elements of democratic traditions.[5] They do not necessarily come together in a particular form of democracy but are valued in and of themselves. This fractional approach takes democracy as a multiplicity of issues and questions; it is bits and pieces of how 'democracy' and 'democratic' have been and are being performed. This does not mean that democracy means everything. It implies, however, that democracy is not a fixed institutional or conceptual point—a model—but consists of various things that are connected to enactments of democracy without necessarily hanging together logically or institutionally. To borrow a phrase of John Law: they are more than one but less than many (Law, 1999: 11–12). In the course of the book I touch on various democratic issues as they emerge from within a security technique and its modulations. They include, among others, legal limits to executive governance, protection of privacy, separation of civil and military institutions, limits to technocratic governing, relative autonomy of citizens and the capacity for reflection on consequences of actions.

I focus on 'democratic practice' rather than the more general category of 'political practice' because the bits and pieces of politics that I look at are somehow connected to two political devices through which democratic issues are brought into the political scene. The first is the use of a constitutive distinction between democratic and authoritarian politics or variations like dictatorship and totalitarianism. In so far as democracy is not a specific sets of institutions but also something that is brought into being through its performance and naming, differentiating between democracy and authoritarian politics has been a central method of asserting 'democracy'. Calling upon the danger of authoritarianism is also a key device through which democratic critique of security practices is mobilised and through which democratic limits are raised in political contestations of insecurities and how to govern them.

The second device is sovereignty, not as state sovereignty but as popular sovereignty. The democratic category is here not one of pluralism between like units, whether states or individuals, but the tension between political autonomy of people and the need for rulers to decide in the name and interest of a people (Walker, 2010: 206). This tension is central to the modern notion of citizenship that is a category of both government and empowerment (Isin, 2002). Instituting citizenship as membership and guaranteed rights is a practice of governing and statecraft. Groups of people are granted rights that others do not receive; some are considered political subjects that can bear upon the polity, while others are enacted as non-political. But citizenship is also a category through which, historically, various groups of people have tried to move from being excluded towards being included in the political scene, from being a part that is seen as not belonging or non-political to a part that is political. The irresolvable tensions that constitute popular sovereignty are related to key characteristics of democratic practice, in particular to claims of equality and fairness, a significant role for popular power in policy decisions and political action, and transparency and accountability in decision-making procedures (Saward, 1998).

These two devices significantly frame what it means to invoke democracy as a stake and at stake in the politics of insecurity. Various ways in which security practice enacts democratic limits and through which a democratic critique is brought to bear upon security practice are somehow connected to them. Although they play an important role in this book, I do not refine them into a set of criteria that together define a model of democracy. As explained, I opt for using a fractional approach of democracy to allow for greater flexibility in bringing out multiple limits and challenges to democratic practice that security techniques are currently enacting.

Conclusion

This chapter introduced a set of key concepts that shape the political interpretation of security practice in the subsequent chapters. It started by introducing a political interpretation of security practice that analyses how security practice does not only render insecurities but also conceptions of politics. Security becomes a technique of securitising and politicising. As securitising, security practice is characterised by its methods of shaping and distributing forms of insecurity. As politicising, it brings conceptions of (legitimate) conduct of politics into play. Securitising refers thus to both security and political techniques.

I am particularly interested in how contemporary security practices make democratic conduct of politics a political and security stake as well as how securitising challenges democratic practice. To foreground this ambiguous and tense relation between security and democracy, I proposed to define security as the technique of enacting democratic limits. The limit of democracy refers to both the limits of democratic responses to insecurities and the dangers security policies pose for democratic politics. More specifically, enacting democratic limits refers to three issues: (a) security is about enacting situations in which democracies threaten themselves, where democracy encounters its own limits; (b) security practice is a danger for democratic politics in the sense that it limits the possibility to act democratically upon security; and (c) security practice challenges limits that democracy sets to the legitimate use of security operations, institutions and technology.

One of the issues that make insecurities a critical issue in politics today is how notions of insecurity, uncertainty, risk and precaution are organising various modes of government and are arranging social and political relations in increasingly diffuse ways through fear, anxiety and unease. The diffusion of insecurities and the techniques through which this diffusion is enacted is receiving increasing attention in international studies. To bring out how diffuse securitising differs from the more traditional conception of securitising in international studies and how it bears upon possibilities for democratic practice, this book works in three steps. The next chapter deals with the securitising technique that works through rendering existential threats. This technique is strongly embedded in the national security tradition and has been central to security studies. I refer to it as 'exceptionalist securitising'. In the following chapter, I introduce how diffuse techniques of securitising differ from exceptionalist securitising. I then conceptualise in Chapters 5, 6 and 7 security and political dimensions of a key technique of diffusing insecurities: the assembling of suspicion. Throughout the driving question is how processes of unbinding security enact democratic limits today.

Notes

1 See Andrew Neal, however, for criticism of this understanding of exceptional situations undermining democratic institutional politics (Neal, 2012).
2 This concept of technique is borrowed from Foucault (Foucault, 1984: 48).
3 Such a political reading cannot start from a particular definition of politics, such as the distribution of values, goods and services in a society, or the distinction

between friends and enemies. It needs to retain a sufficient degree of openness so as not to foreclose the question of the various notions and aspects of politics that security practices bring to bear upon global politics.

4 For a nuanced analysis of how to retain security as a public good while nevertheless retaining the tensions between democracy and security, see Ian Loader and Neil Walker *Civilizing security* (2007).

5 The concept of fractionality is borrowed from John Law (Law, 1999).

3 Insecurity as exception

In international studies security politics is seen at heart to be about the survival of states in an anarchical and violent world. Since there is no highest sovereign authority that has the legitimate and effective capacity to resolve conflict between states, states need to be self-reliant in defending their territorial integrity and functional independence against other states. Global politics is inherently insecure and therefore security policy is central to states. This framing is either taken for granted, leading to the study of strategic interaction driven by a security imperative, or it is challenged by arguing that the anarchical nature of international relations does not prevent long-term cooperation and that international norms do matter.

Less often asked is what kind of global politics and authority legitimating practices are instituted and enacted by declaring an existential threat to one's survival in an anarchical world. How does declaring and enacting national or global security crises structure the political terrain? This chapter argues that playing out existential threats to a polity makes political contestations exceptionalist. Exceptionalism defines the political rationale of a security technique that enacts exceptionally intense conditions that threaten the survival of a state or other political units and their way of life.

This chapter looks at this key security technique in international relations. After introducing the central place of exceptionalism in international studies, the first section explains the main characteristics of exceptionalist understandings of insecurity, especially political intensification and enemy construction. These general characteristics are politically thickened in the subsequent sections. First, exceptionalist politics of insecurity emphasise a radical tension between law and politics, and legality and legitimacy of political action. Secondly, exceptionalist securitising can intensify the violent and repressive capacity of the state and the political role of security organisations, possibly implying a militarisation of politics.

Thirdly, while exceptionalism tends to draw attention to the 'high politics' of 'statesmen', the elite of security organisations, and the judiciary, it is also an intimate security practice working upon people's bodies and their everyday lives. The conclusion brings together different ways in which exceptionalist renditions of insecurity work limits of democratic politics.

Exceptionalist insecurity

International studies founded itself as a special branch of knowledge by declaring the exceptionality of international politics. In Martin Wight's famous words:

> Political theory and law are maps of experience or systems of action within the realm of normal relationships and calculable results. They are the theory of the good life. International theory is the theory of survival. What for political theory is the extreme case (as revolution, or civil war) is for international theory the regular case.
>
> (Wight, 1966: 33)

What makes the difference is the prevalence of insecurity in international politics. Domestically, state authorities organise relations between people and constrain violence. Internationally, no effective highest authority exists and therefore relations between states are inherently insecure. The extreme case of having to focus on one's survival becomes the dominant and normal predisposition in international politics.

In this reading, international politics is exceptional by nature. The contestation of this interpretation and the delineation of the implications for international politics feed much of the core debates in international studies. Is international politics really first of all about survival? Can a policy of wealth creation have precedence over security policies? Under which conditions is long-term cooperation between states possible—if at all? How to limit violence in a condition where there is no effective highest authority?

Wight's quote can also be read as an academic version of political statements that constitute international politics as exceptional by declaring it to be exceptional. The exceptionality is then not the natural condition of international politics but an outcome of the act of defining it as such. Definitional acts like these can then be seen as part of enacting international studies as a struggle for survival in which security takes precedence over other values. Emphasising the performative nature of statements makes enunciations like Wight's an object of analysis rather than a description of the world. International anarchy and the dominance of security concerns between states represent a particular conception of international politics that only exists in so far as it is actioned and reproduced through diplomatic dispositions, procedures of international politics, the teaching of international studies, and so on (Ashley, 1987, 1988). This performative interpretation is important to shift security analysis from focusing on the policies and possible strategies available for creating security in exceptional conditions, to asking how declaring the international exceptional inscribes a particular framing of the nature of political action and its stakes in global politics.

The national security tradition has been a central vehicle for mobilising exceptionalist notions of politics since the end of the Second World War. As Arnold Wolfers noted in his seminal essay of 1952 'National security as an ambiguous symbol' (Wolfers, 1952, reprinted in Wolfers, 1962: 147–65), national security replaced the notion of the national interest to articulate a distinct policy direction. Like the concept of 'national interest', it aimed at defining the key political stakes for the nation as a whole rather than for particular interest groups or mankind. While national interest covered a wider range of social and economic policy issues, national security was specifically used by those who feared that the political elite were underestimating the external dangers that the country faced. Calling upon national security constituted thus a specific demand for giving significantly more political priority to security concerns.

However, Wolfers does not explicitly bring out how calling upon national security mobilises the idea that international politics is a struggle for survival that therefore makes normal politics as conducted domestically impossible. Neither does he bring out that the call upon national security often includes—implicitly or explicitly—a spectre of existential threats to the state (such as nuclear war; destruction of sovereign independence), which are so severe that politics has to be conducted differently. This exceptionalist orientation of the national security tradition has been brought out most explicitly in Ole Wæver's conception of securitisation (and in his joint work in the 1990s with Barry Buzan and other colleagues at the then Copenhagen Peace Research Institute):

> [T]he basic definition of a security problem is something that can undercut the political order within a state and thereby 'alter the premises for all other questions'.
>
> (Wæver, 1995: 52)

'Security' is the move that takes politics beyond the established rules of the game and frames the issue either as a special kind of politics or as above politics. Securitization can thus be seen as a more extreme version of politicization.

(Buzan *et al.*, 1998: 23)

Although I will come back to a specific articulation of the national security tradition later in the chapter (see section on militarising politics), at this stage the central point is that this tradition brings out a particular technique of securitising that works on the basis of constituting an extraordinary political condition through mobilising existential dangers. Given that the international is often presented as, by definition, exceptional, it is important to reiterate that in the interpretation developed here the anarchical condition of international politics is not what makes questions of existential security dominate other concerns. Rather, calling upon the anarchical nature to inscribe the priority of existential threats into political sites is an exceptionalist political move. Exceptionalism consequently changes from a condition that one observes to a strategy of creating exceptions. Now it is possible to ask: what exactly is one doing when mobilising exceptionalist renditions of insecurity in global politics?

An answer to this question requires unpacking two issues:

- The method of exceptionalising insecurities: how does this form of securitising make an issue—like an act of clandestine violence, military recruitment, racial and ethnic identity—into something that can be mobilised to 'undercut the existing order and thereby alter the premises for all other questions'?
- The substantive political thickness of exceptionalist securitising: what does the splitting of normal and exceptional politics consist in? What transformation of politics is enacted in moving towards exceptional politics?

The next two sections focus on the first set of issues; the sections following it deal with the second.

Intensifying insecurity

Let us relocate for a little while from expressions of national security to an example of the globally oriented security discourses at the start of the 21st century. The political rationality of exceptionalism and its method of rendering political stakes are not bound to the national security tradition of the second half of the 20th century. Exceptionalising events can take place in reference to the global security order as well as to individual states.

In March 2003 Kofi Annan, then Secretary General of the United Nations, faced a serious legitimacy crisis of the UN after the US and some allies had decided to intervene in Iraq, despite not having been able to secure a vote in favour of intervention. In his speech he spoke of the end of the global security order that was institutionalised after the Second World War:

> We have come at a fork in the road. ... This may be a moment no less decisive than 1945 itself, when the United Nations was founded.
>
> (Annan, 2003)

Similarly, a few weeks after the attack on the Pentagon and the destruction of the Twin Towers in New York on 11 September 2001, Tony Blair, then prime minister of the UK, marked it as a moment of millennial change:

> In retrospect, the Millennium marked only a moment in time. It was the events of September 11 that marked a turning point in history, where we confront the dangers of the future and assess the choices facing humankind.
>
> (Blair, 2001)

Both are political moves that intensify the political significance of a security event. The decision to intervene in Iraq becomes a moment in which the global security order, as institutionalised in the UN in the wake of the Second World War, faces an existential crisis. September 11 comes to signify an extraordinary event in which violence and the narration of a new threat constitute a historical moment in which global order as well as national security (depending on whether the 'we' is read as the UK or the world) will need to be reorganised.

These two examples show a central characteristic of the form of securitising we are looking at in this chapter. Exceptionalising events intensifies the existential stakes. It increases the degree of intensity of the relation between a political unit and the object of policy, in this case the intervention in Iraq and the attacks on the US of 11 September 2001. The political value of the event, thus, does not rest upon its objective characteristics but lies in the intensity that political action establishes between a political order or unit (e.g. the state, global security order, the UN) and the event (Morgenthau, 1933: 58). From a distance it looks like there is discrepancy between the object and the intensity of the expression of the political will with regard to that object (43–44). Are the particular events of the military intervention in Iraq or the attack on the Twin Towers in New York so consequential in themselves that they constitute a 'fork in the road' or a millennial moment? That exceptionalising has a certain grotesqueness to it (Morgenthau, 1933: 44) can be gauged from arguments that try to limit the intensification by pointing out, for example, that although the event of 11 September 2001 was highly disturbing it is not the case that the US is about to be erased from the Earth, or that although over 3000 people were killed, many more people die of lack of proper health care provision and malnutrition. The point here is not whether the latter statements are right or whether they are relevant but rather to underline that exceptionalist securitising works on the basis of intensifying the political stakes; giving them an importance that does not derive from the nature of the event itself but from the degree to which one relates the significance of the event to the political order or unit.

Both Annan's and Blair's statements concentrate 'everything'—the future of the global security order, the future of humankind—into one particular point in time or into one particular political question. The event poses a test case, the outcome of which 'will frame all future questions' (Wæver, 1995: 53). The intervention in Iraq shifts from a question of its legality to a question of the future of an institutional global security order that was in place for over half a century. The event of 11 September 2001 shifts from a question of whether to change the budgetary priority of security policies or whether to reform counter-terrorism practices to a question of the future of humankind. In everyday politics, exceptionalising is thus a strategy of moving certain issues high up the political agenda, demanding absolute priority because political decisions will have extremely significant consequences.

Intensifying does not work by making a possibility actual, however. Rather it works by a more extreme assertion of 'a real and present possibility'. The exception does not consist in moving from a possibility of war between countries to an actual war, for example. Rather it makes the possibility of war the central decisive issue for understanding relations between countries at the cost of other issues, such as development, economic interdependence, wealth distribution and human rights. When debating in the UN in 2003 whether to agree the possibility to apply military force upon Saddam Hussein's regime if they did not provide the expected information on the production of weapons of mass destruction (WMD), one was not simply seeking to legitimise moving from economic sanctions to actual military intervention—although that was at stake too. One was also seeking to intensify the stakes for Saddam Hussein's regime by the 'extreme accomplishment of ... an already real and already present possibility', namely a military intervention (Derrida,

1997: 124). Rendering existential insecurities intensifies precisely by evoking to a significantly higher degree what is always an already real and present possibility (e.g. that one can be attacked).

Intensification thus requires that the possibility—of war, for example—is indeed understood as a real possibility—not a fantasy—which exceptionalist politics then make present to a higher degree. The almost ritualised repetition of the primacy of a struggle for survival, the anarchical nature of international politics and the impossibility of international political community (Ashley, 1987) does do precisely that. The anarchical view of international relations makes the real and present possibility of war and insecurity the defining characteristic of international politics. It therefore keeps the real possibility of war and political death 'alive' in politics. Exceptionalist security politics then consist in intensifying this real and present possibility that is kept alive in ritualised enactment of realist international studies knowledge and practice. The realist, anarchical reading thus sustains an understanding of international politics as one in which these exceptional moments define the moments when the international political comes into itself, when its real difference from other politics appears. Hence, it sustains the credibility and ever-present possibility for intensifying existential threats and thus the legitimacy of exceptionalist politics.

War and enemy construction

So far, one important issue has been left somewhat under-articulated. Not all intensifications are securitising. For example, a particular painting can be seen as exceptionally beautiful and original, thereby intensifying its significance for the community of artists. Or one can pay an extraordinary amount of money for a painting, thereby possibly intensifying the struggle between those seeing art as a matter of beauty and those seeing it as a matter of investment. Securitising is not in the first instance about intensifying aesthetic value, economic value or moral value. Hence the question: what makes an intensification securitising?

Implicit in the examples so far is that an existential modality foregrounding notions of death and survival in physical or metaphorical forms determines the securitising nature of politics. War, the future of mankind and the 'survival' of a global security order have been the key examples. The existentiality of the intensifying claim can be worked in several ways. Annan's statement works via asserting a moment of radical choice between old and new security orders, for example. The key vehicle of securitising in the national security tradition, however, is mobilising the imaginary of war and enemy construction.

National security does more than asserting a point in time when decisions will affect the survival of the political order. It mobilises an imaginary of war and enemies to make the struggle for survival concrete and acute. For Wolfers the turn to national security signified a particular change in what was the central stake for the US after the Second World War:

> The change from a welfare to a security interpretation of the symbol 'national interest' is understandable. Today we are living under the impact of cold war and threats of external aggression rather than of depression and social reform. ... Unless they explicitly state some other intent, spokesmen for a policy which would take the national interest as its guide can be assumed to mean that priority shall be given to measures of security.
>
> (Wolfers, 1962: 148)

Of interest to us is not to what extent this change was necessary because of the nature of the political situation, or to what extent the prioritising of security was, at least also partly, the outcome of political and bureaucratic choices and struggles in the US (Nathanson, 1988). Of importance is that national security contains and thus mobilises an understanding of politics as a clash between friends and enemies in which war is a real possibility and which demands that one takes sides. For example, US President Bush, Junior, addressing the General Assembly of the United Nations in 2003 (from which I also took Annan's quote in the previous section), states there is no neutral ground; each member needs to decide whether it is a friend or enemy of the US and its allies in the battle against 'rogue states' and 'terrorists':

> Events during the past two years have set before us the clearest divides between those who seek order and those who spread chaos. ... Between these two alternatives there is no neutral ground.
>
> (Bush, 2003)

The central place that enemy construction holds in this method of securitising can be seen from the following quote from then prime minister of the UK, Tony Blair, in the House of Commons debate on Iraq on 18 March 2003.

> The threat today is not that of the 1930s. It's not big powers going to war with each other. The ravages which fundamentalist political ideology inflicted on the 20th century are memories. The Cold War is over. Europe is at peace, if not always diplomatically. But the

world is ever more interdependent. Stock markets and economies
rise and fall together. Confidence is the key to prosperity. Insecurity
spreads like contagion. So people crave stability and order. The threat
is chaos. And there are two begetters of chaos. Tyrannical regimes
with WMD and extreme terrorist groups who profess a perverted
and false view of Islam.

(Blair, 2003)

In making the case for military intervention in Iraq he declares the end
of the Cold War and globalises the security question in terms of interdependence rather than in terms of rivalling superpowers. But equally
central is the move towards the end of the quote from mobilising a
threat of chaos, which can have many sources, to identifying particular
enemies. The tyrannical regime refers of course to Iraq in the context of
this debate.

Enemy construction intensifies the political significance of insecurity
by constituting an emergency in which 'what is held dear' faces an acute
risk of being destroyed if no decisive action is taken. It articulates a
necessity to defend the political entity; there is no choice because the
enemy and its intention to destroy cannot be wished away; enemies can
only be faced, not ignored. By implication, national defence demands
absolute priority. World politics becomes 'a test of will' with the enemy
in which one's 'ability to fend off a challenge is the criterion for forcing
the others to acknowledge [one's] sovereignty and state identity' and
thus to secure one's functional independence and territorial integrity
(Wæver, 1995: 53). If one fails, the state risks ceasing to be independent
and therefore other policy issues can no longer be addressed by the
political community.

This process also contains a demand for speed, which works against
democratic procedures of deliberation that slow down decisions so as to
give different voices and interests an input, and to allow for falsification
of policy proposals in light of evidence, alternative value evaluations, etc.
The requirement of speed derives partly from evoking acute danger.
When politicians evoke the failure of attempts to pacify Germany in the
run up to the Second World War, they do not simply make an argument
against the validity of peaceful conflict resolution but they also say that
time is up for trying to pacify enemies. A decision needs to be taken and
quickly or it will be too late. One can hear the thought: 'we do not
want another world war because of lingering too long with failing pacifi-
cation, do we?' The need for speed is also implied directly in
the imaginary of war that runs through exceptionalist securitising.
'[War] has for ever been a chain of movement, a fabrication of speed'

(Virilio, 1977: 138 (translation mine)).[1] War is not simply a test of will but also a test of one's capacity to manoeuvre quickly and pre-emptively against enemy forces.

National security further implies a demand for political unity. Contest between competing interests and social and political conflict need to be suppressed, or even eliminated, so that the country can stand united against the enemy. National security thus forces a strong identification with the political unit and its leadership (Campbell, 1998).

Wolfers places national security in the international, in a struggle between states. But the Cold War was also an ideological and a power struggle within states about the legitimacy of communist parties and social policies. Securitisation is therefore not driven by an international threat as such but by sharply dividing enemies and friends within and between political units and also the narration and enactment of imaginaries of war.

Thus far I have looked at the way in which exceptionalist securitising enacts insecurities through making issues an existential stake for political units and political order. Intensification and enemy construction are its central mechanisms. Yet the key question I am interested in is which conceptions of politics does this technique of securitising enact and, more specifically, how does it enact democratic limits. The next sections tackle this demand for politically thickening exceptionalist securitising by looking at different modes through which it renders politics and its democratic contestation.[2] I start with a constitutionalist modality of politicising in which securitising does political work by intensifying tensions between law and politics.

Insecurity between law and politics

The starting point for the political reading of exceptionalist securitising is that intensification through enemy construction is not only a mechanism for rendering insecurities but also for authorising transgressions of 'normal politics'. But what exactly is being transgressed by enacting exceptionalist securitising? What are the 'normal politics' that exceptionalist securitising postpones or transgresses? What kind of politics does it constitute instead? These questions move the analysis from the security to political rationality of exceptionalist securitising; they draw attention to its enactment of conceptions of the nature of political power and its legitimate exercise and contestation. This section deals with how this security technique enacts a constitutional concept of politics in international relations. The limitation of arbitrary politics by instituted normative limits and the legitimacy of political transgressions of these limits are its defining stakes. Transgressive politics here works the tension between law and politics or, in more constitutionalist terms, between legality and legitimacy (Dyzenhaus, 1997). In the next section, I will introduce another modality of rendering the transgression of normal politics that is closely connected to the national security tradition: transgressions of the subordination of military and policing power to civil political power.

Let us return to then Prime Minister Tony Blair's defence in the House of Commons (18 March 2003) of his decision to join the US in intervening in Iraq without the backing of the UN Security Council:

> This is the time for this house, not just this government or indeed this prime minister, but for this house to give a lead, to show that we will stand up for what we know to be right, to show that we will confront the tyrannies and dictatorships and terrorists who put our way of life at risk, to show at the moment of decision that we have the courage to do the right thing.
>
> (Blair, 2003)

The combination of identifying an existential threat with a call for a decision has been dealt with in the previous section. Here I want to focus on what is politically invested in this call for a decision. With 'political investment' I do not refer in the first instance to the fact that Tony Blair was trying to find support for the highly controversial decision to go to war but rather to what the decision is about, to what it means to say 'we will stand up for what we know to be right'.

After the UK and the US failed in obtaining legal backing through a resolution of the UN Security Council, international legal grounding of the intervention remained an important part of debate. One of the key elements was the question whether 'what is right' necessarily meant a legalistic 'right' or whether it could be morally 'right'—e.g. freeing people from a dictatorial regime or helping people in need—that transcends legal grounds. The justifications and their criticism were not strictly dichotomously formulated as an opposition between legal criteria and extra-legal (i.e. non-legal) criteria of political decisions. All kinds of mixed arguments were used. Of interest here, however, is that the securitising move is connected to enacting limits of legality. Blair's call for a decision and his reference to the notion of what is right—rather than legal—aims at transgressing the principle of legality in politics.

The principle of legality is one of the defining principles of liberal democratic politics. It refers to the subordination of political decisions to the rule of law (Weber, 1978: 812, 882; Kirchheimer, 1996 [1932]: 46; Dyzenhaus, 1997: 172). The latter restrains the arbitrary exercise of political power by means of a generalised system of rules and a system of checks and balances between the authoritative functions of the state (i.e. executive, legislature and judiciary). Only exceptional conditions can legitimise a disproportionate increase of executive power and other transgressions of the rule of law beyond what would be normally acceptable within the constitutional framework. Among the classic examples of such transgressions are rule by emergency decree, state of siege and suspending parliamentary decision making in case of war.

The relation between law and politics remains inherently ambivalent, however. If law constitutes political power, then who constitutes legal power? The democratic answer is politics, rather than theology, for example. Political authority finds itself placed between being a legally constituted power and being a law constituting power. Law and politics are thus mutually constitutive with the one practice limiting the power of the other. Extra-legal grounding of political authority—i.e. the legitimacy of law-constituting political power—is immanent to democratic notions of politics. Most systems of law also recognise that there will be situations when political authority needs to be exercised beyond the legal framework. War is one of them. The problem of exception here refers to this problem of the legitimacy of the extra-legal exercise of political power immanent to democratic normative systems. Tony Blair's call for a decision based on what one knows to be right, mobilises this particular problematic of legality and legitimacy.

The political question of legality is thus not, in the first instance, the relevance of law and its effectiveness in global politics. The central point is not to come to an evaluation of the general capacity of law to constrain political power globally, or of its capacity to effectively increase predictability and thus reduce transaction costs in international relations. Nor is the question of the limits of legality one of legal scepticism that declares the bankruptcy or non-relevance of law in global politics. What matters for the political reading of insecurity is that exceptionalist securitising inserts legal reasoning and legal circumscriptions of the legitimacy of political authority into the political field. By linking the question of the limits of legality to an existential threat, it makes the tension between legality and legitimacy and between legal and extra-legal grounds of political authority an intense political stake (Huysmans, 2006a).

It is tempting to limit these political effects of securitising international dangers to domestic politics (for example, to domestic debates about the legitimacy of foreign policy decisions) under the assumption that it requires a highly institutionalised legal system. That would be a mistake, however. Similar framings of political authorisation operate in global security politics; for example discussions of the legality of humanitarian intervention in the 1990s (e.g. Reisman, 1990, 1999) and the legitimacy of torture and extraordinary renditions after 9/11 (e.g. Mayerfeld, 2007; Liese, 2009).

The debates following the events of 11 September 2001 and the interventions in Afghanistan and Iraq are an informative illustration of how securitising frames politics around the question of the limits of legality in global politics. The validity and nature of international law featured heavily in global debates on the 'war on terror' as David Greenwood, among others, points out:

> To some observers, the attack can only be regarded as an entirely new phenomenon falling wholly outside the existing framework of international law with its emphasis on (horizontal) relations between states and (vertical) relations between state and individual. For the members of that school of thought, a challenge on this scale by a non-state actor to the one superpower calls for entirely new thinking about the nature of international law. ... The fact that the events of 11 September may demonstrate a need to re-examine some of the assumptions on which the international legal order rests does not mean that those events occurred in a legal vacuum.
>
> (Greenwood, 2002: 301)

One of the political stakes in these debates was the authorisation and limitation of the global exercise of military and counter-insurgency powers by the US. In 2002/2003 Robert Kagan provocatively argued (2002, 2003) that however much Europeans support the international rule of law in contemporary global politics, the international legal order can only exist because the US deals with events that threaten it. By implication the US cannot be continuously bound by international legal obligations:

> [A]lthough the United States has played the critical role in bringing Europe into this Kantian paradise [to exist within a peaceful international legal order], and still plays a key role in making that paradise possible, it cannot enter the paradise itself. It mans the walls but cannot walk through the gate.
>
> (Kagan, 2003: 75–76)

Why is that? How does Kagan authorise the US to sit on the walls? The answer lies with a global application of the constitutional theory of decisionism that posits the continuing need for a universal sovereign in global normative orders (Balibar, 2003).

Decisionism poses that the proper functioning of legality necessarily requires the existence of a sovereign power that transcends legality so as to decide on the exceptions (Schmitt, 1985 [1922]). Normative orders require a sovereign who is included in the normative order as the guardian of its legal form but who cannot be restrained by that order. The essence of the legal form is to come to a decision and enforce it. That is how the gap between the generalised nature of law and the particularity of events is closed. In normal circumstances judges close this gap according to the established procedures of judgement. The limit of legality is a situation in which normal procedures cannot close the gap properly and thus a decision and its enforcement is lacking. For the legal order to secure its continuity it therefore needs to include a 'highest, legally independent, underived power' (Schmitt, 1985 [1922]: 17) that has the actual capacity to decide on these exceptions. This sovereign power cannot be bound by legal principles because it needs to be able to decide when and where an exception exists and what the right course of action is in a situation where the legal procedures cannot decide. Does the act of clandestine violence in the US on 11 September 2001 indeed constitute an exceptional condition for the global security order? If so, is intervening in Afghanistan and Iraq the right course of action to protect the global security order?

The decisionist notion of sovereignty is personalised. The main focus is firmly on who decides and not on the objectified process through which decisions are reached. It thus reintroduces a subjective competence (the 'who' question) in a normative order that in liberal democratic forms tends to focus on objectified processes (the 'how' question of due process). The essence of decisionism is to legitimise a sovereign power that is simultaneously included in the normative order and excluded from it; a power that indeed 'sits on the wall' that separates the legal paradise from legal chaos.

Kagan's provocation is that 11 September 2001 showed, not the bankruptcy of the post-Second World War international normative security order and the global irrelevance of international law, but the absolute need to have a 'highest, legally independent, underived power' (Schmitt, 1985 [1922]: 17) that projects its power globally for a global normative security order to work; and that in the current situation only the US can take up this role. The events of 9/11 call upon the US to take whatever action is needed if global normative security order needs to be maintained. That is why Kagan can endorse the view that the US 'must live by a double standard'; that the US sometimes acts unilaterally 'not out of passion for unilateralism but only because … [it] has no choice *but* to act unilaterally' (Kagan, 2003: 99).

The political purpose of Kagan's insistence that the US makes it possible for the 'Kantian paradises' to exist is therefore not to deny the relevance and validity of international rule of law but to ground the US as the only power capable and willing to embrace and exercise this particular modality of power globally; what Etienne Balibar called 'universal sovereignty' (Balibar, 2003).

From a decisionist perspective, as the universal sovereign the US can, and in exceptional circumstances must, judge without being judged, disarm without disarming itself, control the authority of the global institution at the heart of the normative order (the UN) without being controlled by it, and impose financial policies without imposing them upon itself (Balibar, 2003: 134–40).

This interpretation of Kagan's intervention helps to clarify that the central contention of his text is not a legal sceptic critique of European support for the international rule of law. As a decisionist, Kagan endorses the value of an international rule of law and respects, to a certain extent, that Europe wishes to remain within its 'paradise'. The central bone of contention is that Europeans, in his view, endorse a normativist reading of the international rule of law that assumes that the international rule of law and multilateral forms of global governance can indiscriminately rule all international politics at the cost of universal sovereignty.

It is now also possible to see that Kagan's argument is not unrelated to Annan's statement that we have reached a fork in the road. Both are accounts of the limits of global legality at the start of the 21st century. They co-exist in the political contestation of the global security order. They draw on quite different views of the limit of legality and thus on the authorisation of political power in global security politics, however. Annan's intervention is ultimately in support of a more procedural and multilateral understanding of the global security order instituted within the UN. He draws on normativist arguments, which have traditionally been the main opponent of decisionism, and the main target of the latter.

Normativist approaches seek to contain political power as much as possible within generalised, legal procedures. Ideally it seeks to eliminate exceptions by proceduralising all possible transgressions of the rule of law. If this is impossible, they will seek to institute generalised rules defining how the universal sovereign should come to decisions on the exception. In the global security order this implies instituting multilateral political decision-making mechanisms, among others (Kelsen, 1967).

Annan introduces a choice between either dealing with the security crisis post-11 September 2001 within at most slightly adapted rules of the instituted global security order or accepting that this framework is not adapted to the new situation. Taking the latter path at the fork in the road is for normativists a highly exceptional moment that creates an interregnum when political power shifts from being constituted by an existing normative order to being constitutive of normative order. Normative approaches of the interregnum do not become decisionist at this point, however. The political powers are only liberated from the normative constraints for the purpose of creating a new normative order. In addition, normativist approaches will seek to develop procedures and principles that reign in the freedom of political power during the interregnum.

What makes Kagan's work fundamentally different from this view of constitutive political power in a normative interregnum is that the exceptional modality of sovereign international power—i.e. it manning the walls, it being simultaneously included and excluded from the normative order—is a necessary and permanent condition of the international rule of law. While normativist visions of international political order seek to limit the assertion of the arbitrary exercise of power as much as possible, and ideally fully submerge it in legal constraints, decisionist visions make the arbitrary exercise of power by the universal sovereign a permanent and immanent condition of normative order.

The securitising of global politics in the wake of 9/11 created debates that are centrally concerned with the authorisation of global political power and not simply with how to address insecurities. The academic debate by Kagan on the role of the US and the political one about the future of the UN were not the only debates in town. Yet, taken together, they illustrate one of the central political techniques in exceptionalist securitising and its calls for decision, whether Tony Blair's in the House of Commons or Annan's in the UN General Assembly: a rendition of conceptions of the political and political community through the politicisation of the limits of legality and normative global order. It is important to underline that this political work of exceptionalist securitising cannot be reduced to an endorsement of legal scepticism, however tempting this may be in international politics. Such a move would eliminate from sight precisely what is a central political dimension of exceptionalist securitising. As argued, this form of securitising is not a move of autonomising politics by radically separating it from law—e.g. by declaring that international law is largely irrelevant in international relations. Instead its political capacity consists in connecting a question of insecurity to an examining of the normative nature of political order and the constitution of political authority in it. This examining of global political authority takes place in a contestation of various views on the constitutive relation between law and politics and, more specifically, the limits of legality. To retain the possibility of this political reading of exceptionalist securitising one needs to keep normative systems and reasoning into the analytical loop rather than eliminating them from it.

I started this section by saying that exceptionalist securitising becomes political by drawing a line between normal and transgressive politics. I then focused on a normative constitutional modality of this contestation and in particular the limits of legality as they play out in international politics. Securitising frames politics as a struggle over the degree to which political decisions and political authority are and can be conducted within instituted normative frameworks that are aimed at containing the arbitrary exercise of political power. Subsuming political power under the rule of law or a generalised normative framework, i.e. a constitutional-like normative order, is a categorical democratic practice. The rendition of existential threats intensifies contestations of what constitutes acceptable transgressions of such a normative framework. This struggle can take many forms, including contestations of the primacy of human rights in international politics, the protection of the right to dissent, and retaining a reasonable balance between executive, judicial and parliamentary power. Yet it is always also a struggle of what constitutes an acceptable political decision and what form of political authority that enacts the limits of the normative order is legitimate. To illustrate this mode of rendering the conduct of politics, I contrasted a decisionist and normativist take on these issues. Decisionists make the presence of a universal sovereign that can act extra-legally when the normative order reaches its limits the necessary condition for a normative order to exist and continue. Normativists argue against the need for such a permanent universal sovereign. They instead seek to capture as many exceptions as possible in generalised procedures and try to limit extra-constitutional political power to short periods—interregnums—when new procedures and rights need to be instituted in response to external developments.

The normative modulation I looked at in this section is only one of the modes in which exceptionalist securitising enacts limits of democratic practice. I now turn to a second political mode of this security technique: the enactment of limits to the political power of the military and police, and their transgression in the name of security.

Militarising politics

The political enactment of exceptional insecurities is not limited to contesting the relation between legal and political power. Exceptionalism also has another historical trajectory: the *coup d'état* (Bartelson, 1997; Agamben, 2002). While the limits of the rule of law are often part of it, this history points to another issue in modern politics: the possibility of the apparatuses of organised violence to bear heavily on or even usurp civilian politics. Democracy and its limits are brought into play in contestations of the political power of the military and the police. This section explores more specifically how the national security tradition includes a mode of securitising that makes militarising politics a stake of the political game. A good starting point is Latin America in the 1960s and 70s.

> The last few years in Latin America have given birth to a new type of authoritarian regime. After Brazil, countries such as Chile, Uruguay, Argentina and Bolivia have contradicted the folklore of the despots, by installing a new form of military government.
>
> (Mattelart, 1979: 403)

Mattelart refers here to a series of *coups d'état* overturning democratising processes in Latin America in the 1960s and 70s, most notably Brazil (31 March 1964), Uruguay (27 June 1973), Chile (11 September 1973) and Argentina (24 March 1976). They instituted states of emergency and military dictatorships (Weiss Fagen, 1992: 42). These military coups were not simply a domestic or regional issue but an element of global politics. Similar developments took place in South Korea, the Philippines, Pakistan and Iran, among others (Mattelart, 2007: 81). Exchanges between national security organisations from various countries and connections to US training schools and security organisations were part of the process. Argentinean military trained counter-insurgency forces and paramilitary organisations in El Salvador, Honduras and Guatemala in the 1970s (Seri, 2010). In the 1960s, hundreds of Uruguayan police and military were sent to training sessions in Washington and the School of the Americas in Panama (Mcsherry, 2007: 21). In addition, intense global sharing of security knowledge took place in the wake of decolonisation wars (especially Algeria and Indochina) and the fight against communism. Intelligence sharing and coordinated cross-border operations were an important part of the institutional structures. Operation Condor, a secret intelligence and cross-border operations system, established officially in 1975 at the First Inter-American Working Meeting of Intelligence in Santiago, is one such example (Mcsherry, 2002). These developments found their rationale partly in the US-led war against communism during the Cold War. In that sense, they were expressions of a national security doctrine and the kinds of operation supported by national security institutions (Mattelart, 1979; Mcclintock, 1992; Mcsherry, 2002: 46; Mattelart, 2007).

The military coups in Latin America were often preceded by societal polarisation and confrontations between the military and small armed left revolutionary groups. They were not evenly matched, though, resulting in the relatively quick neutralisation of the latter. However, these 'wars' were an important vehicle 'through which the military leaders were able not only to seize power but also to establish the security apparatuses that permitted them to hold absolute power' (Weiss Fagen, 1992: 46–47). Three developments instituted the military regimes:

- laws of national security and states of exception displaced judicial protection, due process, and executive accountability;
- the establishment of professional anti-subversive forces and counter-insurgency operations;
- and, the transformation of civil society through restricting social gatherings, applying terror and instituting economic individualism.

(Weiss Fagen, 1992)

This history is of interest here not so much as a case of the imposition of military regimes but as the expression of an important aspect of the political practice of exceptionalism. Intensifying threats to national security brings into political play a tension between civilian political power and the violent coercive capacity of security organisations. Democratic notions of politics pose the subordination of the latter to the former but, given the inherent capacity of security institutions to organise violence against the political class and population, the relations between the political and the security classes remain inherently problematic. Intensifying national security claims can bring this tension into the open.

In Latin America this intensification was expressed in a national security doctrine that defined the parameters of the global military reorganisation of society (Mattelart, 1979: 403). The doctrine was developed in the Brazilian Staff College, founded by officers of the Brazilian expeditionary force in Italy in the Second World War (Mattelart, 1979: 408).[3] This doctrine was a particular Latin American version of national security but with clear links to the US and Europe, among others, as a result of meetings and joint training of security personnel (408–12).

Brazilian Field Marshal Castelo Branco, one of the leaders of the *coup d'état* of 1964 and subsequently nominated president of Brazil (1964–1967), highlights that national security is different from traditional defence:

The traditional concept of national defense places the accent upon the military aspects of security, and consequently, emphasises the problems of foreign aggression. The concept of national security is much more complete. It includes global defense of institutions, and takes into consideration psycho-social aspects, preservation of development and internal political stability. In addition the concept of security, much more explicit than that of defense, takes into account internal aggression, manifested through infiltration, ideological subversion, and guerrilla movements. All of these forms of conflict are much more likely to occur than foreign aggression.

(Field Marshal Castelo Branco quoted by Mattelart (1979: 406))

This statement expresses a relocation of the military from defence and its inter-state orientation to a more global societal reach that includes socio-economic development, the nature of domestic politics, and a vast range of practices of insurgency involving propaganda, infiltration and domestic aggression. It also paves the road for the military to usurp the civilian political field. If the military defines itself as the guardian of political stability while simultaneously redefining the security situation as including political instability, the democratic prevalence of civilian politics over security organisations is being inverted. Civilian politics becomes a threat to the state. The politics of insecurity shift from a political contest over security policies within the political field to a struggle between political organisations, the civilian government, and politically oriented organisations like unions and sections of the security apparatuses claiming political power. In other words, the civilian nature of politics turns into the defining stake of the politics of insecurity.

The necessity for the military to 'come out of the barracks' was partly justified by a theorisation of the limits of politics, and specifically democratic politics. In particular two rationales were politically as well as academically developed—not just in Latin America but also in the US and Europe. The first holds that democracies are vulnerable, more vulnerable than non-democracies, to insurgency. Today, in the wake of the events of 11 September 2001, this argument is picked up again (e.g. Homer-Dixon, 2002; Naim, 2002) but it played a significant role in the 1960s and 70s too and is part of the national security tradition more generally. For example, the Trilateral Commission, a private group founded by David Rockefeller in 1973 and comprising corporation executives and political figures from the US, Europe and Japan, wrote in its expert report of 1975 in which it evaluated the global state of affairs in light of the oil crises of the 1970s:

The more democratic a system is, indeed, the more likely it is to be endangered by intrinsic threats. Intrinsic challenges are, in this sense, more serious than extrinsic ones. ... We have come to recognize that there are potentially desirable limits to economic growth. There are also potentially desirable limits to the indefinite extension of political democracy. Democracy will have a longer life if it has a more balanced existence.

(Crozier *et al.*, 1975)

The second rationale to which Castelo Branco's statement above referred, is that economic development is a national security issue and that in developing countries it requires the intervention of the military because the political classes are too much embedded in factional interests to deliver a truly national development. In Latin America, the military became part of domestic development policy, under the banner of 'civic action', a mode of deploying the military that was granted official status when the US Department of Defense included it in its glossary in 1962 (Mattelart, 1979: 416):

Military civic action: The use of preponderantly indigenous military forces on projects useful to the local population at all levels in such fields as education, training, public works, agriculture, transportation, communications, health, sanitation, and others contributing to economic and social development, which would also serve to improve the standing of the military forces with the population. (US forces may at times advise or engage in military civic actions in overseas areas.)

(DOD, 2009)

In 'civic action' the military positions itself directly as a social and economic policy actor (Mattelart, 2007: 81ff). This is a form of militarism in Martin Shaw's terminology; it is a development in which military organisations and values seep into social structures (Shaw, 1991: 11).

Both these justifications are reflected in academic literature in the 1960s and 70s on the role of the military in transitional political regimes (e.g. Pye, 1962; Wilson, 1963) and the recruitment of social science ideas by the Pentagon in the 1960s. Moreover, the military was not only theorised as an actor contributing to national development—i.e. as an instrument used for civilian governmental tasks—but also as an actor directly intervening in the exercise of state power, as in the idea of military nation building, for example (Mattelart, 1979: 415–17, 2007: 112–15).

This extension and rearticulation of the security reach of the military was connected to a process of intensifying insecurity.[4] Castelo Branco makes this securitising move towards the end of his statement by implying that they are facing a new conflict environment. However, a move from external aggression to internal aggression is not the kernel of the doctrine. Rather, a notion of total war with a global, transnational and domestic reach, taking place not simply between states but within societal relations and comprising a wide arena of violent and non-violent instruments, holds the doctrine together:

> From a strictly military conception, war has now been converted into *total war*, a war that is economic, financial, political, psychological, and scientific, as well as being a war of armies, naval forces, and aviation; from total war to *global war*, and from global war to indivisible war, and why not admit it, permanent war.
>
> (General Golbery quoted in Mattelart
> (1979: 406—italic in original))

Such a conception of war intensifies insecurity by making existential threats global and permanent and by rendering social, economic and personal life part of the security strategy. The distinction between peace time and wartime disappears. Local inimical relations become part of a total conflict between a Western Christian world and an Eastern communist world in which all the values of Western civilisation are at stake (Mattelart, 1979: 406). The war demanded a total response, a mobilisation of society as a whole in the fight against the enemy. Everybody was drawn into the conflict, with no choice left but being either a friend or enemy. Dissenting opinion and practice become inimical to the state (e.g. dissenting world views, especially when socialist or communist, become enemy propaganda). With the enemy being immersed in society, society was fighting itself and therefore justified locating the military from the battlefield to society at large,[5] consequently deleting the distinction between military and civilian categories. At this point, politics becomes a struggle over the militarisation of politics; parties, governments and politically oriented organisations endorse, negotiate and oppose the predominance of the military logic and the colonisation of politics and governance by security institutions. The civilian nature of politics is a defining stake of this politics of insecurity.

The national security doctrine was one element in this exceptionalist securitising. The institutionalisation of counter-insurgency as a technique of involving the military in social control was another (Weiss Fagen, 1992: 55). Militarising politics went far beyond declaring a new doctrine. Particularly important was that the military took on policing roles and know-how and that policing became militarised (Huggins, 1998; Seri, 2010). It resulted in coercive capabilities that deployed military violence discriminately within societies. Policing techniques combined the organised use of violence with a capacity to make people legible so that 'dangerous' individuals can be identified within a wider social milieu that is at war with itself (Seri, 2010). For example, the official repression in Argentina started in 1975 with the presidential approval of Operativo Independencia aimed at eliminating guerrillas. A key element of this operation was the subordination of police and other security forces to the army but it also implied an intensive transfer of know-how from the police to the military (Seri, 2010).

The rearrangement of the security apparatuses also involved changes within each of these institutions in favour of hard-line commanders and officers (Weiss Fagen, 1992: 47). The creation of security forces that would wage war for ideological and political reasons upon the citizens they normally are asked to protect required internal reorganisation and retraining of the armed forces and the police forces. Security forces consist of a plurality of people. To mobilise them as a whole—as an apparatus—for something out of the ordinary, requires work (Weiss Fagen, 1992: 55–56).

The deployment of violence and terror within society is not the exclusive remit of the official security institutions. The Latin American experience is one of many that highlight how the militarising of politics—i.e. when politics becomes dominated by the preparation for and fighting of 'war'—mobilises state terror and violence through paramilitary units. Counter-insurgency implied the institution of 'clandestine and usually irregular organisations, often paramilitary in nature, which carry out extrajudicial executions and violent acts (torture, rape, arson, bombing, etc.) against clearly defined individuals or groups of people' (Campbell, 2000: 1–2). These organisations had an ambiguous relation to the formal state apparatuses. They formed 'a secret structure of the state that was, on the one hand, visible in order to create terror, but on the other hand, deniable by the state officials' (Mcsherry, 2007: 40). The latter was important to reduce the effects of international and domestic scrutiny. Hence, they are sometimes referred to as part of a parallel state, which included 'secret prisons, fleets of unmarked cars and unregistered aircraft, unofficial cemeteries, secure communications and computer systems, false papers and documentation' (Mcsherry, 2007: 16). In Latin America, they targeted political dissent but also more generally instigated terror in society to destroy people organising demands for social and economic justice. (Pion-Berlin and Lopez, 1991; Mcsherry, 2007: 14).[6]

While notions of war defined the exceptionalist securitising in Latin America and the constitution of the national security state, the political stakes were not simply about dealing with violence and insurgency. The securitising moves and the militarisation of politics were a central instrument in the political contestation of social-democratic and socialist visions of justice and socioeconomic policies. The securitising moves and the institution of the national security state were linked to a neo-liberal economic programme favouring the opening of domestic markets to foreign capital and export-oriented production (Mattelart, 1979: 418). This programme existed directly within the security practices. It extended enemies of the state from armed resistance forces, which were often small, to all people potentially supporting demands for economic and social reform. Enemies and friends were differentiated in terms of the socio-economic programme one was associated with. Socioeconomic elements were thus a defining component of the national security practice (Pion-Berlin and Lopez, 1991).[7]

This history helps us understand that exceptionalist securitising also gains political thickness through militarising politics. 'Militarising' can imply the military overthrowing of a civilian political regime but refers in the first instance to the wider process of politics being intensely organised by the logics and practices of national security and counter-insurgency. This securitising is not simply a matter of doctrine, of expressing a high degree of insecurity to mobilise security forces. As mentioned, it involves institutional and operational changes in the security apparatuses. Its key components are the military appropriating policing techniques, mobilising the police and intelligence in the service of national security and counter-insurgency, and organising specific counter-insurgency instruments that operate in the shadow of formal institutions. The militarising of politics also implies that issues of war are intensively driving politics, and that security organisations operate more heavily within and can ultimately usurp civilian politics. War-driven politics can take different forms,[8] and does not necessarily have to go hand in hand with a military *coup d'état*. For example, it can mean that military issues define the kernel of the power system in the sense that those elite dealing with war occupy the centre—the high ground—of the power elite, with those working in other areas relegated to the middle and lower levels (Mills, 1956). It can also take the form of the political elite becoming heavily dependent on permanently referring to war and related security crises for its political legitimacy (Thompson, 1980). Changes in conceptions of war from inter-state relations and contained battlefields to a social milieu at large are an integral part of these institutional and discursive changes.

One of the central implications of these processes is that the military–civilian distinction, which is central to democratic governance, becomes blurred, and that military conceptions and practices drive politics, including an increased legitimacy of violence as a tool of governance. The Latin American experience is one where these developments came together in military *coups d'état*.

Such developments are not limited to regime change and domestic politics, however. As mentioned, the militarising of politics in Latin America was strongly embedded in international cooperations, networks, training exercises and transfers of knowledge, as well as a global conflict between capitalism and communism, liberalism and socialism. Connecting domestic developments to international and transnational operations and networks is one way of bringing out the global political dimensions. Securitising draws here on a global arena. However, the mode of exceptionalist securitising discussed in this section can also take on global dimensions by taking the global as its arena of operations. Securitising then does not simply draw on global developments, conflicts, instruments and relations to locally 'fight' a 'total war'. Instead, it globalises the social milieu itself, thus, making the world as a whole a terrain of war. Such a globalising of exceptionalist securitising has been taking place since the 1990s but particularly intensely since the beginning of this century. It is not the first time, however. The Latin American experience in the 1960s and 70s was part of a similar global securitising. From the 1950s through to the 1970s national security strategies enacted to a considerable degree a global social milieu. The securitising developments were not only part of a globalising struggle between two conflicting political, social and economic projects—capitalism and communism—but also of struggles for decolonisation and post-colonial state formation and international politics. To bring out a little more how the militarising mode of the exceptionalist security technique enacts a global social terrain, I will focus on post-Cold War developments.

Since the end of the Cold War security practices have reached into a vast range of areas of governance. Security shifted from national security in a bipolarised world to a tentacular governmental practice reaching into areas such as migration, environmental protection, natural and human-made disaster relief, humanitarian actions in wars, development policy, etc. Much has been written about this extended reach of security practice and how it differs from the tradition of national security (e.g. Huysmans, 2006b; Duffield, 2007; Dalby, 2009). These developments thus do not necessarily imply exceptionalist securitising but they do contribute to placing security institutions and practices firmly within a global social milieu. For example, the development policy of the

European Union and its member states has become enmeshed with security in terms of both its rationale—its needing to serve security purposes—and security organisations executing development policy and being part of development policy making (Davidshofer, 2009). They create conditions that facilitate the mobilisation of military and police in a globalising enactment of the militarising mode of exceptionalist securitising. Cases of exceptionalist securitising can mobilise these tentacular workings of security in a global war. When the US declared a global war on terror in the wake of the attacks of 11 September 2001 that is what happened to some extent. It intensified insecurities by linking them to a global existential threat, signified by terrorism. The enemy was seen as a loose global network in which dispersed groups would connect but not necessarily in a permanent way. Enemies are seen to operate within transnational economics, hiding in various social milieus and moving across the globe. The war on terror was thus located within a global social milieu. Dispersed sites of violence in Afghanistan, New York, Iraq, the London Underground, Mogadishu, Sudan, a bus in Israel and a house in Gaza are operationally and discursively integrated into a fight against an enemy that is seen to operate globally and to exist in dispersed, loosely connected ways. The enemy is located in neighbourhoods, embassies, mountain ranges, tourism, political regimes, cyber space, etc.

Vivienne Jabri (2007) speaks of a global matrix of war to emphasise that strategies of violence are central but that they are no longer clearly organised in terms of battlefields and a fixed enemy.[9] Instead war functions as a matrix in which a wide range of security instruments, including battlefield wars, counter-insurgency operations like extraordinary renditions, nation and peace building, and intensified everyday surveillance of people, are mobilised to police a global social milieu in a dispersed form. The global matrix of war does not make war the organising principle of all global politics, however; it has not absorbed tentacular security governance in the sense that the main rationale for humanitarian security, peace building, migration policy, etc. is now the global war on terror. Environmental, migration and development policies still function within environmental, migration and development programmes. Rather, the process is one of the war on terror drawing on some of the security instruments like border controls, biometric identification, peace building and military support in humanitarian relief operations that are applied in these policy areas for the purpose of fighting enemies globally within social milieus.

Similar to counter-insurgency practice described earlier, in the global matrix of war military practice meshes intensively with policing. Alessandro Dal Lago (2004, 2008) speaks of global policing as a new type of military intervention.[10] It draws on a wide repository of counter-insurgency instruments in which various modes of violence, ranging from military intervention to incarceration, are legitimised in the name of a global war on terror. Global policing is not a process of policing simply absorbing military practice, however. Rather it refers to how military and police know-how and practice are worked into one another in the global war on terror. In 2003, a war in Iraq was followed by policing streets and people. This policing was partly done by the military.

Militarisation of politics is part of these developments, which is the reason why it makes sense to speak of a matrix of war. Militarisation does here not consist in a military coup or the military taking over from politicians but rather military rationale and knowledge organising security and political operations—politics becomes war—and the use of military violence becoming a legitimate, normalised tool of global governance (interview with Dal Lago in Huysmans and Ragazzi, 2009: section 'Global policing'). For example, Dal Lago characterises the political reaction to the attacks of 11 September 2001 as follows: 'American politicians, while retaining their prerogatives, reasoned almost exclusively in military terms, at the same time as the military tried to operate politically. ... [W]ar defines the political dynamic' (Dal Lago, 2008: 47 (my translation)). Militarisation is here not a military putsch but a reframing of politics around questions of war and military reasoning.

To retain analytical access to the democratic political stakes in these current processes of global exceptionalist securitising, it is important to keep in focus how the assertion of national security doctrine and re-organisations of the security apparatuses towards governing social relations at large led to the serious unbinding of civilian political limits to the political power of military and police in Latin America and other places in the world in the 1960s and 70s. At stake is not necessarily another wave of military *coups d'état*—despite this exceptionalist rationale being closely linked to a history of *coups d'état*—but an intensification of the militarising of politics, the meshing of policing and the military, and the deployment of violence within a global social milieu that put under pressure the democratic primacy of civilian political power.[11]

In this section, I introduced a second process that gives exceptionalist securitising political thickness. In the national security tradition intensifying insecurities does not only give rise to the question of the political limits of legality but also the militarising of politics. In the latter case, securitising enacts limits of democracy by raising the political and governmental significance of the military and police, and by making the subordination of the official apparatuses of organised violence to civilian politics a stake of the political game. Regime change—a move from democratic to non-democratic military regimes—can be part of this security technique, as was very explicitly the case in some Latin American countries in the 1960s and 70s, but does not necessarily define it. Currently of more immediate concern are the meshing of military and police powers and the militarisation of civilian political power in the enactment of a global matrix of war that extends military and counter-insurgency operations across a heterogeneous, multifaceted and loosely connected global social milieu.

Intimacy and resistance

The previous two sections dealt with how the technique of exceptional securitising enacts questions of political authorisation and limits of democracy. They focused on two modalities in which existential intensifications of insecurity are brought to bear on political relations: (a) raising the limits of legality and (b) enhancing the political presence of apparatuses of violence, in particular the military and police, and the militarisation of politics. Both techniques also enact an elitist view of politics. They define political strategic interaction in the first instance as a matter of professionals, politicians, security professionals and the legal profession in one case, and politicians, military, police and paramilitary in the other. Focusing on elite politics, however, has a drawback. It tends to reduce the visibility of the pervasive presence of exceptionalist securitising in everyday life and intimate relations. Less elitist sites and modes of political contestation easily move into the background of the analysis, if they are not simply ignored. This section aims at correcting the reproduction of an elitist view of the politics of insecurity that are enacted in exceptionalist modes of securitising. It does this by drawing on examples of protests to security actions that make public how security practices and actors pervade everyday relations and intimate spheres of life. In doing so, these protests do not only allow us a more detailed view of the workings of exceptionalist securitising but also show that the politics of exceptionalism are not limited to negotiations and struggles between elites.[12]

Exceptionalist security practices deploy legal, military, policing and political resources, and rhetoric in conflict and wars but they also deploy these to govern the intimacy of everyday practice in the name of global or national security. As Juliana Ochs states in her ethnography of security and suspicion in everyday life in Israel: 'Security is a set of military strategies and political beliefs, but it is also a guiding force for daily experience. ... Security is a national discourse and partisan rallying cry that also assumes social, material, and aesthetic forms in daily life' (Ochs, 2011: 3). If aspects of everyday life are part of exceptionalist security practice, does this then not imply that the intimacies of everyday practice can become sites of political contestation themselves? If security practice works the intimacy of everyday life through violence, extensive prohibitions and extended surveillance, it embeds itself in intimate and everyday relations, thus allowing resistance to emerge that draws on these relations. This enveloping of security practice in the everyday (Huysmans, 2009) is most visible when exceptionalist securitising displaces insecurities from the battlefield to social milieus, when the enemy is understood to operate within everyday practices of crossing borders, working for a labour union, and eating with friends and family. The counter-insurgency strategy of dividing up cities and neighbourhoods into small quarters and organising the movement of people by means of various checkpoints is one way of pervading the everyday practice of people. In the decolonisation struggle in Algeria, the French security forces used it to control the Algerian armed resistance in the capital Algiers. Someone was *hors-la-loi* (outside the law) when they were not back in their quarters at the time they should be. Simply being outside the area at the time of the curfew made the person subversive and therefore a legitimate target of security forces (Mattelart, 2007: 103–4).[13]

Border controls are another example. For Mark Salter (2006) the border is a permanent state of exception. Borders are sites where individuals encounter the discretionary power of political authorities represented by border guards. At the US border the defence of the national territory prevails over the protection of the individual and their rights. Individuals, including citizens of the US, thus find themselves at the border checkpoint in a state of postponed rights. What is of special interest is the intimate nature of this condition of exceptionality. The individual directly faces a three-fold relation of authority in what is in many ways an intimate encounter with the bodyguard. They are rights holders but their rights are to some extent suspended until the legality and safety of their passage is established. They are placed as subjects needing to confess their status and intentionality to the authorities. They are subjected to the judgement and discretion of border guards. In this complex site, collective notions of danger and suspicion are worked onto individual bodies and through confessionary narrations in which individuals have to 'confess' why they are coming to the US. Salter speaks of 'a confessionary complex' in which security becomes an intimate 'corporeal documentary affair' (Salter, 2006: 181).

Yet is this confessionary encounter really an enactment of exceptionalist securitising? Not all confessionary encounters at the border constitute necessarily a site of exceptional securitising. For that to be the case the intimate everyday confessionary interaction between the border guards, the routines of profiling and the individual traveller need to operate within an intensified enactment of insecurity. Exceptionalist securitising does this by integrating the intimacy at the border into a conception of 'war'. The exceptional status of the border becomes enacted not in terms of a routinised defence of the territory but the routines are deployed in and come to symbolise a fight against violent enemies that pose an existential threat to the polity. That is what counter-terrorist policies did to encounters at the border after 9/11 and is also one of the reasons— but of course not the only one—why border studies became a growth area in security studies.

Governing through intimate relations also makes intimacy a political resource. Intimate everyday elements of life can be drawn on and linked up to other visions of collective political life as a way of questioning the legitimacy of securitising authority. I want to briefly draw on two examples to illustrate that interpreting the politics of exceptional insecurity does not have to start necessarily from the power elite and from unpacking the technique and political thickness of securitising. It can also start from practices drawing on the intimacy of everyday encounters to contest exceptionalist securitising.[14]

The first example is Machsom Watch in Israel (Naaman, 2006; Halperin, 2007; Braverman, 2008; Carter Hallward, 2008; Levy and Mizrahi, 2008). Machsom Watch was founded in 2001 by peace-activist Israeli women to protest against the Israeli occupation of Palestinian territories and the repression of the Palestinian people (www.machsomwatch.org/en). Their main activity consisted in monitoring checkpoints in Israel and, in particular, in the Westbank ('machsom' means 'checkpoint'). The documentation is not in the first instance about spectacular events (e.g. when somebody gets shot or when a crisis emerges) but about the everyday conditions and practices of people moving and of border control in the name of national security. Most of it is banal.

> Bethlehem (300): close to ('Jerusalem Envelope') Wall in north Bethlehem, cutting West Bank off from East Jerusalem. This checkpoint which is the only entrance to Israel for residents of southern West Bank, Hebron and satellites, has a sophisticated terminal.

> Bethlehem (300), Etzion DCL, Tue 30.4.13, Morning

> We asked the people crowding out on the sidewalks: how is it going today? The answer is—not well. Inside the terminal it is packed, four windows are slowly operating. One group passes and then there is a break. And then again in comes a new wave of

people. It seems that people cross in groups, which slows the pace. Odah, the police officer at the crossing enlists to assist with the checking. The officer tells us the number of people using the CP increased significantly because it includes people who bypass the Kalandia Checkpoint whenever it's possible. By 7:10 AM the crossing has been completed, and a total of 5,000 people had passed.

(www.machsomwatch.org/en/reports/checkpoints/
30/04/2013/morning/23091 [Accessed 2 May 2013])

Bethlehem (300), Fri 19.4.13, Morning

Three windows are open. Many Palestinians are passing but according to their reports the passing doesn't take long: they say that there are not many people on the Palestinian side and that it takes about 15 minutes to pass. Towards the end of the shift an ecumenical volunteer passed and reported it took her 25 minutes. A strange event at the beginning of the shift: an older woman passed along with two men, all of a sudden soldiers run toward her claiming she was not checked in the sleeve on the Palestinians side and had surpassed it (how is that possible?). They took her back, checked her and demanded her to return to the other side and go through the security check. Eventually she came back and crossed over to Jerusalem. By the end of the shift: a 45 year old man presented his permit and was turned down. When I asked the soldier at the window why he was refused passage, the soldier said that the permit was no longer valid. The man stood there between the windows, probably hoping for a miracle. A few minutes later, a security guard led him into an inner room. 5 minutes later the security guard came out apparently summoned by a soldier in window 1 and asked, 'Where is the illegal guy?' They pointed at a disheveled young man 25 years old and led him through the same door to an inner room. 15 minutes later he came out with the two men, wagged his finger, rebuked them, and warned them lest they try again to infiltrate, and followed them to make sure they return to Bethlehem.

(www.machsomwatch.org/en/reports/checkpoints/19/04/2013/
morning/23004?checkpoint=320 [Accessed 2 May 2013])

Checkpoints are instruments of Israel's security policy controlling and restricting the movement of Palestinians partly in the name of exceptional security threats posed by suicide bombers. Machsom Watch documents that they are sites of asymmetrical power relations where the Israeli state asserts its power over the everyday life of Palestinians.

Bethlehem, May 9, 2010:

07:15 1500 have crossed. There are still hundreds of people on the Bethlehem side.

The humanitarian line was opened only at 05:25. The CP was opened at 04:45. One metal detector only was operating and this caused major uproar. A second one was put in operation and about 500 people passed quickly. Then one of them again went out of order and it took Alex from the DCO Etsion to put some order back. Workers tried to use the humanitarian line and had to be brought back, they tried to use the turnstile in the wrong direction and had to be disciplined, etc.

07:30 2044 have crossed. 07:45 2164 people crossed. In other words, 664 people crossed in half an hour. But it was at the wrong time. By now the laborers have lost an hour or two of work.

(www.machsomwatch.org/en/reports/checkpoints/23/05/2010/ morning/15508 [Accessed 2 May 2013])

Checkpoints can be suddenly closed, people can be detained for hours or minutes. As a result many everyday activities, like family visits, going to the market, and working across borders become unpredictable and ultimately severely restricted.

In documenting the practices that take place at the checkpoint, Machsom Watch seeks to partly displace the image of the border as a site of confrontation with the image of it being a site of everyday human interaction. People queue and talk, they are on their way to visit family, to see a doctor, to trade goods. Soldiers and police interact with the people passing through the checkpoint in various ways. By bringing out the intimate work of soldiering and checking, they work against the idea that security policy dealing with exceptional threats is all that there is to checkpoints. Danger, security and the discretionary exercise of sovereign power are submerged within a complex set of interactions, many of which have nothing to do with existential security but with banal everyday mobility and its regulation (Carter Hallward, 2008).

This political practice seeks to dislocate the legitimacy and taken-for-granted necessity of security practices by means of a method of counter-monitoring that is confrontational but somehow also very mundane and therefore not that easy to justifiably shut down. It turns a security practice that seeks to impose exceptionality on everyday social practice on its head. It starts from the very banality of practices at the checkpoint to show that the security practice is submerged within the complexity and diversity of everyday practices (see also e.g. Constantinou, 2008) and therefore cannot claim to just do security—i.e. defence against exceptional threats—but has all kinds of disturbing and dehumanising effect on the way in which people conduct their everyday interactions. It brings this out in minute and repetitive detail in a continuous stream of reports. In that sense Machsom Watch is a political activist translation of the intimacy of borders and checkpoints.

Their political activism inserts a practice of counter-gazing (Braverman, 2008)—or counter-monitoring—in sites that are established to monitor 'the others'. By monitoring the monitors, Machsom Watch disrupts the regime of visibility instituted at checkpoints; it brings into view what normally is left invisible. The activists do more than monitoring, however. They become an active third party that mediates and interferes in various situations that arise.

> 06:10   A'anin checkpoint 25 April 2013
>
> Husni, the redhead, approached us—his 8-year old grandson has a blood disease. He has an appointment this coming Sunday at Hadassah hospital in Jerusalem, but they haven't yet been able to obtain an entry permit to Israel. With Chana Barg's help we learned that the appointment doesn't yet appear in any hospital's registry. We explained to Husni what he must do; let's hope he manages to complete the complicated arrangements by Sunday.
>
> (www.machsomwatch.org/en/reports/checkpoints/25/04/2013/ morning/23040 [Accessed 2 May 2013])

The political effects of these interferences remain ambivalent. Within Machsom Watch this has been a point of debate, especially whether humanitarian actions risk marginalising the political challenge to the checkpoints themselves and their securitising of the relation between Israel and Palestinians. Does one become complicit in the security policy one opposes by trying to mitigate its negative effects? This issue is not easy to resolve and requires careful negotiating, especially in a form of activism that partly draws on showing intimately the human cost of checkpoints (Huysmans and Angel Eye Media, 2010). It partly arises precisely because Machsom Watch upsets the institutional regime of checkpoints by introducing a third party, which monitors the monitors and mediates situations directly, in a site that is typically dichotomously defined as a confrontation between a people or their soldier representatives and their potential enemies (Braverman, 2008).

The political mobilisation of counter-gazing demands that documenting the intimacy and everydayness of what happens at the checkpoint is connected to a more general questioning of the collective stakes in security policies. Bringing out how the intimacy of exceptional securitising forcefully inscribes dichotomous collective boundaries between Israelis and Palestinians on bodies and whole populations, and suggesting their possible counterproductive effects because they reinforce the alienation of Palestinians is one way this is done. Machsom Watch also politicises the dehumanising subordination of people by connecting the documenting of series of complex practices of humiliation and discretionary assertions of power to questions of human rights, claims of justice and demands of respect for the memory of the Holocaust. By sometimes framing the practices at the checkpoints as a violation of the memory of the Holocaust, for example, it draws on a central aspect of the self-identification of Israel to challenge the exceptionalist policies of instituting checkpoints (Carter Hallward, 2008: 23–24).

This politics of insecurity draws on the intimacy of the security practice to open up a struggle over the collective stake of the living together of Israelis and Palestinians that exceptionalist securitising seeks to push aside in the name of the necessity to prioritise security. Such a political contestation is never simply about the collective stakes as such but also about who has the authority, and on what grounds, to frame what is collectively at stake. In the securitised context of the checkpoint, Machsom Watch's counter-gazing is a claim to authority, to legitimately contest among others how security practice renders living together, Israel's identity and relation to the Palestinians, and justifications of collective violence. In addition it seeks to make everyday practice and grassroots activism an inherent part of what is often an elitist politics of insecurity by challenging the exceptionalism of the situation.

Machsom Watch is only one example of political activism drawing on intimate relations to challenge the institutionalisation of exceptionalist securitising.[15] In Latin America another such politics revolved around the disappeared—the people who were killed by the security agencies and whose bodies they made disappear, thus instigating a doubt or ambivalence about their death. Through disappearances, the security agencies expressed the power they hold over individuals and, through the terror they thus create, over society (Garcia Castro, 1996–97). The absence of the bodies, however, also excluded mourning to be completed for the relatives. They could not reach closure. Hence the disappeared remained subjects of strong emotional attachment and were therefore in a sense more intensely present than those who died but were properly buried (Garcia Castro, 1996–97: paragraph 4 online version). This potentially makes the disappeared into a resource for political action and prevents forgetting (Frazier, 1999: 110). Jenny Edkins (2003), in her analysis of traumas in Western wars, speaks more generally of trauma-time—i.e. a time where things are disrupted, do not run their expected course—as moments where political questions emerge.

The disappearances gave rise to a particular form of resistance. Women organised to find out about disappeared relatives and friends, resulting in movements such as the Mothers of the Plaza de Mayo in Argentina and the Association of Families of Detained-Disappeared (AFDD) in Chile. The AFDD publicly expressed the search for knowing about what happened to their sons, daughters, husbands and friends by dressing themselves in pictures of their disappeared relatives and friends. They also performed a traditional dance in a way that retained the empty place of the disappeared dancing partners (Garcia Castro, 1996–97: paragraph 13 online version). Their opposition drew on a continuous affective link to the disappeared. This practice was not one of classical armed resistance or mass demonstrations but mobilised the intimacy of everyday relations and emotions against the way in which coercive power seeks to create fear and political docility (Garcia Castro, 1996–97: paragraphs 3 & 7 online version).

To make the action politically relevant, the women needed to give their personal bonds and loss relevance for Chilean society as a whole (Garcia Castro, 1996–97: fn 15). Finding out what happened to disappeared relatives opened a window into what they did (e.g. being a member of a union). Understanding the reason for their disappearances revived the political ideas they enacted and for which they were disappeared (Garcia Castro, 1996–97: paragraph 10 online version). The women's protests therefore mixed manifestations of personal loss with discontent over the vision of Chilean society that the military regimes instituted and enacted. Their dances, marches and silences also reinserted traces of democratic politics by making the workings of military governance visible, reiterating the violence security forces perpetrated on Chilean society, and more generally by seeking a disruptive voice in a highly constraining political situation. Like in the case of Machsom Watch, these protests were a struggle over who has the authority to speak for Chilean society and to decide the values that this society represents. That is one of the reasons for their continuing political relevance after the return to democratic government; they remain a struggle over who can legitimately speak for Chile and Chile's past (Garcia Castro, 1996–97: paragraph 3 online version).

Both these examples draw a more complex picture of the politics of insecurity. They support two important analytical points that question an exclusive focus on political and security elites for understanding securitisation and its contestation. First, besides constitutional changes, transgressions of legality and the militarisation of politics, exceptional security practice works itself into intimate and everyday relations. This is most visible in cases like the military coups in Latin America and decolonisation struggles when the military becomes mixed with policing and focuses on social milieus as theatres of operation. But the intimate work of exceptionalist security practice can also be encountered in less spectacular settings like changes in border controls since the events of 11 September 2001 when routine body searches and confessional demands intensified as part of a war on terror. The second analytical point is that an analysis of exceptionalist securitising and its political contestation can, rather than focusing on elite politics, analyse how people are affected in their intimate and everyday relations and how they and activists draw on it to contest the securitising policies and the claims of authority that are made in the name of exceptional threats. As a technique, exceptionalist securitising is never simply an acting out of its rationality but also is shaped by how it enacts a field of political contestation. That field and the determination of the legitimate limits to transgressions of democratic governance are not the exclusive remit of political, judicial and security professionals.

Both these analytical points are not present in most security analyses in international studies, which tend to lock security practice into inter-state and diplomatic relations, notions of battlefield and more generally elite politics.[16] As feminist security analysis has argued, this comes at the cost of a distorted understanding of how power relations and political contestation work. In reproducing a separation between an elite politics and everyday, intimate, private relations that security policies govern but that remain outside of that which is called politics, such an analysis reiterates a delimitation of the political as the privileged realm of the political and security class. This is especially problematic when exceptionalist security practice itself explicitly silences how it is enveloped by and works security forcefully and often violently into intimate, everyday relations. Retaining a place for the politics of intimacy and the everyday in security analysis is crucial to avoid reproducing in the analytical set up the authorisation claim, which is immanent to exceptional securitising, that security politics is for an exceptional class and especially so under the circumstances of intense existential insecurity. Developing a concept of the intimate politics of exceptionalist insecurity provides an important opening to a more complex and adequate understanding of how exceptionalist securitising works on societies and polities and how it is politically contested.

Conclusion

This chapter dealt with a particular technique of securitising, which authorises exceptional political practice on the grounds that the political community faces an extraordinary security crisis that normal politics cannot cope with. By intensifying the threat of enemies and the possibility of war, it shifts the political terrain to a contest of the need for and limits of transgressing democratically instituted restraints of governmental power, including the degree to which security institutions can take on political functions. As a political technique, exceptionalist securitising thus enacts—both in the sense of acting out and bringing into being—conceptions of distinctions between normal and exceptional politics, limits of infringing normal politics and demands to transgress these limits. In the context of this book, the focus is in particular on how securitising exceptionalises democratic practice by enacting limits to democratic politics and seeking to authorise transgressions into extra-democratic or non-democratic practice (like dictatorship).

A significant proportion of international studies has ritualised such an exceptionalist reading of politics by sharply separating the domestic from the international. In its conception of international politics, insecurities can be held in check domestically but the lack of an overarching global authority and an effective international rule of law make international politics one big security problem. This notion of the international reiterates the ever-present possibility of being conquered by other political units as the constitutive political stake that defines international politics. Insecurity therefore needs to be dealt with before anything else can be considered. Compared to domestic politics in modern states, the international thus emerges as an exceptional political site; the international is the limit of normal politics.

Exceptionalist securitising intensifies this ritualised rendition of international politics by identifying acute existential threats. In other words, rather than ritualistic enacting a distinction between normal domestic and exceptional international politics, securitising creates an exceptional situation in which the survival of the political unit, whether state or international order, is critically threatened. In such moments the sharp distinction between domestic and international often significantly blurs and gives way to a transversal deployment of the boundary between the normal and exceptional. In other words, although the ritualised rendition of the international reproduces exceptionalist political moves by defining the international as the realm of exceptional politics, the political work of securitising is not a more dramatic expression of the distinction between a domestic realm of harmony and an international struggle for survival. In the case of the national security tradition, the intensification of insecurity often explicitly places the boundary between the normal and exceptional also within the domestic, thereby blurring the differentiation between an international exceptionality and the domestic normality. The idea of the internal communist enemy, linking inter-state war to war in a social milieu and organising politics in terms of civil war is one example of how the political work of exceptionalist securitising cannot be captured by reproducing a distinction between the international and the national but needs to be thought of in the first instance, in terms of how it constitutes political terrains through conceptions of boundaries between normal and exceptional politics, and how it modulates demands for and resistance to transgressions of normal and, more specifically for the purpose of this book, democratic politics.

Because exceptionalist securitising asserts special insecurities that make the normal business of democratic politics problematic, it is tempting to read securitising as a secondary phenomenon that works upon an already given form of normal democratic politics. However, such a reading misses that exceptionalist securitising also defines what counts as normal or democratic in the very act of identifying what is considered abnormal or non-democratic. Constituting what is normal through practices of identifying what is abnormal is quite a widespread method. We define exceptions all the time to constitute our normality—through defining madness we define what it means to be mentally sane, through defining deviancy we define law abiding, etc. It raises an important point, however. The political question of securitising is not simply one of transgressing an existing political condition; it is also a question of how securitising renders what constitutes normal democratic practice. Exceptionalist securitising is therefore never simply the imposition of exceptional rule but always the opening up of a political terrain of contestation of democratic political organisation and authorisation. This politics of exceptional insecurity brings into play various conceptions of both democratic and transgressive politics; and it retains some place for those who defend the 'normal side' of democratic politics against exceptionalism.

The boundary between normal and exceptional is not a sharp line between two fixed substantive conceptions, one of democratic politics and another of dictatorial politics. It is a murky and fractioned political terrain in which specific definitions of the limits of democracy are enacted and define the substantive political issues. The chapter explored two modes of rendering limits to democratic practice that give the exceptionalist technique of securitising political thickness by placing it into a contest over substantive criteria of the authorisation of political authority and legitimate methods of governing. The first was the limit to constitutional normative restraints on executive political power.

Democracy emerges as government under the rule of law, and securitising takes on political dimensions when the mobilisation of existential
insecurities implies a contestation of the limits that generalised normative
arrangements set to politics. Exceptionalist securitising challenges democracy through enacting limits of the democratic principle of legality that
demands the subordination of arbitrary political power to the rule of
law. It includes principles like the primacy of fundamental rights, checks
and balances between judicial, executive and legislative power, and defining
generalised procedures for decision making and the conditions and procedures for transgressing them. In the chapter, I extended this principle
of legality to quasi-constitutional or generalised normative arrangements
that are to be applied across cases in international politics. The judicial
profession, diplomats and professional politicians are key actors in this
political terrain. The central issue is not an evaluation of the validity
and relevance of law in global politics but more specifically of whether
and how lawyers, judicial institutions and legal reasoning become
embedded in the politics of insecurity through demands for transgressing
normative arrangements. The relations of domination and subordination
between lawyers, judges, diplomats, politicians and the security institutions in a struggle over the authorisation of constitutional and legal reasoning in global politics and the limits of normative restraints on political
power, both in the form of constitutions and international normative
arrangements, define this political terrain. Analysing the exceptional
politics of insecurity in terms of the politicisation of the limits of legality
draws attention to sites like parliamentary debates on the legality of
intervention, debates in the UN Security Council, the interpretation of
fundamental rights in the constitutional court in the US, the constitution
of transnational legal networks and the International Criminal Court. In the
chapter, I focused on debates related to the intervention in Iraq in 2003
to illustrate how this mode of exceptionalist securitising enacts constitutional conceptions of politics and brings them to bear upon international
politics.

The second substantive limit of democratic politics that I looked at was
the limits of civilian power and the militarisation of politics. Securitising
here enacts the expansion of political functions of the military and police,
and the encroaching of a military rationale on politics in the name of
limits of civilian politics. Intensified existential threats are mobilised together with narratives of the limits of civilian, democratic politics (for
example, for delivering effective economic development) to justify
demands for a more central political role of the military and other
apparatuses of organised violence. Enacting the limits of civilian politics
includes more than military *coups d'état* and other forms of the military

encroaching on the political field. The chapter touched on, among others: the military and police working more closely together and intensifying exchanges of operational know-how; internalising external enemies in the form of fifth columns and terrorists hiding in society; and defining society as a whole as a milieu from which to extract dangerous elements. These are significant developments that unbind democratic limits to the political use of organised violence and the political function of the military and other security apparatuses. I used the notion of militarising politics for this mode of substantively opening a political terrain through exceptionalist securitising. In some way, the issue is not simply about the role of the military but about opening a political terrain in which Clausewitz's dictum is inverted. This mode of securitising more generally shifts the political debate from taking war as the continuation of politics and thus positioning civilian politics as dominant, to taking politics as the continuation of war and thus sustaining the pervasion of the political field by professionals of the conduct of war. Military–civilian relations as well as the organisation of counter-insurgency practice by and within democracies are an important inroad into analysing this particular politicisation of the limits of democracy.

At stake is the authorisation of political power of security apparatuses and the structuration of the political field through military and policing rationales, thereby legitimating excessive use of violence. The relations and power struggles between civilian politicians and security professionals are one important issue to look at. Another is whether intensifications of definitions of war signify a restructuring of security apparatuses so that they can enact social milieus globally, with special attention to the arrangement for counter-insurgency operations. Evaluating whether legitimacy in civilian politics has become strongly dependent on an imaginary of war and a military rationale, is a further one. In the chapter, I took the development of a national security doctrine and military rule in Latin America as the key example to introduce this mode of securitising. I extended the analysis to more contemporary reflections on how war is becoming a modus operandi for acting on a global social milieu in the war on terrorism and how this re-enacts the pervasion of military and other security apparatuses in society and subordinations of politics to war.

Both modes of exceptionalist securitising draw attention to political negotiations and struggles between elites—especially political, security and juridical elites. Yet the political contestations and negotiations of exceptionalist securitising and its enactment of democratic limits are not only defined by elite politics but also by grassroots protests, social movements and multiple other forms of political action. In the final section of the chapter, I introduced this aspect by looking at how protests against exceptional securitising draw on everyday and intimate effects of securitising. It allowed me to correct the often-given impression that exceptionalist security practice is, in the first instance, a matter of high politics and security of the state. The narrative of exceptionality thrives on the constitution of situations that claim to be of higher concern than the immediate matters that people routinely negotiate in their everyday lives. In such cases, showing how exceptionalist securitising often works the boundary between the normal democratic and the exceptional into intimate and everyday relations and thus has a serious impact on how people can go on with the usual business of life is an important analytical and political correction. Keeping such intimate work of security practice in view sensitises the analysis of insecurity to practices that resist securitising. It shows how the excessive effects of securitising on everyday life can lead to political action that questions the authority of security organisations and the legitimacy of exceptional security practices. In the chapter, I looked in particular at the activism of Machsom Watch (Checkpoint Watch) in Israel and also briefly at protests by the Association of Families of Detained-Disappeared against 'disappearances' in Chile.

Although the exceptionalist security technique is the most familiar one in international studies and continues to render insecurities and politicisations of democratic limits, there is another important technique of securitising that has been on the rise, governs an increasing variety of issues and raises distinct challenges to democratic practice. Different from exceptionalist securitising, it unbinds security and its democratic limits in a non-intensive way and by dispersing insecurities transversally across various areas of life. In the next chapter, I develop the notion of 'diffusing insecurities' to introduce this non-intensive technique of unbinding security.

Notes

1 Original French text: ' ... la guerre est depuis toujours un chantier de movement, une fabrique de vitesse'.
2 For an excellent and more extensive analysis of the political dimensions of exceptionalism and a critical method of approaching questions of exceptionalism in the context of counter-terrorist policies, see Andrew Neal's *Exceptionalism and the politics of counter-terrorism* (2010).
3 The Brazilian General Golbery do Couto e Silva was one of the leading figures in developing and systematising the doctrine.
4 For an analysis of the internal deployment of military forces and exceptional securitising outside Latin America, see issue 56 of the journal *Cultures et conflicts* on Northern Ireland (Bigo and Guittet, 2004).
5 This development reflects the French military's evaluation of why they lost in Indochina—and later in Algiers—despite material military superiority (Mattelart, 2007: 100ff).

6 Paramilitary forces are not a phenomenon limited to military regimes. They can also operate within democratic regimes: see, for example, Emmanuel-Pierre Guittet's excellent analysis of post-Franco Spain (Guittet, 2006).

7 For an example of how paramilitary violence operates in a local community, including after the end of a military regime, see Nancy Scheper-Hughes's chapter on paramilitary violence in her ethnography of violence in everyday life in Brazil (Scheper-Hughes, 1992: 216–67).

8 For a succinct and insightful discussion, see Martin Shaw's *Post-military society* (Shaw, 1991: 64–108).

9 Others criticise using war in this way. David Chandler, for example, argues that such a conflict is not a war because there are no clear internationally defined stakes and because there is no strategic calculation possible without having a fixed enemy (Chandler, 2009).

10 Alessandro Dal Lago's notion of global policing is not limited to the war on terror but expresses a more general shift he observes in how the US practises global hegemony and how the use of violence shifts from traditional notions of war and intervention in an inter-state setting to a more continuous use of a wider range of violence in global politics—e.g. wars are not declared and territorial state boundaries do not organise the theatres of war. See Dal Lago and Palidda, 2010, and for a different take on similar developments in war: Dillon and Reid, 2009.

11 I did not have space to include another key element of this process of securitising eating into civilian political power: the rise of global assemblages of private military and security companies (Leander, 2005; Abrahamsen and Williams, 2010; Leander, 2010, 2013).

12 For a work that takes this point much further than I can do here, see Cynthia Enloe's interpretation of how eight women enact and are immersed in the politics of the Iraq war (Enloe, 2010).

13 Gillo Pontecorvo's movie *The Battle of Algiers* remains a classic in showing the intimate nature of security practice and the close relation between everyday life and the violence of decolonisation wars.

14 In international studies, feminism in particular has played a crucial role in showing how everyday, intimate relations are entangled with the exercise of power (e.g. Enloe, 1989; Sylvester, 2002; Wibben, 2011).

15 The politics of Machsom Watch are more complex than I have been able to set out in this short section. It includes among others gender politics, the re-appropriation of critical politics by the state and the limits of humanitarian arguments. For more on these and other aspects, see, among others, Braverman (2008), Carter Hallward (2008), Levy (2008), Halperin (2007), Huysmans and Angel Eye Media (2010) and Naaman (2006).

16 There are some notable exceptions, of course, most importantly feminist security studies (for an overview: Wibben, 2011) and anthropologically inspired works like *Cultures of insecurity* (Weldes *et al.*, 1999).

4 Diffusing insecurities

In attempting to discourage consumers from buying pirated copies of DVDs in the UK, in around 2006 a flyer was inserted in DVD cases that presented piracy as part of a wider criminal activity with serious human costs. The flyer said:

> Immigration Crime. By rejecting DVD piracy you're helping us tackle it. You may remember the 21 Chinese illegal immigrants who tragically lost their lives whilst picking cockles in Morecambe Bay. Investigations by Lancashire Police led to the houses of the men responsible for their deaths. There they found over 4,000 counterfeit DVDs and computers containing counterfeit material. Lin Liang Ren and Lin Mu Yong were charged with 21 counts of manslaughter, perverting the Course of Justice, assisting and facilitating illegal immigration and manufacturing of false work permits. They received a total of 23 years imprisonment between them. DVD piracy costs too much. Don't support it. Report it. 0845 60 34567.[1]

Migration, international crime, criminal justice, copyright piracy ... .The flyer seems to have taken us miles away from international relations, the anarchical condition of global political life, and the rendition of existential threats to states and societies. It highlights global societal processes, policing, consumption and individual deaths; people, as immigrants, criminals and consumers, enacting a complex set of transversal relations. No immediate presence of the strategic practice of states, the assertion of national security and exceptionalist enactments of global politics. The flyer does mobilise insecurities but without being exceptionalist in its technique of securitising. The death of immigrants is not an emergency or even something out of the ordinary. Seeking to escape the structures of the inter-state system comes sometimes at a high cost for the individuals involved but it does not in itself constitute a national or global security crisis. The same can be said about international criminal networks. They are part and parcel of the global labour market and trade relations. The events are concluded with the British criminal justice system having been able to exert justice through its normal institutional practices.

Both the method of circulating insecurities by means of a flyer in a DVD and the mode of connecting insecurities in the discourse of the flyer gives us an opening to explore a form of securitising that differs from the exceptionalist understanding of insecurity set out so far. Insecurities are clearly circulated through the flyer but they do not come together in a collective catastrophe or in an urgent societal security threat. For the latter, one is better off watching some of the movies like *Superman Returning* in which Superman returns to save the world once more from a catastrophic security threat unleashed upon the Earth by an evil person and his minions. In contrast, the flyer inserts insecurity in non-spectacular and unexceptional modes into the everyday lives of consumers. Buying a counterfeit DVD is not a national or global emergency but connects the consumer to trade relations that are saturated with insecurities. By buying such a DVD one gets involved in the danger of picking cockles, the death of Chinese immigrants, trafficking of people, trading counterfeit DVDs, fraudulent identities and disregard for the justice system. Consumers find themselves connected to a network of insecurities.

This chapter develops the concept of diffusing insecurities to create an opening towards studying similar securitising practices that unbind security and that work limits of democratic practice through associative dispersing of insecurities in non-intensifying modes. 'Diffusing' means both 'scattering' and 'making less intense'. While the flyer provides a nice opening to diffusion and its distinctness from exceptionalist securitising, diffusing insecurities is a more general process. I will illustrate this by drawing on a wider range of examples throughout the chapter. In the first section I start from changes in NATO's strategic concept to look at how scattering of insecurities took place in the period after the end of the Cold War. The section introduces that the combination of a move from defining existential threats to risk and uncertainty and a related blurring of divisions of security labour are central to diffusing insecurities. The second section looks at how diffusing insecurities challenges limits of security by turning limits into more ambivalent and porous boundaries and by creating insecurity continuities. In the final section, I pick up the associative mode of rendering insecurities and its non-intensifying characteristics. The section briefly introduces how the mere circulation of insecurities securitises without enacting the intensifying rationale of the national security tradition; practices, statements, subjects

and things are security associated rather than aggregated into an existential
threat.

Taken together, the three sections introduce key characteristics that
make diffusing insecurities different from exceptionalist securitising. In
the next chapter I will pick these up in more detail by narrowing the
analysis from the more general processes to a particular but powerful
technique of diffusing insecurities that enacts democratic limits in multiple ways: the assembling of suspicion through enacting risks and
uncertainty.

Insecurity without limits?

Since the 1990s, Western security practice has dispersed insecurities,
linking up policy issues and agencies that during the Cold War
were kept significantly more separate from one another (Buzan, 1991;
Haftendorn, 1991; Bigo, 1995; Buzan *et al.*, 1998; Bigo, 2000; Sheehan,
2005; Huysmans, 2006; Huysmans *et al.*, 2006; Fierke, 2007).[2] Security
was shifted from national security in a bipolarised world to a diffusing
governmental practice reaching into areas such as migration, environmental protection, natural and human-made disaster relief, humanitarian
actions and development policy. Security appeared to be without limits.
Under the label 'human security', the United Nations Development
Programme (UNDP) inserted security as a key issue in development
policy. The UNHCR deployed the same concept in relation to refugees, connecting individual vulnerability with socioeconomic inequality
and larger scale violence. Wood and Shearing summarise the diffusing
nature of securitising nicely in their analysis of the governance of human
security:

> [T]he governance of state security—i.e. coercive capacity including
> military might—is decentred. Space is made for other sources of
> knowledge and capacity to be identified, developed and deployed in
> producing arrangements for global governance that serve to form
> bonds or links between otherwise distinct problem spaces.
>
> (Wood and Shearing, 2007: 74)

The European Union created an internal security approach that linked
economic free movement, terrorism, transnational crime and migration
to the abolishment of internal border controls. NATO deployed resources
in natural-disaster relief operations and refugee camps, indicating a wider
attempt to diversify the functions of military capacity.

Defining uncertainty as the 'new' security question and instituting practices of risk management have played a central role in this process of breaking down the instituted hierarchies and divisions of insecurity. NATO offers a particularly interesting example. With the disintegration of the Warsaw Pact and the Soviet Union between 1989 and 1991, a discourse of a dramatically changing international security environment dominated in NATO—and other political and academic security debates. With its main enemy gone, the security of the Western alliance was perceived to have significantly improved. Two years after the Berlin Wall came down, however, NATO foregrounded uncertainty and risks as the new security issues.

> The historic changes that have occurred in Europe, which have led to the fulfilment of a number of objectives set out in the Harmel Report, have significantly improved the overall security of the Allies. The monolithic, massive and potentially immediate threat which was the principal concern of the Alliance in its first forty years has disappeared. On the other hand, a great deal of uncertainty about the future and risks to the security of the Alliance remain.[3]
>
> (NATO, 1991: paragraph 5)

With communism nearly completely discredited, the Soviet Union falling apart and the global system rapidly moving away from a bipolar structuration, it is not surprising that Cold War security institutions expressed uncertainty about the future.

Throughout the 1990s concepts of risk and uncertainty were reiterated to identify the security environment that NATO enacted. For example, in April 1999 NATO published an update of its strategic concept. Paragraph 12 reads:

> The Alliance operates in an environment of continuing change. Developments in recent years have been generally positive, but uncertainties and risks remain which can develop into acute crises.
>
> (NATO, 1999: paragraph 12)

And paragraph 20 states:

> The security of the Alliance remains subject to a wide variety of military and non-military risks which are multi-directional and often difficult to predict.
>
> (NATO, 1999: paragraph 20)

This reiteration of the language of uncertainty and risks does not merely express the loss of a bipolar security script focusing on threats from an inimical military alliance that organised security thinking for over four decades. It enacts uncertainty as an organising principle of international politics. NATO was not simply saying 'we are uncertain about the security environment and what to do' but rather 'uncertainty is the new security problem'. The expression of uncertainty and risk is thus not descriptive of a state of affairs but a securitising move defining the security framing through which the Alliance develops its role in global politics (Coker, 2002; Rasmussen, 2006). The security priority was no longer to manage a global enemy but to govern risks, which referred to a multiplicity of often not yet known insecurities. The security register on which NATO could act became wide open. In a world in which uncertainty is the security problem, everything can potentially be enacted as a security question. Security potentially scatters in all directions and becomes unlimited in terms of the policy issues security agencies can act upon. NATO indeed diversified its actions. It converted military power and expertise in collective defence into a capacity to operate in global conflict zones, disaster management, peace-building operations, policing and humanitarian action.

This scattering of existential insecurity and a military-capable enemy into uncertainty about the future, and multiplications of risks also implied the dissolution of established divisions of security labour for NATO. For example, policing and military operations overlapped in conflict zones. Humanitarian and judicial actions intertwined with military operations, resulting in interference in military actions and justifications by legal professionals, humanitarian NGOs and development professionals. Changes in NATO are only one of several developments in which instituted differentiations between various security functions—policing, military operations, criminal justice, counter-insurgency and intelligence—partly dissolved and were renegotiated. The European Union has been another institutional site in which such repositioning of security professionals and encroaching of security actions on a variety of policy issues took place.

Equally important to security professionals repositioning themselves vis-à-vis each other (e.g. the military and police in peace-building operations) is security professionals taking up positions in a wider range of policy areas, including development, migration and the environment. Multi-positioning of security professionals makes security knowledge and techniques 'travel' and scatters securitising across governmental practices. European Union development and aid policy (Davidshofer, 2009) is one example of a policy area in which security professionals started playing a prominent role; EU migration and neighbourhood policies (Jeandesboz, 2011) are two other prominent examples in the EU.[4]

These developments indicate how in Europe in the 1990s international security opened up from a quite specifically defined terrain of military and political managing of relations with an inimical alliance of states to a potentially unlimited enacting of insecurities as risk and uncertainty. Although I mainly used European institutions, the brief overview of changes in security strategy after the Cold War introduced a general key characteristic of diffusing insecurities: mobilising uncertainty and risk as a distinct language and technique of defining and governing insecurities. I will come back extensively to governing risk and uncertainty in the next chapter but for now the important point is that it is a technique that dissolves insecurity into a potentially unlimited set of issues on which security institutions can act. I also introduced that the scattering of security is not just rhetorical in the sense of a discourse of refocusing security tasks to multiple new dangers in situations in which the enemy one focused on for a long time has gone. It also involves the repositioning of security professionals and institutions in relation to one another and in relation to other policy professionals. Such repositioning plays a significant role in the breaking down of instituted limits to security.

Limits, boundaries, continuities

In security studies, the dispersal of insecurities has been mirrored in the so-called widening debate (Buzan, 1991; Walt, 1991; Krause and Williams, 1997). Rather than limiting security to military relations between states and the threat of military occupation and destruction, security studies shifted focus to a wider range of possible insecurities in the 1980s and 90s. It included expanding what needs securing from the state to society, human life as such, and individual needs and rights. It also extended the kinds of threat security studies would deal with from a focus on military threats by other states to a range of security sectors, including weak political legitimacy (weak states), migration (societal insecurity), environmental degradation, and so on. Each of these insecurities was seen as a particular sector that deserved to be studied as a security issue of equal importance to military defence of the national territory.

At the heart of the widening debate was a contestation over where and how to place the limits of what counts as a security question and what not. Those arguing for a narrow definition that continued focusing on military interactions between states and on intra-state and inter-state wars clashed with those who argued for a much broader understanding of what could count as a security question, including environmental degradation, poverty, global health and migration. For the latter, security is a pervasive and multifaceted practice that cannot be easily delimited to military defence. Yet the issue of the limits of what counts as security remained. If everything is security, then the concept loses its analytical value; if only a limited set of issues can be called security, blind spots can easily emerge.

One of the most original moves in this debate was to not seek to limit the range of security issues themselves but rather the definition of the securitiness that is invested in them. The notion of securitisation originally referred precisely to such a limitation of security (Wæver, 1995; Buzan *et al.*, 1998). Securitisation was defined as an existential framing of phenomena, rendering them an exceptional threat to the survival of a unit (referent object) that legitimates the deployment of emergency measures and the transgression of normal democratic political processes. Securitisation can thus in principle be applied to any issue as long as the issue is framed according to an exceptionalist rationality. In the next chapter I will introduce more extensively that diffusion of insecurities does require us to think about the security specificness differently—the security thicknesses that is enacted, that makes diffusion a securitising practice, is not an existential one. But in this section it is the issue of how we should understand the breaking down of limits that is central.

Although the debate focused on limiting the extension of security, the processes of expanding insecurities that the widening debate reflected on actually introduce a boundary question. While 'limits' refers to a sharper and clearer dichotomous marking, i.e. drawing a line in the sand, the concept of boundaries expresses a more fluid—or greyish, if one prefers colouring—delineation of insecurities. Although diffusion makes securitising potentially unlimited, in practice security did not change from a set of sharply delineated problems to something with no limitations. The process was rather one about security practice challenging instituted limits by turning lines into zones where clear distinctions between security and non-security are challenged by the introduction of continuities that stretch the meaning of security and that make it more ambivalent where security ends. 'Boundaries' is a better term than 'limits' here because it expresses that the practice of scattering insecurities delimits the reach of securitising but does it in a process that opens existing limits and expands the coverage of insecurities. Anastassia Tsoukala illustrates this process in the case of the securitising of football hooligans in Europe. The Council of the European Union Joint Action of 26 May 1997 provided for the collection and exchange of data on 'all sizeable groups that may pose a threat to law, order and security when travelling to another Member

State to participate in a meeting attended by a large number of persons' (Tsoukala, 2009: 106). The notion of 'meeting' embeds football hooligans in a wide range of events, including rock concerts, demonstrations and protest campaigns. Its core register still remains within criminal justice but through the Joint Action, football violence is connected to an expanding range of ordinary events. Besides blurring the borderline between delinquency and deviance, which is a central distinction in criminal justice, the Joint Action makes the relation between deviance and ordinary behaviour more continuous. This allows for an expansion of criminalising and policing into areas of ordinary practice where this would otherwise not be legitimate. Not anything can be enacted legitimately because the expansion remains tied to the policing of cross-border mobility. The reference to and European developments in policing of football hooligans delimit the expansion but it does this in a process of breaking down existing limits.

Marieke de Goede (2012) observes a similar challenge to limits of security practice when counter-terrorist policies targeted terrorist finance in the wake of 9/11. Rather than membership of a known terrorist network or active involvement in a terrorist act, one started identifying terrorist involvement through financial transactions that could be associated with supporting terrorist organisations. The required link was not necessarily to give money directly to support violent actions but could be of a humanitarian nature, like funding hospitals in Gaza that then are presumed to free up money for terrorist activities by Hamas—as was the case in the prosecution of the Holy Land Foundation for Relief and Development (HLF) in the US (de Goede, 2012). Terrorism by association considerably extends the range of activities that are connected to terrorism. It also blurs what are the limits of convicting someone by association in the criminal justice system. This unbinding of limits to security practice is further increased by a more outspoken move towards pre-emptive security and 'anticipatory prosecution'. This is a development that seeks to convict people on increasingly widening notions of what are credible criteria that someone is behaving suspiciously and what counts as convincing evidence that someone is preparing a terrorist attack. The key issue here is not that counter-terrorist policies move from the military area into areas of financial security. Although the latter is also part of what is going on—targeting finance is sometimes defended as the less violent approach to counter-terrorism compared to military interventions and drone attacks—the point of interest for the discussion here is the process of unbinding legal limits to criminalisation, which gives security an expanding reach into society, resulting in the criminalisation of humanitarian aid to certain regions, for example.

Another challenge to limits of security practice can be observed in the document that presents the first results of the security theme of the EU's Seventh Framework Programme for Research (FP7) 2007–2013: 'Towards a more secure society and increased industrial competitiveness'. It contains several projects where the security industry is undoing limits of security practice among others by promoting monitoring technologies. For example, ADABTS (the Automatic Detection of Abnormal Behaviour and Threats in Crowded Spaces) promises algorithm-driven automated detection of abnormal behaviour. The promise of protecting citizens, infrastructure and property is put up front.

> ADABTS aims to facilitate the protection of EU citizens, property and infrastructure against threats of terrorism, crime and riots by the automatic detection of abnormal human behaviour.
>
> (European Commission, 2009: 6)

Yet it is not at all clear on what criteria the monitoring and thus the protecting will be organised except that the system will somehow be able to capture a range of 'abnormal'—rather than simply inimical or criminal—behaviours. These definitions will be worked through the development of algorithms. The definition of who is going to be protected against whom, which citizens against which other citizens is kept rather vague. Yet the reach of the monitoring is defined in a very elastic way.

> ADABTS aims to develop models for abnormal and threat behaviours and algorithms for automatic detection of such behaviours as well as deviations from normal behaviour in surveillance data.
>
> (European Commission, 2009: 6)

In doing so, distinctions between criminal behaviour and inimical practices that are subjected to public order or national security policing and other forms of disturbance are deconstructed. Stretching abnormalities within a security technology, as suggested here, substitutes porous boundaries and continuities for limits. Breaking apart limits is here connected to security industries seeking to open an internal security market by implicitly challenging existing methods of governing insecurity (Dal Lago and Palidda, 2010: 8–9).

This way of understanding the dispersal of insecurities differs significantly from looking at it in terms of widening, which analytically dissects a process that seems to be more about connecting. Let me briefly return to the flyer we used at the start of the chapter to explain. Using a widened security concept, one can demonstrate that the flyer mixes human security, the criminalisation of migration and international policing of transnational criminal networks. The different insecurities mentioned are thus dissected into discrete security concepts or sectors. The problem with such a dissecting approach is that it takes apart analytically what in the flyer functions by being brought together. Separating the various insecurities destroys the synthetic technique of securitising that is deployed in the flyer. The flyer creates insecurity precisely by drawing the various events and developments and the insecurities they signify together. Separating them out for analytical purposes then misses the securitising work that is performed by relating—rather than separating—various insecurities. In a different way the flyer does something similar to ADABTS and the Joint Action: it works by letting security language and practice slide across issues; it works through connecting what are treated as discrete or separate issues in widened security studies.

The next section picks up on this connecting work that characterises diffusing insecurities. The main contribution of this section to the definition of diffusing insecurities is that insecurities do not scatter by making everything insecure but rather by displacing security limits with boundaries and continuities in which distinctions between objects of security practice and those falling outside the security realm are rendered ambivalent. When dissolving, security does not expand necessarily infinitely but rather disperses by making limits porous and thus turning relatively clear-cut lines separating in and out into more ambiguous boundaries that allow for security technologies and practice to slide into a wider range of areas of life than before.

Associative securitising

So far I have focused on how the notion of diffusion refers to a scattering of insecurities. It works by displacing existential threat with uncertainty and risk and relaxing instituted limits of security by displacing them with continuities and boundaries. Yet diffusion is not simply a process of scattering insecurities in all directions. The securitising practices simultaneously reconnect sets of phenomena and policy issues discursively, institutionally, technologically, and through informal cooperation. This connecting works slightly differently from existential intensification, however. I use the term 'associative securitising' to characterise diffuse modes of connecting. Associating is a horizontal mode of connecting in which the multiplicity and diversity of what is brought into relation is rearranged without stacking up or hierarchising the various elements so that they aggregate into an existential urgency. Let us return to the flyer with which I introduced the chapter. Unlike exceptionalist securitising, it does not mobilise a particular threat, a sense of emergency, or an imaginary of war. Although individual events that are included are dramatic for the people involved, the flyer does not really create a spectacle around a national or global security threat that demands swift and unusual action. On the contrary, according to the flyer the criminal justice system worked its normal course leading to the conviction of the perpetrators of crime. The patchwork of insecurities securitises more through circulations of a sense of unease rather than an existential concern, both within the discourse and visualisation of the flyer and in the everyday life of consumers reading it.

Unlike the integrative work of existential intensification that is so central to exceptionalist securitising, associating retains significant degrees of diversity and multiplicity in the insecurities that are connected. An example of integrative work of exceptionalist securitising is how trade in dual-use technology, nuclear science knowledge, anti-nuclear weapons protests and liberation struggles were constituted as manifestations of or as contributing to a global communist threat during the Cold War. The flyer, on the other hand, is a good example of associative work. The flyer simply brings into relation a set of statements that talk about various insecurities. Their juxtaposition rather than their unification under a meta-discourse creates security meaning. Simultaneously, it is a device that connects consumers with the wider political economy of DVD production and distribution, counterfeiting and precarious migrant labour, as well as the criminal justice system. The connecting is largely associative, keeping a multiplicity of discrete elements in play. Disagreeing with this reading of the flyer, one could point out that ultimately it does aggregate the various insecurities into one particular threat that connects all of them: migration. After all, the eye-catching heading of the flyer places 'migration' and 'crime' in bold capitals with an image of a DVD disc as the background. However, such an interpretation misses how the leaflet creates a closeness of texture by circulating various sources of unease without unifying them under one major threat. Traditional security readings would miss this production of insecurities by indeed looking for a particular threat to a society or state under which the various issues can be brought together. Migration can fulfil this aggregating function but usually it goes hand in hand with mobilising warring or emergency semantics of invasion, fifth column or flood, which is not the case here. Events and insecurities are connected in the flyer but without locking them in a linear causal chain that lets the death of immigrants culminate in a global threat posed by international criminals. The flyer keeps the relation between these horizontal; they are netted together rather than placed in a causal chain and hierarchy.

To give a sense of the variety of associating, let me introduce another example. In 2003 the then Minister of Citizenship and Immigration Beverly Hughes justified the need to introduce ID cards in the UK:

> We are not in the same position that we were 50 years ago. In today's world, correct identification has become imperative in a way that we could not have foreseen. We face new threats and increases in the scale and sophistication of illegal immigration, organised crime and terrorism, but there are also new opportunities and new improvements in the technology of biometrics. Crucially, such improvements offer the opportunity to link an identity record to an individual with a high level of security. That record can then be used to verify a person's identity and immigration status, show entitlement to work and do some of the other things on which Members have touched.
>
> (Hughes, 2003)

The statement places organised crime, terrorism and illegal immigration next to one another without formulating any relation between them beyond ID cards being a useful instrument for tackling them. Policies are not justified by creating an acute threat that aggregates the different insecurities into a single existential threat to a given referent object. Instead the statement develops a general context of societal insecurities by naming various sources of unease (Bigo, 2002; Huysmans and Buonfino, 2008). Like in the 'immigration crime' flyer the statement constructs a close but multidimensional texture relating various elements by putting them side by side. Rather than increasing the degree of the existentially dangerous quality of a particular development, it extends the circulation of insecurity connotations and denotations by increasing the number of units that are included in the text.

Both examples also show that various insecurities are associated by simply juxtaposing them discursively and by the materiality of a device—the flyer and the ID card. Hughes associates terrorism, illegal immigration, identity theft and welfare fraud because they can be managed through the same technology—ID cards and the related databases. The link between them is therefore instrumental, in a literal sense of depending on an instrument or device. The applicability of the technology brings them together rather than the similarity of danger they pose (Huysmans and Buonfino, 2008). Moreover, causally connecting different sources of unease is not important in this process of securitising. Compare Beverly Hughes' statement and the flyer to the following analysis of possible security effects of overpopulation to see the difference: 'projected rapid growth of population, most of it in the poorest regions of the Earth, will exacerbate regional disparities, fuel resentment, and possibly give rise to more terrorism' (Cassils, 2004: 187). Unlike Beverly Hughes' statement and the flyer in which insecurities seem to vaguely circulate through one another, here a dual linearity is introduced. The first is a causal one in which population growth causes conflict and terrorism. The second linearity transfers insecurities of terrorism and regional conflict back to population growth. It introduces a linear transfer of security connotations back to the phenomenon one is securitising. Rather than circulating insecurities between one another by simply juxtaposing them, Cassils performs a more traditional global threat construction—i.e. the inscription of an existential threatening quality on a global phenomenon like population growth. Cassils' approach further intensifies the security modalities of population growth by ending the series with the global security threat of terrorism.

The two examples further indicate another characteristic of associating insecurities: there is no real centre that is insecure, or at least it is not foregrounded in such a way that it organises the securitising associations. Securitising by association does not pull the different elements into a cohesive relation to a given political or social unit that is under threat of a collective agency. Instead multiple referent objects are associated, fluctuating, and working through and into one another. Neither public order nor human security prevails in the flyer; neither the state nor individual life holds the flyer together; they simply co-exist. Its acentric nature contrasts sharply with exceptionalist securitising that centres the world onto a referent object, often the state, with the threat being an environmental factor that endangers its 'survival'. Rudolph's national security analysis of migration is a good example of the centring that takes place in security studies by integrating multiple dimensions of migration into national security calculations of the state. First he looks at conditions under which forms of immigration are a national security threat. For example, he formulates the hypothesis that sudden influxes of large numbers of people produce demographic changes that threaten stable identities. In addition, he identifies migration as a factor in the national security strategy. For example, he expects that geopolitical threats lead to a more open labour migration policy because migrant labour is needed to support defence (Rudolph, 2006). The different aspects are held together by their relation to a state and its strategies for survival in an anarchical world. Although issues like migration can be securitised through national security calculations, diffusion of insecurities points to a process that is far less fixed on how people movement affects the survival of one political or societal unit. In the example of the technological securitisation of behavioural patterns that I used in the previous section the issue is not simply the protection of the state and its citizens. ADABTS connects behaviours and people through patterning degrees of normality and abnormality that can then be acted on from various interests, including national security, security in shopping malls, ordering public spaces, and so on.

Its acentric nature is also another reason why diffusion cannot be analysed in terms of security sectors, which have played such an important role in organising the widening of security in security studies. The seminal categorisation is Barry Buzan's. He organises insecurities into five sectors: military, political, environmental, societal and economic (Buzan, 1983, 1991; Buzan *et al.*, 1998). Each sector is characterised by a specific kind of threat to a specific kind of referent object. Distributing associated insecurities according to sectorial characteristics places each in relation to a specific entity that is threatened—e.g. society, political regime or environment—consequently connecting issues by establishing a similarity between them in terms of what they endanger (e.g. analysing migration and European integration as both issues of societal insecurity because they are threatening national identity (Wæver *et al.*, 1993)).

One last point that needs emphasising is that although diffuse securitising dissolves limits of security—i.e. the idea of a quite strict distinction between where security begins and ends—and sectorial distinctions, the listing of insecurities is not accidental or random. In Beverly Hughes' statement the key elements of organised crime, terrorism and illegal immigration—in other debates supplemented with identity theft and welfare fraud—mirror the European internal security agendas that have been developed at least since the mid-1980s. The associative work of the flyer combines victimising and criminalising, which is also at work in other securitisations of migration, most notably human trafficking. Diffusion is to a considerable degree embedded in institutional developments, existing circulations of security knowledge, changes in the field of security professionals, mediatisation of events, and technological developments. Associative modes of connecting insecurities are enacted in an already busy world. Although distinct from exceptionalist securitising, the associative work taking place in the diffusion of insecurities is not more free-floating or contingent than national security strategies.

Conclusion

Taking developments in security practice and studies since the end of the Cold War as a starting point, this chapter introduced the concept of the 'diffusion of insecurities'. The concept draws attention to processes that scatter or disperse insecurities and do not reconnect them by existentially intensifying a situation. It thus brings into view processes of securitising that are significantly different from the exceptionalist security technique developed in the previous chapter. In particular, I defined diffusion as combining three processes. First, I introduced the scattering of insecurity and how it makes security potentially limitless. Although diffusion is not exclusively linked to a turn towards risk and uncertainty, the displacing of a global enemy construction with defining uncertainty and risks as the security problem has played a significant role in diffusing insecurities. Secondly, I discussed how the scattering of insecurities is in practice not really limitless because diffusion works by turning limits into continuities and boundaries that make the parameters of where security begins and ends ambivalent and contested but not disappear altogether. It thus allows security practices to travel beyond its previous limits but not everywhere all the time. Finally, I introduced the associative nature of diffusion. Diffusion is a form of scattering that reconnects elements through associating rather than existential intensification. Multiple elements, insecurities and relations are brought together, creating associations that retain multiplicity and heterogeneity in the securitising process and that decentre security. In that sense diffusion is a non-intensifying way of connecting insecurities horizontally; it relates insecurities without subsuming them under a national security calculus that aggregates issues into an existential threat to a given unit.

The discussion of diffusion cannot be left at this point. Although the concept of diffusion prepares the ground for exploring non-exceptionalist techniques of securitising, in itself it does not answer the question of what makes diffusion a matter of security—of what defines the security thickness of modes of governing that do not enact acute existential threats. Neither does it answer how diffusing security techniques enact democratic limits. The next three chapters pick up both questions in relation to a key technique of the contemporary diffusion of insecurities: the assembling of suspicion. The next chapter introduces key elements of this security technique that combines the associative work of risk governance and surveillance. The emphasis is on its security thickness but the chapter also already opens up important political dimensions of this technique. The following two chapters focus more directly on how assembling suspicion brings limits of democracy into political play and challenges some categorical democratic practices.

The reason for introducing the notion of diffusing insecurities is not that exceptionalist securitising has become irrelevant or that it cannot co-exist with diffusing security techniques in particular sites. Neither do I introduce this difference for the sake of simply getting international studies to include events and developments that otherwise would be dealt with in other disciplines, like criminology and police studies. The reason is rather that the contemporary diffusion of insecurities is configuring significant security sites and processes that are forcefully enacting limits to democracy but that cannot be fully understood in terms of exceptionalism.

Notes

1 The flyer was sponsored by the Foundation Against Copyright Theft, which is a trade body representing the interests of the UK film and broadcasting industry, the Industry Trust for Intellectual Property Awareness, which promotes copyright and has film studios and retailers as members, and the Trading Standards Institute, which represents trading standards professionals in the UK and overseas.

2 Diffusing insecurities is not something new and exclusively related to the watershed in global politics in the early 1990s. Especially, the dispersal of insecurities and security practices has been part of exceptionalist securitising too, as we indicated in the case of the national security doctrine and practice in Latin American military regimes in the 1960s and 70s as well as in the matrix of war that is taking shape in the war on terror. Yet dispersion in itself is not the same as diffusion and not all moments and cases of diffusion are the same, as Duffield (2007) has extensively argued in the case of the contemporary insurance-based technique of securitising development and its difference with the securitisation of development in the 1960s. Analysing change in terms of a watershed moment, however, is never simply a statement of fact but mostly also a rhetorical move. One of the reasons for drawing attention to the 1990s is that it was taken over by 11 September 2001—9/11—as the marker of the fundamental turning point—the moment after which nothing was the same—in global security history. One of the consequences is that exceptionalist enactments of insecurity have partly displaced the focus on diffusion in international studies. The counter-terrorist discourse and strategies have been quite successful in reconstituting global security politics by connecting various acts of violence and political protest to a global existential threat—terrorism—and war—the war on terror. Discourses on 9/11 reassert that securitising is ultimately about existentially intensifying politics through enemy construction and instituting a political contest of the legitimacy of deploying extraordinary security tools. The 1990s then easily emerge as a prolonged moment of uncertainty, a moment of flux waiting for a new global enemy to emerge. Already during the 1990s, security studies articulated the post-Cold War in these terms. Some authors declared that sooner or later international politics would return to balancing power in a multi-polar world (e.g. Mearsheimer, 1990). Others accounted for foreign policy as a practice seeking to fix a new enemy that can define a new global security order with relatively clearly defined global security cleavages and challenges (e.g. Campbell, 1998, 2002). Making 9/11 the rhetorical marker of contemporary security practice tends 'to proof these interpretations right' and partly remove from sight a process of securitising that works through diffusion rather than intensification; a process that was strongly articulated in international studies in the 1990s. Drawing attention to the end of the Cold War is a method of sustaining the continuing importance of taking diffuse

securitising seriously in international studies. The 'end of the Cold War' marks a site of debate in which processes of diffusion were most explicitly discussed in international security studies and institutions.

3 The Harmel Report (1967) was a key document that reasserted NATO's basic principles in the second half of the 1960s. It introduced a dual-track strategy that combined maintaining adequate military defence more explicitly with a political strategy of seeking a relaxation of tensions between East and West.

4 This development is theorised in an excellent way by Didier Bigo's conception of security field, drawing on Bourdieu's work, and Anastassia Tsoukala's use of the notion of multi-positioning of security professionals (Bigo, 1996, 2000, 2002; Tsoukala, 2004).

5   Assembling suspicion

The previous chapter introduced the enacting of insecurities in dispersing and non-intensifying modes and its difference from mobilising exceptional and existential insecurities. Introducing diffusion in this way provides an opening towards understanding how security practices that unbind insecurities operate but does not embed diffusion into particular techniques of rendering insecurity. To move from these more general observations on diffusion to specific understandings of diffusing security practice, I draw on work in surveillance studies and the governance of risk in policing. This literature introduces a security technique that assembles and circulates suspicions through surveillance technology and risk communication. The assembling of suspicion is not the only modulation of diffuse securitising, but it does introduce a persistent method of unbinding security today.[1] Homing in on this technique is thus more than an illustration of what it means to thicken the idea of diffuse securitising. Modes of policing that combine risk communication and surveillance to technologically assemble and circulate suspicion have been increasingly seen as a key form of governing that unbind security and raise a wide range of pressing political and social challenges (e.g. Bauman and Lyon, 2013).

The first section introduces Ericson and Haggerty's work on policing as risk communication, which I am using as a springboard to explore a process of diffuse securitising that challenges exceptionalist securitising as well as the understanding of policing as social control. The next sections develop the concept of assembling suspicion as a diffusing security technique. They look at the main categories through which I conceptualise this technique: surveillance, risk, suspicion and assembling. In this chapter the focus is on what makes assembling suspicion a diffuse *security* practice—i.e. its security thickness. The next two chapters introduce further political thickness to this security technique by looking more extensively at ways in which assembling suspicion enacts limits of democracy.

Security as communications work

In 1997 Richard Ericson and Kevin Haggerty (1997) published an influential book *Policing the risk society*. It drew attention to a range of policing practices that in the understanding of policing as a coercive practice of social control, sustaining public order and crime control disappear in the background. Although the police spend plenty of time filling in forms, logging data on computers, and providing information to public and private agencies, these practices are more often than not presented as a deviation from proper policing. Ericson and Haggerty, however, argue that these 'deviations' are central to contemporary policing practice that govern various issues through risk management. They demonstrate that form filling and data gathering is a far more serious practice than often assumed. It makes visible how policing is, to a considerable extent, defined in terms of its information function in multiple networks of organisations that require information to be able to determine insurance premiums, risks of walking or cycling to school, and so on. I use Ericson and Haggerty's analysis to introduce key categories that define the diffusing technique of securitising that I want to develop in this chapter: the assembling of suspicion. Their work gives the categories contextual thickness to which I will return throughout the chapter.

Ericson and Hagerty start their book by summarising the view of policing they seek to challenge:

> The police pervade contemporary social life. They are seen daily on the streets. Their presence is felt even more strongly through hour-long television shows that feature cathected scenarios of their heroics. They are turned to for help when people experience personal troubles, accidents and criminal victimization. They are present at community ceremonies, sporting events, parades, and demonstrations. They are featured in full-dress uniform on postcards and souvenirs, standing for what is noble about the community and nation-state. In all of these manifestations the police simultaneously reproduce and represent order. They embody central authority, peace, order and good government.
>
> (Ericson and Haggerty, 1997: 3)

In the next paragraph they call for a fundamental reassessment of this view of policing. From extensive research on police practice they conclude that the police, most of the time, do something very different. 'We argue that policing and the society in which it takes place are best understood in terms of a model of risk communication' (Ericson and

Haggerty, 1997: 3). The police are first and foremost knowledge workers who gather, modulate and distribute data that support risk analysis, rather than guarantors of public order. 'Patrol officers worked very hard to patrol the streets and keep the peace. They also worked very hard, and for much longer durations, to "patrol the facts"' (Shadgett, 1990: 72—quoted in Ericson & Haggerty, 1997: 21). Policing units collect information on car accidents, illegal migration, burglaries and money laundering to name only a few. These data are subsequently used by organisations such as government agencies, international organisations, charities, insurance industry and building companies to assess risks that inform insurance premiums, building criteria, infrastructure projects, strategies for supporting resilience, and so on. Policing as data gathering is not limited to police patrols. In the financial sector in Europe, for example, Financial Intelligence Units were created in the 1990s in response to a European Directive that required reporting of suspicious financial transactions (Thony, 1996: 258). James Sheptycki summarises their activities as follows:

> Financial Intelligence Units amass information from the financial sector, collate it (sometimes with reference to other forms of criminal intelligence) and disseminate it among a network of similar institutions.
> (Sheptycki, 2000b: 152)

In defining policing as knowledge work, Ericson and Haggerty do not simply state the obvious: the police spend a lot of time filling in forms and thus producing data. Their interpretation challenges the under-standing that the police are primarily an agency of social control.[2] 'We argue that society is organized less in terms of deviance, control and order, and more in terms of risk, surveillance, and security' (Ericson and Haggerty, 1997: 448). As a social control, policing reproduces and sustains cohesive, consensual conceptions of order through the control of deviancy. The police, together with the courts, are seen as the coercive arm of the state, on occasions mobilised under international agreements, that imposes order on society. Deviancy is framed in generalised moral terms as the behaviour that breaks consensual rules that define orderly living together, such as prohibition to steal or damage someone else's property, prohibition to kill, prohibition of collectively organised violence and demands for justice when legally recognised harm is inflicted. The emphasis is on coercive and punitive control to secure public order, including defusing potentially violent situations and supporting the criminal justice system. As can be seen in the paragraph quoted at the start of this section, social control is a more diverse and rich practice than simply using coercive force. It includes helping people with personal problems, keeping order during events, solving crimes and symbolising the nation-state. Critical criminological analysis has shown that social control institutions, together with the media, also generate anxieties, social order problems and categories of crime (e.g. Hall *et al.*, 1978; Cohen, 2002 [1972]). Taken together, these various aspects of social control concern the production of order defined through set norms and foreground the coercive work of state institutions, rather than gathering data and supporting risk analysis.[3]

Policing as social control also functions internationally. For example, in the late 19th and early 20th century a number of European governments sought to coordinate police action to control prostitution—or, what they referred to as 'white slave traffic'. In 1904 in Paris they signed the International Agreement for the Suppression of White Slave Traffic. The agreement specified, among others, the repatriation of prostitutes to the country of origin when requested by the authorities, and the policing of railway stations and ports (Deflem, 2002: 68–69). Policing as social control and public ordering is also part of peace-building operations and military interventions. Operations in Afghanistan following the 2001 intervention are one example (Pineu, 2009); NATO's policing operations in Kosovo in the late 1990s and after are another (Coker, 2002).

As risk communication, however, policing is not primarily about maintaining order. Instead, policing seeks to guarantee usable categorisations of riskiness. It gathers data to establish links between sets of data and bodies, things, transactions and/or sites that can be configured into risk calculus. For Ericson and Haggerty, risk refers to external dangers, like natural disasters and threatening behaviour, and to the 'rules, formats, and technologies that institutions develop to deal with the danger they identify' (Ericson and Haggerty, 1997: 17). Risk is thus not simply another name for danger. The second part of the definition implies that the modalities of rendering the danger are equally important. In that sense, risk refers to a set of practices of making dangers intelligible in specific ways. I will return to this notion of risk later in the chapter. For now the key point is that Ericson and Haggerty introduce two concepts to mark a distinct practice of policing: knowledge work and risk. I will conceptualise the former more specifically as surveillance, in the next section, which, when combined with risk governance, creates suspicion as a mode of practice and government.

For Ericson and Haggerty, risk and knowledge work mark a way of policing that enacts insecurities differently from social control. As indicated in the previous chapter, however, risk language also functions as a marker of a technique of securitising that works differently from exceptionalist securitising. Let us take Frontex as an example. Frontex, the external border agency of the European Union, was established in 2004 to strengthen security at the external borders. It can be called on by member states to help with controlling migration emergencies, among others. For example, in 2011 Italy called Frontex into action to deal with Tunisian and other North African migrants arriving in Lampedusa during the political crises in Northern Africa. Although called on for assisting with what was politically rendered as an emergency, the operations in Lampedusa in February 2011 had a strong risk component. The mission included 30 experts and also Italian and Maltese aerial and naval support. The experts debriefed and interviewed migrants. According to a press release from Frontex, their mission included: 'to gather information necessary needed for analysis, to make assumptions concerning migrants' nationalities, and to enable early detection and prevention of possible criminal activities at the EU external borders'. Frontex was also tasked to provide risk analysis experts to evaluate security risks at the southern boundaries of the EU (Boundary News, 2011). Contributing to risk analysis is part of Frontex's mode of operation. Rather than being mainly a coercive instrument that seeks to tackle migration as a matter of closing borders or stemming an invasion, Frontex's operational remit is significantly geared towards migration management and, more generally, information gathering and supporting risk assessment (Neal, 2009: 351):

> Based on a common integrated risk analysis model, the Agency should carry out risk analyses in order to provide the Community and the Member States with adequate information to allow for appropriate measures to be taken or to tackle identified threats and risks with a view to improving the integrated management of external borders.
>
> (Council of the European Union, 2004)

Although the use of risk techniques can be framed within a language of national emergency and combined with coercive control, its modalities of operating are distinct. They defuse existential and exceptional renditions by placing migration crises within a more continuous managing of cross-border mobility that requires refining and renewing information about risky mobilities (Neal, 2009). To bring this distinctness out requires shifting attention from security practice as a technique of coercive control of existential threats to methods of data gathering and the production and enactment of risk knowledge; in other words, it requires moving the spectacle of police boats chasing vessels carrying migrants to the background, and the far less spectacular processing and exchanging of data to the foreground.

Besides risk and knowledge work, there is another category that is important for the type of policing that Ericson and Haggerty highlight. As knowledge workers, the police operate as an information hub in multiple networks of agencies that require information about society and people. This way of working is defined through transaction flows rather than the police mediating between the state and society. At this point, the central unit of analysis is no longer the police as such but information exchange relations and how they connect various agencies, data, knowledges, interests and so on. Policing becomes partly detached from the institution of the police and starts referring to a more general associative practice of assembling risk knowledge, technologies and agencies into networks that govern through rendering and distributing risks. This mode of policing thus implies a dispersed set of agencies and practices that are brought together through communication flows. 'Assembling' is a key category for understanding this dispersing mode of rendering insecurities that Ericson and Haggerty introduce, and the one that I will use for developing an understanding of diffusing renditions of suspicion in this chapter.

This section briefly introduced a form of policing that securitises by enacting flows of risk information. Although policing organisations also solve crimes, support the criminal justice system, patrol borders and impose public order (e.g. during demonstrations or drinking-related disturbances), much of their work consists in putting information into forms that organise it into data that can be used by various agencies to associate sites, bodies, transactions and behaviour in risk narratives and calculations (Ericson and Haggerty, 1997: 39–42). This form of policing can work against a background of references to existential threats and emergencies but its operational mode is mostly diffusing. The focus is on routine practices of data gathering and risk-information distribution. This modality of policing practice is the thick contextual background from which I now seek to conceptualise in more detail the diffuse security technique of assembling suspicion; a technique of which the practice of policing that Ericson and Haggerty analysed is a particular enactment.

Surveillance

Data gathering is central to the policing practice that Ericson and Haggerty introduce. Yet it covers a wide range of practices, from simply recording arrests or complaints to proactive intelligence gathering of financial transactions. In itself, data gathering is not connected to diffusing insecurities. Exceptionalist intervention as well as public order actions rely on data gathering too. When seen as a force that unbinds insecurity, data gathering is mostly understood as surveillance and, in particular, technologically driven digital surveillance spreading through many areas of life.[4] So, what is surveillance and how does it diffuse insecurities?

Haggerty and Samatas define surveillance as 'assorted forms of monitoring, typically for the ultimate purpose of intervening in the world' (2010b: 2). By emphasising that surveillance is about gathering and processing data through various forms, they move us away from focusing simply on CCTV, spying, hidden cameras, satellites or distant audio recording. Recording daily activities on forms, a census, or gathering consumer data through loyalty cards are also assorted forms of monitoring. Monitoring is a proactive gathering of data and not a passive recording. The forms are not simply devices of registration but they are an element in the processing of data so as to make them usable for policy decisions (Walters, 2002).

The mode of operation of surveillance, in David Lyon's terms, is 'to seek out factual fragments abstracted from individuals' (2001: 2). Surveillance is not about individuals watching other individuals in close proximity, like spying on one's neighbours or gossip in villages. It is a routinised reporting practice that translates an encounter between a migration officer and a migrant or a monetary transaction, for example, into information that is compatible with similar information of previously registered encounters and transactions. The standardising of reporting practices facilitates internal homogeneity and uniformity between data (Walters, 2011). Individuals and their practices are detached from the immediate context and the specificities of the encounters and transactions. They are reconfigured into usable information that can be turned into knowledge about violent crime risk, poverty risk or predisposition to illegal immigration, for example. Haggerty and Ericson summarise this logic of surveillance:

> [The systems operate] by abstracting human bodies from their territorial settings and separating them into a series of discrete flows. These flows are then reassembled into distinct 'data doubles' which can be scrutinized and targeted for intervention.
>
> (Haggerty and Ericson, 2000: 606)

'Data doubles' refers to an individual assembled as a set of data connections— for example, connecting bank transactions, registered passing of borders and sites of mobile phone calls to construct the travel pattern of the individual. This pattern can then be translated into a risk profile of terrorism or of the transfer of a virus, for example. What matters in policing as risk communication is this disembodying of individuals and their actions into standardised data fragments that can be exchanged in a network of institutions, and that institutions can appropriate for their own interests and objectives. Virtual data gathering, however, does not erase the body. The data are often gathered from bodies and their transactions, and are re-inscribed on bodies at the points of control or service delivery (e.g. Ball, 2006; Campbell, 2006). The disembodying work takes place at the level of the data itself. Data gathering abstracts information by erasing the thick context in which the body or transactions are situated. The data retain little, if any, traces of the embodied situation from which they are extracted. Understanding the person's specific situation, motivation and personality are at best secondary concerns (Poster, 1997; Lyon, 2001). This thinning of information into data makes its circulation through various networks and its use in assembling various data doubles possible.

The Schengen Information System (SIS) is an example of the abstracting work done in surveilling mobility in the European Union. It has been set up in the 1990s as a core monitoring system that collects and exchanges information about persons, objects and vehicles, mainly for the purpose of migration and border control, after the abolishment of internal border controls between participating states. It is a European information system that collects information from member states and makes them available to authorities in other member states. A central database in Strasbourg and identical databases in each of the member states are the central devices of the SIS. A majority of the persons entered in the databases are unwanted aliens (Bonditti, 2007: 102). The following personal data are stored: (a) surname and forenames, any aliases possibly entered separately; (b) any specific objective physical character-istics not subject to change; (c) first letter of second forename; (d) date and place of birth; (e) sex; (f) nationality; (g) whether the persons concerned are armed; (h) whether the persons concerned are violent; (i) reason for the alert; and (j) action to be taken (The Schengen Acquis, 2000: art. 94). Access and use of the data is constrained by the legal terms of use but, like other databases, it abstracts people and objects, reconstructing them as data doubles on the basis of the information obtained. At that point, they take on a virtual existence that is con-stituted by the rules of access and the practical uses of the data. One of the consequences, as Florian Geyer notes, is that because of the multiple uses and transfer of the data in the EU databases, the recognition that individuals should be able to oversee what information is kept cannot really work in practice.

Although there are provisions that intend to ensure that the individual is duly informed and that grant access rights to personal data held, these instruments might be insufficient to establish how the personal information has been actually used, interlinked, and, especially, with which authorities it has been exchanged, and how these authorities have further used and exchanged it.

In this respect it is interesting to note, for instance, that data processed in SIS II [Schengen Information System II—upgrading of the first SIS] shall, in principle, not be transferred to third states or international organisations (article 54 SIS II-decision). At the same time, however, Europol [European Police Office, the European law enforcement agency] and Eurojust [EU judicial cooperation body] do have partial access to SIS II data and these two bodies are in fact allowed to communicate the information obtained to third countries and third bodies, only provided that the member state that entered the data has given its consent (article 41(3) SIS II-decision). Whether or not the concerned individual must give his consent or be at least informed about his member state's consenting decision is not regulated by the SIS II-decision.

(Geyer, 2008: 7)

The multiplicity of institutions involved makes it virtually impossible for individuals to retain some control over the information the surveillance devices hold on them. The data have a life of their own. Once extracted, they can circulate across institutions and in multiple virtual worlds of information flows that are disconnected from the continuing embodied existence of the individuals from which they were extracted. When that happens, keeping in touch with one's data becomes virtually impossible. The European Union currently contains a whole set of databases and seeks to facilitate inter-operability, which means that the data can flow more easily and extensively thus also facilitating the multiplication of its uses (Geyer, 2008).

In the process of abstraction, surveillance thus 'dislocates insecurities'. It takes subjects, objects and transaction out of the intensity of the immediate and thicker context in which they take place. The diffusing power of surveillance follows from this systemic decentring and disembodying of intentional subjects into fragmented data that are assembled in terms of statistical proximity, similarities of profile and, more generally, the logics of comparison that institutional interests inscribe in the risk analysis. This abstracted circulation of insecurities as risks is a process of diffusion both in the sense of reducing intensity and dispersing security.

Insecurities are dispersed through data circulating in a multiplicity of information flows. The data do not circulate as individual monads. They enter technological and professional systems that relocate them into virtual spaces and moments of comparison where they are rendered alike (Haggerty and Ericson, 2000: 608). These spaces of comparison are sites where insecurities are associatively created, i.e. where numerous disparate elements are brought together in risk calculi and narratives. As the example of the Schengen Information System illustrated, the circulation can be legally constrained. Yet that does not necessarily mean that once the system is in place it will not expand its circulation, de facto or after being given new functions. Moreover, given the difficulty for individuals to track which data are circulated to whom, enforcing the legally circumscribed containment is not easy.

Such processes often also take the emergency out of emergencies. It is not always straightforward, but the dispersal and associative work of risk communication not only detaches the data from the individual bodies and experiences but also from the immediate intensity of events. As briefly illustrated in the case of Frontex in the previous section, policing and surveillance systems can indeed be politically mobilised through intensification—by calling the arrival of immigrants an emergency situation. These intensifications can also be politically mobilised to sustain an assertion of sovereign control—over borders, for example (Neal, 2009: 351). Yet the mode of operation of surveillance linked to risk communication—i.e. its extracting of data from bodies, objects and transactions, and placing them in virtual spaces of comparison—mostly diffuses intensities and exceptionalities. It detaches their significance from the immediate intensity of events. The significance of the data depends not on the emergency but on how they can be and are related to other data in the future and on the mode of comparison that the data and knowledge systems generate.

From risk to suspicion

Surveillance operates in a wide range of practices. Monitoring can have various purposes, among others: entertainment (e.g. in reality TV), the effective distribution of welfare benefits, disciplining behaviour in shopping malls, policing financial transfers, controlling border crossings and profit (e.g. tracking consumption patterns). The question therefore arises whether all surveillance is securitising. Is surveillance by definition a security practice? The different monitoring practices are not necessarily disconnected, but defining each of these practices in themselves as security practice may weaken the analytical leverage of the concept of 'securitising'.

This is not a call for fixing the meaning of securitising but rather for being more explicit and specific on what is implied by speaking of monitoring as a security practice. In Ericson and Haggerty's *Policing the risk society*, the orientation towards risk calculation placed within a policing perspective defines the securitising nature of surveillance. However, the mode of generating insecurities that I want to introduce here is not simply a mix of surveillance and risk but one in which this mix creates suspicion as a principle of relating, as a mode of arranging social relations and data flows. I will first look at the conception of risk and then introduce the notion of suspicion.

Creating risk categories is a mode of enacting worlds; a mode of knowing, representing and engaging that does not simply interpret given worlds already full of risks but brings worlds of risks into being. For example, migration or money flows are not simply an economic activity but are defined in terms of various risk calculations and governed through risk management techniques. Risk analysis is not the same as data gathering. Risk analysis refers to particular ways of connecting data. 'Risk' is currently used in various ways in security studies.[5] The one I am interested in here is the risk language that shifts attention away from the focus on war and violence and geopolitical renditions of inimical relations in international security studies, and towards a much wider range of forms of risk governance and technologies (Aradau *et al.*, 2008b; Lund Petersen, 2012). The key change, however, is not in the first instance one of subject areas of security such as changing the analysis from military invasion to migration. The latter can equally easily be rendered through security strategies that foreground notions of invasion, fifth columns, creation of violent domestic instability, and so on. Rather, the important issue is that risk language introduced a rationale of securitising that differs from the national security framing. Therefore, the interesting question is what modes of rendering insecurities is risk analysis.

Risk is mostly conceptualised as a technique of making uncertain dangers—contingencies—calculable. In this understanding, danger is the residual category of insecurity—the insecurities one is not consciously aware of, or insecurities that have not been brought within human control. Risk then is a mode of making such dangers intelligible to humans so that they can take them into account when making decisions to travel, to buy something, to live somewhere or to invest (Beck, 1992; Daase and Kessler, 2007; Luhmann, 2008 [1991]). Risk calculation often combines the probability calculations that something dangerous will actually happen with an understanding of the scale of 'destruction' or 'harm' if it happens—for example, the risk of a nuclear accident and the level of destruction it will generate; or, the risk of particular people to be trafficked and the level of harm implied. Among others, this calculus underlies the idea that responsible people base decisions on weighing the level of risk they are prepared to take against the level of harm their action might cause. It also informs insurance-premium calculations in which the level of compensation that might be required is measured against the level of risk that the harm or destruction occurs.

The concept of risk is not always used in this actuarial definition with its focus on making uncertainties calculable, and instituting the distribution of compensations, however. It has started also referring more generally to techniques of governing that make the future actionable in the present.[6] Although the idea of controlling the future is central to the current debates on risk, one of the key issues that informs the growth in risk literature is the observation that the possibilities of risk calculations and adequate compensations for harm are currently severely challenged. Paradoxically, the growing intellectual and institutional interest in risk is taking place at a time when the actuarial methods of risk calculation of the past are being challenged. Risk governance is now applied to messy areas of life like medical operations and mobility that function differently from the economic and welfare systems. In addition, risk management is applied to catastrophic events in which the consequences of failure of control are so devastating (e.g. nuclear catastrophe) that rational calculation of taking risks becomes meaningless (Beck, 1992; Adam *et al.*, 2000; Aradau and van Munster, 2011). As a result, risk has become a fluid concept that refers to techniques of making future events knowable so that they can be acted upon in today's decisions.

Governing through risk creates sets of comparison that distribute populations, sites or actions in terms of levels of risk. Certain areas are classified as more crime prone than others. Migrants are classified according to the relative risk of overstaying, of becoming irregular. Instead of unifying migratory movements into a single force threatening an 'invasion', risk disaggregates them in terms of various degrees of risk that they pose to welfare, to being trafficked, to generating irregular migrants, etc. The existential intensity of 'invasion' is broken apart into a series of risk calculations that hold individual units (e.g. a migrant or a group of migrants) in relation to a total pool (e.g. the population of migrants crossing a border). In distributing degrees of riskiness, risk governance simultaneously constitutes 'a population' (e.g. migrants passing through a border checkpoint) or 'site' (e.g. a city) and pools of varying insecurities within them (e.g. neighbourhoods varied according to propensity to violent crime; migrants varied according to propensity to irregular border crossing). This distributive logic differs from securitising by means of binary distinctions between friends and enemy, good and evil, or peace and war that are a key characteristic of exceptionalist securitising. Governing risks breaks down binaries by distributing insecurities in terms of degrees rather than aggregating them into an inimical force (Aradau *et al.*, 2008a).

Governing through risk analysis does not simply distribute degrees of riskiness but also stratifies units by categorising tolerable and less tolerable riskiness. The riskiness of migration, for example, is defined against more and less tolerable levels of pressure on welfare services, contribution to the economy, terrorist dispositions, etc. The spaces of comparison that risk techniques create are thus spaces of stratification, of the formation of hierarchically organised layers or groups. In the case of cross-border movement of people, this manifests itself in the degree of control and inhibition individuals are subjected to. Some require no visa to enter a particular country, others do; some will be given a visa easily, while others are subjected to linguistic or physical obstacles, etc. The issue is not whether you can move or not but how one is allowed to move. Securitising practice changes from a relatively simple dichotomising between the wanted and unwanted, the friends and the enemies, the normal and the abnormal, and the included and the excluded to a practice of governing through constituting multiplicities of modes of moving. Governing mobility as risk is not about blocking movement but about channelling and controlling speed and modes of movement (Bigo, 2008; Jeandesboz, 2011). For example, analyses of detention camps for migrants show that many immigrants will be allowed to enter the country after a while. Instead of being an end point, or a point of return, they function more like speed boxes that slow down mobility for certain categories of people and are part of a regime governing mobility by differentiating speed of border crossing in terms of the risk definition ascribed to categories of people (Papadopoulos *et al.*, 2008; Andrijasevic, 2010). Another example of this differential mobility regime is the fast lanes for pre-registered passengers that have been created at airport security checks.

When turning dangers or contingencies into risks, surveillance makes suspicion an organising principle of relating (Amoore and de Goede, 2008a: 17; Aradau and van Munster, 2008b: 26). During an encounter with a border guard a passport is a document identifying the traveller but also a potentially forged document that helps criminals, irregular immigrants and terrorists enter the country and potentially cause harm. The travellers are suspects until risk evaluation clears them. Suspicion is here not in the first instance a psychological phenomenon but a mode of connecting passports, the passenger at the border desk, computer databases, the queuing travellers waiting to be checked and border guards; it is a mode of relating. The idea of suspicion being an organising principle of relating does not imply that suspicion is necessarily the main glue connecting people, things and practice. Passengers share experiences, they carry shopping, the passport can signify a coming home, or a border guard and passenger crack a joke. The point is rather that rendering suspicion into a mode of connecting ordinary, everyday practice requires the particular work of surveillance and its enactment of risk knowledge. It requires surveillance that actions suspicion as its operational principle.

This mode of surveillance enacts suspicion in a dual way. Most immediately visible in everyday practice is that not everyone is equally suspicious. Surveillance inscribes suspicion on particular bodies or transactions and not on others. Data doubles are connected back to particular bodies (e.g. particular migrants as terrorist risks) and sites (particular neighbourhoods as having a high risk of car theft). Yet this mode of surveilling also does something else: it makes suspicion the background condition against which it maps risks. It is a practice of making suspicion the default position from which to render and evaluate transactions, bodies and mobilities; they are suspicious until cleared. Nothing can be trusted; 'everyone is assumed to be 'guilty' until the risk communication system reveals otherwise' (Ericson and Haggerty, 1997: 449). Policing turns into a technologically mediated practice of intelligence gathering in worlds where in principle nothing can be trusted and everything is potentially suspicious.

How does the rendition of suspicion as a generalised principle function within everyday policing practice that links data back to suspicious practice and bodies? Surveillance and risk governance use generalised data that place individual bodies within abstracted connections and situations. For example, someone being in a site that is identified as 'dangerous' has a higher chance to be stopped by the police than when not in this site. This identification has nothing to do with the individual having dangerous intentions or having committed a crime. Suspicion is generated through the general categories rather than the individual actions in that particular context. The example I used earlier on how risk profiles are created by connecting travel patterns, income, method of payment, nationality, citizenship status and so on works in a similar way. Suspicion is lodged in the generalised patterns that are rendered through connecting certain data. When an individual body falls within the profile or is present in a particular site the suspicion generated within the data connections is transferred to the individual. In a sense the process is one of contamination.[7] Bodies performing certain actions find themselves contaminated by the suspicion that the generalised risk analysis and surveillance generates. As Juliana Ochs argued, however, arranging suspicion as a form of relating is not simply a 'systemic' practice of data sets being applied upon individual bodies. As she illustrates in great detail in her study of the everyday embodiment of suspicion in Israel, individuals internalise suspicion as a mode of acting, for example on public transport and in relation to Palestinians and certain objects. Moreover, some individuals will also externalise their suspicion by taking on explicitly the role of 'guard' or 'soldier' and acting proactively upon situations or encroaching upon another body on grounds of suspicion (Ochs, 2011: 79–98).[8]

This enacting of suspicion is not a question of certain practices being about distributing goods and services and others about dispersing suspicion. Both these can co-exist in the same practice. Yet the securitiness of monitoring practices and the circulation of data and knowledge that they develop derives from inscribing suspicion as a mode of relating in situations. What it inscribes as insecurity is not enmity or exceptionality but circulation of suspicion. Observing how anomalies are identified in the wake of the July 2005 bombings in London, Amoore and de Goede summarise this as follows: 'the exception … is both deferred into expert algorithmic calculations and diffused into ordinary everyday suspicions' (Amoore and de Goede, 2008a: 17). Risk communication and management enact trust (and distrust) through a more continuous and multiple set of distinctions that works gradations of trust against a generalised background of suspicion, rather than through mobilising existential notions of heavily destructive ruptures and dichotomous renditions of the world based on sharp distinctions between friend and enemy, war and peace, or catastrophe and normality. Surveillance is a technology that can be used to police particular dangers connected to existential threat, e.g. money laundering related to terrorism. Yet it securitises in the first instance by circulating and instituting suspicion, e.g. in the relation between banks, clients and government in the case of money laundering (Favarel-Garrigues *et al.*, 2009) or in operational procedures of policing institutions like Frontex in the case of migration.

Of interest for analyses of securitising are the specific modes of surveillance through which suspicion is enacted. Suspicion is not simply a generalised condition making distrust rather than trust the actionable principle of practice. The dispersion of suspicion takes on different forms depending on the situation in which it is embedded (Ochs, 2011) and the mode of surveillance that renders it. For example, much attention has been given to changes in the modulation of surveillance from prevention of known enemies and dangers to pre-empting yet unknown dangers (Garland, 2001; Johnston and Shearing, 2003; Daase and Kessler, 2007; Aradau and van Munster, 2008b; de Goede, 2012). The latter requires a proactive 'invention' or 'imagining' of dangerous bodies or sites. The focus shifts from people with a trajectory in crime or sites with relatively high levels of violence to imagining propensities to crime, violence or catastrophic actions on the basis of behavioural patterns that are evaluated in terms of deviation from a median, irrespective of whether there are clear motivational indications of committing a crime. Motivation and individualised surveillance is not what immediately matters. Instead, subjects are placed in pools of riskinesss by technologically linking fragments of practices and biological and cultural characteristics.

In some cases policing shifts from policing the probable to policing the possible. Instead of rendering suspicions through the creation of statistical probabilities translated into algorithmic connections, one seeks to pre-empt rather than prevent criminal practice. Pre-emptive surveillance enacts the idea of capturing criminals before they even thought about committing a crime.[9] Speculation and imaginative processes trying to somehow produce knowledge about the unexpected so it can be acted upon facilitate the dispersal of suspicion across a wide range of practices.[10] Anastassia Tsoukala (2009) has argued that in European governance of football violence football supporters have become a locus of suspicion irrespective of whether they have committed a crime or not. Bans on travelling to football games have been imposed without individuals having a past conviction. Evelyn Brouwer refers similarly to a proposal to include 'troublemakers' in the Schengen Information System in the EU:

> The purpose of this proposal is to share information on persons 'whom certain facts give reason to believe that they will commit significant criminal offences'. The proposal gives no definition of 'significant criminal crime' other than that this should fall within a category higher than that of petty crime that is likely to disturb public peace and have a considerable effect on the public's sense of security. With shared information, persons, including EU citizens, could be barred from certain events by refusing them entry to the territory of the EU member state in question.
>
> (Brouwer, 2009: 17–18)

Although the emphasis in this example is on biographical information, suspicion is also rendered through gathering and connecting transactional data. Transactional data are data that are not linked to a person as such but to particular transactions that have taken place and which are then possibly but not necessarily connected to bodies involved in the transactions.

While biographical and biometric data are principally used for the purposes of identification standardization and verification, transactional data track the movement and conduct of subjects. Governing agencies are ever more interested in utilizing transactional data, which are generated routinely as a by-product of everyday activities.
(Ruppert, 2011: 221)

In this case surveillance creates risk patterns on the basis of telephone calls to particular countries, money transactions in different parts of the world, travelling to places and buying certain products, for example. In doing so, surveillance not only extracts data from everyday practice but also inscribes suspicion across a wide range of ordinary transactions (for example, financial transactions above a certain amount).[11]

Much more can be said about how various practices of surveillance render insecurities and, in particular, modulate and disperse suspicion. The main point for the purpose of this book, however, was to indicate that there are different ways in which suspicion is brought into existence as a mode of organising relating, and how it is dispersed in and through mundane situations and transactions. Although they are sometimes linked to national security framings as in the case of counter-terrorism strategies, the key element through which surveillance renders insecurity is not the enactment of an existential threat but the multiple ways in which it disperses suspicion and makes it an organising principle of relating.

So far I have looked at how surveillance, risk management and the enactment of suspicion diffuse insecurities in the sense of both diluting the existential exceptionality of insecurities and dispersing insecurities as suspicion. Yet something more needs to be said about the mode of association that takes place in these processes of rendering insecurity. As indicated in the previous chapter, diffuse securitising works through associating rather than aggregating and centripetal connecting of issues that characterise exceptionalist securitising. In *Policing the risk society*, Ericson and Haggerty captured such horizontal organisation of policing through the notion of networks that organised information flows. It is to this question about the organisational forms of connecting that I turn now.

Assembling

In Ericson and Haggerty's study, policing is not the prerogative of the police. The police are an agency within a network of knowledge producers and users. They play a pivotal role in providing the kinds of data that are being used to modulate riskiness but the modulations themselves and their circulation and implementation are taking place in the relation

between institutions. For example, a district manager of police organisation 'defined community policing as "a satellite, kind of going around
the rest of society" and allowing the police to function as "conduits of
information and facilitation"' (Ericson and Haggerty, 1997: 185). As a
conduit, they work with a variety of institutions, including businesses,
housing corporations, schools and real estate agencies. The community
they address is not seen as one but consists of diverse communities (e.g.
various business communities, neighbourhoods and offices) that are defined
in terms of the specific information they demand, and the risk categorisations they raise (Ericson and Haggerty, 1997: 185). The police are
experts at gathering data but the network of institutions defines their
reach as risk communicators and the modulation of the data into
actionable risk knowledge. As Ericson and Haggerty summarise:

> The police are part of interinstitutional networks in which claims to
> expertise pertaining to a given type of risk and the need for knowledge
> about that type of risk among the relevant institutions determine the
> police jurisdiction in the given field.
>
> (Ericson and Haggerty, 1997: 17)

A few years later they introduced the notion of 'surveillant assemblage' to sharpen the implications of their analysis of policing for the
understanding of contemporary surveillance practice (Haggerty and Ericson,
2000). In particular, the concept of assemblage brought into focus the
corrosion of the boundaries between sites and moments of surveillance
and those free from surveillance. The various institutional demands
made on the data often lead risk knowledge and surveillance to spread
beyond the specific site or problem for which monitoring was introduced.
For example, when CCTV cameras were introduced in Athens to
guarantee security during the Olympic Games, they were retained
afterwards for supporting other data gathering and policing.[12] Speeding
up travel on the London Underground by introducing an electronic
payment card that one just swipes across an electronic node produces
data that are used in counter-terrorism actions and other productions of
risk data.

'Assemblage' is a conceptual instrument for analysing this multiplicity
and heterogeneity of usages that makes the boundaries between surveillance and non-surveillance porous and that inserts surveillance into various
areas of everyday life.[13] As Marcus and Saka explain, the concept of
assemblage—and assembling—combines the idea of heterogeneity,
multiplicity and emergence with remnants of the social scientific interest
in structures. An assemblage is not a structure—it does neither have the

fixity and coherence of a structure—but it retains a methodological focus on that what is more than the sum of the parts. It provides a relational view of sites, things, subjects and practices—i.e. bringing them together in an 'assemblage'—while retaining their heterogeneity, multiplicity and decentring qualities (Marcus and Saka, 2006).

As assemblages, suspicion and insecurities are created through a dispersing, relatively unbounded process of associating. Yet diffuse techniques of securitising do not simply disperse, fragment or scatter insecurities. They connect data, bodies, institutions, devices and knowledges. Unlike the exceptionalist security technique, the securitising connecting is here not a process of intensifying insecurities; a process of increasing the acuteness and degree of presence of dangers, which works in particular through existentialising issues. Instead, securitising works in the first instance through densification; it does not enhance existing degrees of insecurity but works by bringing together more units and insecurities in a network of signification that creates a texture of suspicion. An analysis of densities would normally look for multiplications of elements within a given volume or container. The flyer on DVD piracy used earlier in this book can be read as a container. It is a piece of paper containing a combination of statements and graphic representations that bring a variety of insecurities and issues together. Yet the flyer can also be read as a device that gains its significance not simply from its statements but also from its physical circulation, thus connecting film companies and consumers to a world of crime and exploitation, the printers, the police, the distributors, pirated copies and so on. As a device enacting multiple associations both in its discursive content and its physical production and circulation, the flyer creates density not by holding a multiplicity of units in a container but through a multiplication of enacted connections.

Although increasing degrees of an existential insecurity quality is not necessarily absent from these processes (e.g. through references to terrorism or a catastrophic future event), intensity is not the defining characteristic of this technique of securitising. Assembling insecurities works against fixing or subsuming a variety of relations to a particular existential threat relation by keeping multiple issues and relations dispersed in heterogeneous associations. The overall logic is one of multiple and heterogeneous connections that cannot be reduced to a single insecurity. For example, the national security threat of terrorism has been an element in debates about the use and dispersal of CCTV surveillance. Yet CCTVs are not primarily driven by a national security concern but have a different history and function precisely as a device through which multiple insecurity concerns are addressed, from bullying in schools and security in shopping malls to border controls. Similarly in the UK, migration policies became hooked into counter-terrorism after the terrorist violence in the US on 11 September 2011 but neither did migration issues dominate counter-terrorism debates nor was counter-terrorism the central issue in migration policy debates (Huysmans and Buonfino, 2008).

As Ruppert highlights in her analysis of governmental database devices, this implies more contingent relations than linking issues to one particular relation, which in security practice often comes down to privileging relations to a particular enemy or natural existential threat:

> 'What is assembled then is not the product of any one relation or performance but numerous ones such that the enactment of both the subject and population is more precarious, indeterminate and unpredictable'.
>
> (Ruppert, 2012: 126)

In line with this observation, suspicion is not given density by simply increasing risks and surveillance technologies in a bounded space such as a particular institution (the police or the insurance company), a particular policy area (welfare benefits or migration) or a particular site (shopping mall, neighbourhood or territorial border between two states). Suspicion as a social texture is thickened through multiplications of interstices created by the associative connecting of policy areas, institutions and sites in the practice of monitoring, data circulation and knowledge production. Boundaries between realms and times of surveillance and non-surveillance are blurred, and surveillance is dispersed across a range of devices and agencies that does not exist as an institutional centre that commands the what, how and who of monitoring.

Bauman and Lyon (2013) speak of 'liquid surveillance'; Haggerty and Ericson (2000: 614) of rhizomatic surveillance. Deleuze and Guattari (2004 [1980]: 3–28) differentiate practice resembling rhizomes from tree-like practice. The latter exists as a set of branches springing from a root (e.g. the government or a police institution) that holds them firmly in place. When you cut the root, the branches will disappear too. Rhizomes, in contrast, are plants, like certain weeds and grasses, that grow in surface extensions of horizontally expanding roots. Rhizomic surveillance can be cut off at some point but will spring up elsewhere or later. It will grow independently from its point or site of origin. In its rhizomatic forms surveillance is thus acentric, neither springing from a single centre nor depending on an original 'patch'. The fragility that Ruppert refers to above now appears as a strength. It makes surveillance versatile and difficult to contain or abolish.

Its rhizomatic nature makes assembling suspicion different from bureaucratic organisation of surveillance that emphasises central information storage and supervision, and that played a significant role in the formation of the nation-state. Bureaucratic surveillance is an administrative practice of statecraft that concentrates authoritative resources for disciplining populations and individuals in the state (Giddens, 1985; Dandeker, 1990). This mode of surveillance works from a centre upon a dispersed field—from a state upon society—while producing and sustaining the power of the centre. It is tempting to refer to George Orwell's dystopia '1984' and thus link this conception of surveillance to the formation and practice of authoritarian states and institutions. Yet, as Giddens (1985) and Dandeker (1990) argue, bureaucratic surveillance has played a key role in the formation of nation-states and, more generally, in centralised bureaucratic governance, whether authoritarian or not. Bureaucratic surveillance is an instance of social control through which the state interferes in society. In this form, policing actions the state's claimed monopoly over the legitimate use of violence; it is a method of imposing order on society through coercive means for the purpose of reducing societal violence and for bringing to justice deviancy from instituted norms. The bureaucratic form also contained methods for limiting surveillance. In particular it combined general legal and functionally defined limitations to what each bureaucratic section could do and how it could link up with other sections. While bureaucracy is often seen as an apparatus of power, it is also a method of limiting how this power can be exercised. In its Weberian sense it constrained the arbitrary exercise of power through instituting generalised procedures and role definitions.[14]

Ericson and Haggerty's understanding of surveillance differs in important respects from this bureaucratic mode of surveillance. They share with Giddens and Dandeker that surveillance is a mode of monitoring for the purpose of intervention and that it generates power resources for institutions through the formation and storing of knowledge and by transforming the latter into a capacity for intervention. Yet, in Ericson and Haggerty's understanding, surveillance is centrifugal rather than centralising. The networks of risk data and knowledge circulation do not exist as a pseudo-state; they do not come together in one big entity, i.e. a governing network, organised around a coherent or consensual notion of order. The risk categorisations work incoherently; different interests, organisational missions, and entrepreneurial imperatives drive and organise them.[15] As de Goede summarises in the case of the financial sector: 'This fosters new assemblages of governing between regulator, private institutions, risk assessors and software programs' (de Goede, 2008: 101; also

Amicelle, 2011).[16] Securitising is then not a matter of centralised imposition of order by state institutions but of diffuse interventions that
depend on the particular interests and knowledge that are formed in
dispersed heterogeneous associations between various bits of information
and multiple agencies.

Didier Bigo (2008) in his analysis of transnational policing and Julien
Jeandesboz (2011) in his analysis of the governance of mobility in the
context of the EU neighbourhood policies introduce the concept of
ban-optical control of movement to express such a differential, heterogeneous form of surveillance.[17] Although one used to speak of a 'Fortress
Europe' in identifying the EUs immigration and border policies, this
Europe is in fact not a fixed, bounded set of relations that can be identified through separating inside from outside. EU mobility policies do
not really constitute a fortress at all but enact assemblages of policing
practice that brings into play multiple sites, people, public and private
agencies, databases, forms, and other things. The heterogeneity can be
observed in:

> bodies of discourses (on threats, immigration, enemy within, immigrant
> fifth column, radical Muslims versus good Muslims …), of institutions
> (public agencies, governments, international organizations, NGOs …),
> of architectural structures (detention centres, waiting zones and
> Schengen traffic lanes in airports, integrated video camera networks
> in some cities …), of laws (on terrorism, organized crime, immigration,
> clandestine labour …), and of administrative measures (regulation
> of the 'sans papiers', negotiated agreements between government
> agencies vis-à-vis policies of deportation/repatriation, 'common'
> aeroplanes specially hired for deportation …).
>
> (Bigo, 2008: 32)

The ban-opticon thus governs mobility through 'a network of heterogeneous and transversal practices' (Bigo, 2008: 32) that do not 'look' at
and act upon mobility from a central point of authority. The ban-opticon
is a technique of channelling mobilities and modulating the speed and
mode of movement through a surveillance assemblage that spreads in
various directions—that is, cut off at places and springing up elsewhere—
and that reconfigures itself quickly in light of changes in hardware,
problem foci, personnel, market conditions, and so on. Unlike a fortress,
the ban-opticon does not stop movement—immigrants are rarely
completely stopped—but rather stratifies by differentiating nature (business,
tourism, refuge, trafficking or studying) and speed of mobility (Jeandesboz,
2011: 394).

Such diffuse modes of securitising do not imply that state and public international policing agencies are no longer relevant but rather that their modes of operation and their relations to other security providers and various other surveilling institutions are quite diverse and cannot be reduced to more centralised state conceptions of social control and surveillance. For example, Wood and Shearing, drawing more on the notion of networks than assemblage, propose that although this dispersing form of surveillance and policing, which they refer to as nodal governance, challenges traditional conceptions of state bureaucratic governance (among others in favour of marketisation), the result is often a more hybrid form of governance in which market and state, networks and centralised state bureaucracy co-function (Wood and Shearing, 2007). Similar points have been made in relation to privatisation of security. The development towards security assemblages and securitising being organised through markets is not a straightforward cutting away of state and public forms of governing insecurity but often implies various combinations of both (Olsson, 2003; Abrahamsen and Williams, 2010; Hönke, 2013). Also studies of 'plural policing' that look at relations between public police and private agencies, for example in the case of CCTV use, have shown the great diversity this relation takes as well as that at times it is cooperative, at others conflictual (McCahill, 2008).

Forms of bureaucratisation are present in these assemblages too but work in a more diffuse way than the centralising bureaucracy that is captured through the notion of Big Brother and the modern conception of statecraft. As Hibou (2012) has argued, dispersed bureaucratic processes of formalisation and abstraction are a form of social power. It is a form of power that is not in the first instance an institution or an organisational structure but sets of formalising rules and procedures that are internal to societal practices rather than imposed on them from the outside. They exist in the form of demands within organisations, and in the regulation of relations between them, to systematically log activities, set KPIs (key performance indicators) and report against them, and so on. Abstracting realities into often quantitative measures against which one can measure proper performance are central to a formalisation of processes that is claimed to create capacities to act fast, and be effective and transparent. Amicelli discusses this form of bureaucratisation in relation to financial surveillance:

> The accountability of the regulated institutions depends on the enforcement of risk-management systems that are based on technologies and procedures aiming at demonstrating conformity. … [T]echniques of

traceability systematically store information to make it possible not
only to 'follow the money', but also—for the regulator—to follow
internal procedures and to scrutinize the decision-making processes of
regulated institutions.

(Amicelle, 2011: 173)

As a technique of governing, this practice does not depend on a centralised organisation or structure that imposes constraints and discipline
on society but on dispersing certain managerial methods of measuring
performance across society and the many activities people engage in (for
example, registering mobile phones, passing through borders demanding
a particular behaviour, and checking financial transactions). For Hibou,
these dispersed managerial modes of abstracting and formalising enact
mechanisms of accountability that produce indifference and subordinate
substantive value meaning of practice (e.g. eradicating poverty) to for-
malised measures of efficacy (e.g. the poor becoming part of a calculus of
the performance of governmental and non-governmental organisations)
(Hibou, 2012: 109–40).

The main point that the concept of assembling introduces is one of a
mode of practice and not that state and international public agencies can
be discounted as irrelevant. As risk communication, policing disperses
across a multiplicity of institutions and networks and is at least partly
delinked from coercive statecraft. It displaces the vertical power relations
between state and society with horizontal relations between institutions
that are associated in the circulation of risk information and knowledge.
It also challenges the institutions and methods that are used to define the
limits to surveillance in its statist bureaucratic mode. Assembling suspicion implies not only that insecurities are dispersing through decentred
forms of organising surveillance. It also raises questions about how to
constrain, call to account and democratically modulate the exercise of
power in these assemblages of suspicion when centralised Weberian
bureaucratic mechanisms are challenged by heterogeneous, decentred but
nevertheless bureaucratised modes of organising surveillance.

Although Ericson and Haggerty's work is embedded in national case
studies, the logic of policing they describe is transversal. Technology
abstracts the bodies, practices and things from their environment by
turning them into data that are connected and reconnected in knowledge
transactions that are organised in terms of the 'interests' (e.g. insurance
profits, price setting of real estate, etc.) for which risk communication is
arranged (Ericson and Haggerty, 1997: 109). National boundaries and
territoriality are only important in so far as they exist within a risk calculus
as a unit of analysis or site of data extraction (e.g. mapping neighbourhoods

rather than individuals in terms of risk of poverty or risk of car theft; travelling to certain countries as factor in algorithms calculating terrorist risk profiles; border crossings as points of data gathering and risk control). Territories, like bodies, circulate as data rather than as boundaries that constitute and frame the conduct of policing as either national or international. Philippe Bonditti speaks of the pixelisation of borders in this digital world of data transfers:

> We can observe a sort of pixelization of borders as they shift from a line to a set of points of connection distributed around the earth—points of connection at which people are controlled through connections to a central database, with the capacity to determine whether or not people are acceptable for entry.
>
> (Bonditti, 2004: 478)

This transversality of surveillance is partly a technological phenomenon (Marx, 2007):

> Modern technology permits social relations across vast spaces. Instantaneously mediated communication through sound, pictures, texts, and film links the world in a continuous web of stimuli, information and imagery.
>
> (Manning, 2000: 180)

Yet the central element of assembling is not the technological reach and the shrinking of distance as such but the enactment of life as associations of data, as information. Time becomes more important than spatial distance. It is the speed of information exchange and the capacity to adapt the information quickly that is crucial. The flow of information depends more on the media through which information is assembled and transferred than on national territorialised boundaries (Virilio, 1977; Der Derian, 1992; Dillon, 2003; Dillon and Reid, 2009).

The transversal logic of assembling suspicion is not the same as transnational policing. The latter refers to understanding policing 'on the global stage by reference to state action as non-state factors and processes in world politics condition it' (Sheptycki, 2000a: 6). It refers to a world stage that is 'crowded with actors, many of whom are relatively autonomous from the state-system and often do not act in the interests of states' (Sheptycki, 2000a: 7). The main difference between transversal and transnational is that the latter retains borders between states as a key principle for understanding policing and links between police bureaucracies. Transnational police are national police forces working together across states. Assembling suspicion operates internationally, transnationally and nationally but its mode of operation is not primarily organised by distinctions between national, transnational and international, and the political territorial borders that organise these distinctions. Transaction of information—often digitalised—is its first principle of organisation rather than (re)producing state and inter-state units. This allows for greater heterogeneity, acentric operations, and the blurring of dichotomously structured boundaries and limits. The multiple internal security practices of the EU today police the external borders of the EU and organise risks territorially. Yet EU policing mobility cannot be reduced to territorialised conceptions of control. Its instruments of surveillance are varied, work at a distance, or are spread out across the territory. Examples of its instruments are: visas, detention centres, neighbourhood policies, databases retaining and circulating individualised data, and categorisations of mobility such as refuge, business, trafficking, tourism and clandestine labour. Territorial identity of the EU and borders separating a territory of free movement from a territory of controlled movement is mostly only a particular factor in the surveillance of mobility.[18]

This section introduced the concepts of assembling and assemblage as a tool for understanding a diffusing method of associating through which insecurities as risk and suspicion are created and circulated. Although one also uses the idea of network and networking, surveillance does not always diffuse insecurities through a network with clear nodal points and relatively stable lines of connection. It can work at times more like a 'chaotic' rhizome, a set of relations that spread in various directions, that is cut off at places and springs up elsewhere, and that reconfigures itself quickly in light of changes in hardware, problem foci, personnel, market conditions, and so on. 'Assembling' expresses this possibility for rhizomatic diffusion that unbinds security by dispersing surveillance and risk into many areas of life, thus spreading suspicion as a mode of governing and relating. It also brings sharply into view how contemporary forms of surveillance challenge modern bureaucratic surveillance that functioned as a method of statecraft and a centralising tool of social control. At this point, the question about the political implications of this rhizomatic technique of securitising through surveillance and the rendition of suspicion as a mode of relating starts to loom large. This question is the topic of the next two chapters.

Conclusion

This chapter introduced assembling suspicion as a technique of diffuse securitising and its unbinding of security. I drew extensively on Ericson and Haggerty's analysis of policing as risk communication. They present a practice of policing that consists mainly in registering and processing data and assembling risk knowledge. Data are exchanged between institutions for the purpose of a more continuous managing of various subjects, objects and transactions as risks. This form of policing governs a great variety of issues including insurance, neighbourhood safety, money laundering, rogue states and migratory mobility. Their work functioned as a case study that brought into view a distinctive technique of securitising in which technologically mediated surveillance combines with the governance of risk to assemble suspicion as a mode of relating. Intensification, which is so central to exceptionalist securitising, is displaced by more continuous and less spectacular distributions of degrees of riskiness and in enhancing insecurity density. Instead of dichotomist enactment of friend–enemy and inside–outside distinctions in exceptionalist securitising and of state–society distinctions in social control, the assembling of suspicion connects in more continuos and heterogeneous ways various data, mobilities and bodies thus traversing the boundaries and limits that are established in these dichotomies. It translates a multiplicity of relations and data into sites and profiles through which gradations of risk can be inscribed on places, bodies and actions. Suspicion functions both as the operating principle of this technique—nothing and nobody can be trusted until cleared—and as a distinct mode of relating and stratifying that the technique inscribes upon social relations and subjects. This mode of diffuse surveillance has places and moments where information is grabbed and control exercised. Yet the centres and moments of appropriation remain dispersed and do not constitute a process of accumulating resources of authority into one central apparatus that is the main hub (e.g. nation-state or the EU) that disciplines bodies and sites (e.g. society or EU neighbours) it is surveilling. In this fluid and heterogeneous mode of existence surveillance resembles rhizomes that contrast sharply with the hierarchical and contained organisation of bureaucratic surveillance in modern statecraft. To capture this fracturing characteristic of securitising and to emphasise its horizontal organising of a multiplicity of relations, rather than its decentralising nature, I used the concept of assembling.

On occasions assembling suspicion can seem to be subordinated to or function largely within exceptionalist securitising. The expansion of variations of risk analysis and surveillance can be driven by a political and corporate mobilisation of emergencies, existential threats and worst-case scenarios. Political contestation of surveillance is often organised in terms of trade-offs between protection of privacy, fundamental rights and freedoms, parliamentary oversight and judicial accountability on the one hand, and the need for securing territorial integrity, infrastructure and personal protection of citizens on the other. Especially following the renewed focus on global terrorism after 11 September 2001 and the subsequent bombings in Bali, Madrid, London and various other places, the risk of authoritarian, executive government, the increased institutionalisation of arbitrariness, and global militarisation have been central to a political intensification of risk governance, surveillance and pre-emptive security practices.

Yet justifications for assembling suspicion often also do not claim to protect democratic life against an existential threat. Much of this technique of diffuse securitising works in relation to routinised public order practice, risk evaluations and administering deviancy. In addition, surveillance is tightly hooked into optimising service delivery, the welfare of populations, responsiveness to consumer desires and managing various contingencies of life. Assembling suspicion is a continuously developing process characterised by relatively small changes and adaptations. It thus depends less on existential crisis points and is strongly embedded in— and, driven by—non-exceptionalised activities. It also moves easily across and between security and non-security practice. It would therefore be a mistake to reduce assembling suspicion to a function within exceptionalist securitising. The main purpose of this and the previous chapter has been to introduce a conception of security techniques as diffusing, to avoid such reductive reading of securitising in international security studies.

Much more can be said about the rendition of insecurities as suspicion, and the particular workings of assembling. However, this chapter aimed at introducing basic categories through which to understand a particularly powerful and highly present technique in contemporary global politics that unbinds limits to security by diffusing insecurities through enacting, as its organisational principle, suspicion rather than existential threats. Rather than further detailing this technique of securitising, I now want to change focus and move from the security reading to a political reading of assembling suspicion.

Notes

1 The literatures I draw on are best seen as a case study of a particular process of diffusion. Another interesting case is the literature on cultures of fear (e.g. Furedi, 2002), which would bring out slightly different modulations of diffusion, not disconnected from developments in surveillance and risk management but emphasising the constitution of fearful subjects through a wide range of media and governmental programmes. Similarly, the case of the incorporation of the molecular revolution in the biosciences and informatics in conceptions of war would also modulate security diffusion differently (Dillon, 2003; Reid, 2006;

Dillon and Reid, 2009). The insertion of risk governance and uncertainty into the military strategy of NATO (Coker, 2002; Rasmussen, 2006) is again another case, though an ambivalent one given that risk is here often read back into a geopolitical world view and strategies reconfiguring collective defence.

2 See also Peter K. Manning's work on information-led policing (Manning, 2000: 196).

3 More extensively on social control: Cohen, 1985.

4 There are important differences between face-to-face, analogue, 'fiche' recording and digital surveillance. Although this chapter focuses on technologically mediated surveillance as different from frace-to-face monitoring, it does not develop in a sustained way the difference digitalisation makes. On the latter, see for example: Marx, 1995; Norris, 2003; Bonditti, 2004, 2008.

5 Compare for example Coker (2002), Rasmussen (2006), Amoore and de Goede (2008b), Daase and Kessler (2007) and Aradau and van Munster (2007, 2008a). For an excellent overview and discussion of the various uses of risk in the context of security studies: Lund Petersen (2012).

6 For a discussion of the various conceptions of uncertainty and risk analysis: Daase and Kessler, 2007.

7 I am indebted to Henning Koch for mentioning this idea of 'contamination' when I presented an earlier version of this chapter at a seminar in CAST (Centre for Advanced Security Theory) in Copenhagen (14 December 2011).

8 See also Janet Chan's analysis of lateral policing that generates a generalised suspicion—in particular in the context of calls for vigilance and peer-to-peer surveillance in counter-terrorism (Chan, 2008).

9 One of the standard references is the science-fiction novel *Minority report* (Dick, 2002 [1956]) in which a crime unit works on the basis of reports from three subjects who predict who will commit what crime, when and where.

10 For an analysis of a pre-emptive enactment of suspicion in the financial sector, see de Goede's work on terrorist financing (de Goede, 2008, 2012) and Amicelle's work on financial surveillance (Amicelle, 2011).

11 This move towards institutionalising speculative security (de Goede, 2012) and imagining insecurities (Aradau and van Munster, 2011) has been a key part of the war on terror. For example, a group of science fiction writers 'Science Fiction in the service of National Security' joined the Department of Homeland Security in the war on terror (Aradau and van Munster, 2011: 69). This example also indicates that the security technique I am introducing in this chapter and the exceptionalist security technique are not mutually exclusive practices. They can operate together in particular situations.

12 On surveillance and mega-events like Olympic Games: Boyle and Haggerty, 2009.

13 Several concepts can be used to express the decentred and non-linear connectivity: networking, patching, collating or assembling, for example. Although networks and collage are not exactly the same as assemblage, the finer differences between these concepts are not central for the purpose of this chapter. Here the main issue is to introduce a concept that helps to perform an analytical move from connecting in hierarchical, aggregative and centring modes to associating in diffuse, flatter and decentring modes of securitising. 'Assembling' and 'assemblage' express best the diffuseness I am talking about.

For a more detailed unpacking of network and assemblage: Collier (2006); Marcus and Saka (2006); Phillips (2006); van Loon (2006); Venn (2006).

14 I am indebted to Vibeke Schou Tjalve for pointing out the relevance of this power-limiting aspect of bureaucracy in its Weberian conception.

15 Ericson and Haggerty speak of 'fragmentation'. I prefer the notion of 'incoherence' because fragmentation is too often read as the opposite of social integration. Ericson and Haggerty explicitly argue that fragmentation is not undermining social integration but simply changing it by locating integration in the circuitry of risks and institutions and the logic of risk categorisation and communication (Ericson and Haggerty, 1997: 120).

16 For an excellent and detailed analysis of the technological practice of risk analysis and the relations between various actors in the related but distinct area of the fight against money laundering: Favarel-Garrigues *et al.*, 2009.

17 The ban-opticon identifies current surveillance and control practices that differ from those that work in pan-optical ways. In the pan-opticon, the group under surveillance and the group being controlled are the same—e.g. prisoners in a closed penal institution. In the ban-opticon everyone is subjected to surveillance but only particular groups are targeted for control—e.g. everyone is under surveillance at the border but only the mobility of particular groups is limited.

18 Didier Bigo (1996, 2008), Julien Jeandesboz (2011), and much of the work done in the European Commission-funded FP7 project CHALLENGE (the Changing Landscape of Liberty and Security in Europe) have shown this in great detail (Huysmans and Ragazzi, 2009; Bigo *et al.*, 2010).

6   Surveillance, democracy, privacy

Having set out key elements of diffuse techniques of securitising, and in particular assembling suspicion, and its difference with exceptionalist securitising in the previous two chapters, this chapter and the next concentrate on introducing political thickness by asking how assembling suspicion enacts limits of democracy. Rather than summing up a range of themes, I will focus on two issues. In this chapter, I focus on surveillance and the intrusion of privacy. In the next chapter, I deal more explicitly with the impact of technology. Between them they bring into play two of the most central tensions through which modern democratic practice and its limits have been contested and given form: the right to privacy and public interests, and the relation between technology and technological reason, and deliberative politics and value reasoning.

This chapter will draw mostly on analyses of surveillance. In so far as surveillance refers to the technological extraction of information on persons and contexts, not all surveillance assembles suspicion, e.g. businesses gathering data on consumer preferences. Yet surveillance is a key technique in assembling suspicion. Therefore discussions of the tensions between surveillance and democracy give us an insight into how diffuse securitising enacts limits of democracy. In this chapter, I start with a short introduction to how the diffuse organisation of security raises challenges to democracy, followed by an overview of how assembling suspicion through surveillance enacts various limits of democracy. To bring out democratic challenges of surveillance in more detail, I then turn to the protection of privacy, which is one of the central issues that is mobilised to limit the unbinding of security in surveillance practice. In particular, I ask two questions: (a) how does surveillance, and its assembling of suspicion, enact the limits of democracy through enacting the limits of privacy? and (b) what are the limits of a political critique of surveillance based on the protection of privacy? The aim of the chapter is not simply to introduce privacy as a stake in the democratic politics of assembling suspicion. I also want to explore how assembling suspicion poses quite radical challenges to democracy by undermining key processes through which one often tries to recapture democratic politics in relation to surveillance. To that purpose, I introduce how surveillance limits the capacity for reflectively engaging the assembling of suspicion and its implications for conceptions of resistance.

Diffusion and democracy

The diffuse nature of surveillance, policing and risk governance challenges central mechanisms of democratic control and distribution of power (Wood and Dupont, 2006; Haggerty and Samatas, 2010a). The rhizomatic aspects of assembling suspicion delimits the bearing that core institutions exercising democratic control, aggregating values and expressing the demands of the wider community of people have on these processes. Ian Loader raises this issue in relation to the networking and pluralisation of police providers:

> The questions—pertaining to legitimacy, effectiveness, equity, human rights and so forth—that have long vexed discussions of police policy and (mal)practice in liberal democratic societies press themselves with renewed force under the altered conditions of plural policing. The precise value and purchase of [the] received democratic lexicon under such conditions remains, however, both unclear and underelaborated. How—if at all—can public interest considerations be made to count in shaping the diverse network of policing providers that is presently emerging? On what basis might citizens be able to seek a 'fair' share of, or voice their concerns about, the multiple policing forms that increasingly impact upon the quality of their lives? How might the plurality of agencies and agents that now constitute the policing field locally, nationally and transnationally adequately be rendered responsive to democratic audiences?
>
> (Loader, 2000: 324)

The main political issue that arises here is not that different from the concerns with how to exercise democracy in a transnationalising world in the 1960s and 70s (Kaiser, 1969, 1971). Growing interdependence and transnational practice was seen as posing two related issues for democracy. How to bring to bear political demands arising from domestic democratic processes of interest articulation and common value determination upon transnational processes that work across national jurisdictions and political institutions? And, how to organise demands arising from transnational social relations into a democratic process of interest and value articulation and how to make decision makers in transnational processes democratically accountable? In the 1960s and 70s the response focused very much on adapting statist political processes and possibilities for scaling up politics from the state to regional polities and supranational organisations. Studies on regional integration and especially on European integration were at the forefront of these debates in international studies.

These responses retained a sharp distinction between societal developments and political rule, and favoured institutions acting upon society through more or less centralised forms of governance. The democratic problem arose because the societal took on transnational dimensions, while the political remained strongly territorialised. The political answers were based on the understanding that the democratic issue was to somehow align political institutions of the state with the transnational society so that democratic political decisions and controls could effectively act upon transnational processes. Hence, the interest in regional and global political integration. In scaling up the democratic political organisation of power to supranational levels, one sought to increase the leverage politics could have upon transnational societal organisations and processes. It was a 'politics of scale' in which political arrangements largely replicated state-level (democratic) political processes at the supranational level.

The diffuse nature of assembling suspicion undermines a central building block of such a politics of scaling up democratic institutions, however. As indicated in the previous chapter, the rhizomatic nature of assembling suspicion questions the capacity of modern centralised state-like governance arrangements to exercise adequate control onto a dispersed field of agencies. Rhizomatic modes of surveillance enact horizontally organized and dispersing relations between agencies, and between data flows and their re-inscription into bodies, sites and transactions. The dispersing of agencies makes it relatively difficult to assign critically significant actions to particular actors or to aggregate sets of actions into a limited group of actors who have the capacity to create and control an assemblage of security, and therefore to be called to account. When the organisation of vertical relations between people and rulers, society and state fracture into multiple networks, the democratic leverage that can be exercised through centralised bureaucratic arrangements is limited (Loader, 2000: 323). Organising constraining measures through juridical oversight or political legislative and quasi-legislative practice become more complex in these situations, as Haggerty and Ericson note:

As it is multiple, unstable and lacks discernible boundaries or responsible governmental departments, the surveillant assemblage cannot be
dismantled by prohibiting a particularly unpalatable technology. Nor
can it be attacked by focusing criticism on a single bureaucracy or
institution.

(Haggerty and Ericson, 2000: 609)

When state institutions are increasingly just one among many agencies in
highly dispersed networks of power, their capacity to intervene in the dispersed societal developments as the guardian of democracy and sites for
the development and expression of common values and interests is
undermined. This does not imply that there are no power asymmetries
and relations of domination and subordination being played out and
reconfigured. It does imply, however, that the democratic question
cannot be limited to bringing state like political institutions in line with
the transversal nature of practice. The democratic stake includes the
more open question of what democracy can possibly be in a rhizomatic
enactment of power and security. The next section deals with some
elements of this question in more detail by looking at how assembling
suspicion and in particular surveillance enacts limits of democracy, and
what resistant responses to diffuse modes of surveillance can be.

Surveillance limiting democracy

The democratic issues that surveillance practice engages and challenges
are wide ranging. As explained above, its diffusing mode raises particular
issues for democracy. Dispersal of decisions across a wide range of sites
and instances with no clear understanding of which decisions make a
key difference seriously limits the possibility to regulate surveillance
agencies through established democratic institutions. It also makes it
difficult to institute accountability for decisions and processes of decision
making, and exacerbates the lack of transparency that is often already
limited in instances of security practice (Huysmans, 2011). For
Wood and Shearer, of particular significance is that diffusing security
techniques—or, what they refer to as the 'nodal governance of security'—
further limits the bargaining power of weak actors, which raises a more
general issue:

[W]hat possibilities might exist for governing democratically within
a nodal world in ways that ensure that common goods will continue
to be provided to a whole variety of different constituencies[?]

(Wood and Shearing, 2007: 151)

Other authors have highlighted how developments in surveillance practices are not simply limiting the power of the weak but are eating away at the possibilities to participate in collective decision making more generally. For example, Haggerty and Samatas (2010b: 6) point out that the capacity to disaggregate populations in evermore specific segments, as developed in targeted marketing practices, now operates in both electoral engineering and security practice. Surveillance draws distinctions between ever-smaller segments within a population. In elections this means identifying specific segments of the electorate that, when successfully targeted, can shift key votes from one party to another. In doing so, surveillance fractures the enactment of an aggregated public and therefore undermines the political need to aggregate various demands, interests and concerns into an expression of public will (Haggerty and Samatas, 2010b: 6). This segmentation can also be seen at work in security practices increasingly insulating small segments of a population that will be subjected to more intrusive surveillance and coercive security measures. Similarly, precautionary surveillance pre-empts demands, decisions, dangers and needs, thereby removing the need for public discussion and contestation to establish common interests and demands. The agencies claim to know the needs, demands and intentions of people better and in greater detail than the people themselves (Ball *et al.*, 2010). Moreover, as Aradau and van Munster (2008) argue, precautionary risk governance displaces social antagonism, which is another key element of democratic politics. Others again have highlighted that assembling suspicions undermines trust between citizens, which is for some a necessary condition for engaging in deliberative politics (Los, 2006; Haggerty and Samatas, 2010b).

The uneasy relationship between democracy and surveillance is not limited to deliberative and antagonistic politics, however. Risk governance and surveillance practices are also understood to transform central pillars of legal practice. For example, pre-emptively assigning criminal intent or predisposition is challenging the criminal justice system. In 1940, Otto Kirchheimer (1996 [1940]) strongly argued how certain changes in criminal law and the penal system are a central part of both the breakdown of liberal democratic political systems and the institutionalisation of authoritarian government. Some of the main changes he identified as key indicators of the hollowing out of the democratic organisation of (criminal) justice have a cunning resemblance to current developments. Among the main changes he identified in his essay are:

- a demand for greater self-control of the individual and taking criminal intent as the main object of offensive action, which facilitates pre-emptive suspicion and convictions of crime that depend on the type of person or the personal history without a crime actually having been committed (pp. 172–75);

- unifying moral and legal order to broaden the scope of penal law by blurring the difference between what is morally defined as unacceptable and what is a legally defined criminal act; such broadening makes it possible to extend criminal justice practices to new fields in line with moral rather than legal definitions of crime (p. 174);
- the disappearance of the unified nature of the criminal justice system by granting special penal competences to administrative organs (pp. 178–79), which leads to turning the penal system into an administrative technique that often makes due process rules less constraining upon the authorities (p. 185);
- the prevalence of the protective needs of the community over the personal rights and duties of the offender, which reinforces the reliance on criminal types rather than precise legal definition; a crude form of social protection becomes the main content of criminal law (p. 183).

Many of these resonate with key characteristics of how assembling suspicion based on pre-emptive criminal justice operates. Criminal intent is the basis of pre-emptive criminal justice but the intent has been objectified through mapping predispositions on the basis of behavioural patterns and individual trajectories. By deconstructing the boundaries between deviant, criminal and abnormal practice, criminal justice is extended to other fields. As Kessler and Werner have argued, turning extrajudicial killings into a form of risk management in the war on terror has gone hand in hand with administrative processes bypassing the key legal rationalities that govern the capture and killing of individuals, i.e. responsibility, immediate threat and institutionalised danger (Kessler and Werner, 2008). Moreover, as Marieke de Goede and Beatrice de Graaf have argued under the heading 'sentencing risk', counter-terrorist practices focusing on pre-emption and risk profiling have been incorporated into criminal legal practice and the law itself (de Goede and de Graaf, 2013).

These and other potential consequences of assembling suspicion on the democratic legal order indicate that the spectre of authoritarian and totalitarian government remains relevant in understanding how diffuse securitising is not simply compromising democratic practice and institutions but can be a serious threat to them. However, in relation to diffuse securitising today the issue is not in the first instance the institutionalisation of an authoritarian and totalitarian state but rather how authoritarian and totalitarian forms of governance operate within and through a transversal and diffuse practice of surveillance and risk management (Bell, 2006; Los, 2006). Maria Los, for example, articulates in detail how key elements of totalitarian governance in communist regimes are at work in contemporary surveillance practices but without necessarily hooking them together in an ideological state project and without considering them to be driven by centralised powers. Some of the key processes are the construction of files, the inscription of suspicions in social relations and the creation of a 'fearing subject' by having people enacting themselves as 'beings under surveillance'. Her argument is that the fact that surveillance works in a diffuse mode, in which the role of state bureaucracy is much less clear-cut, has not eliminated these key techniques through which governing practices seek a totalising reach that constrains freedom by means of surveillance. She concludes that dropping the spectre of totalitarianism altogether would imply that certain key characteristics of how contemporary surveillance enacts limits of democracy are lost from sight. For her the challenge is rather to use the spectre of totalitarianism to check if and how surveillance configures key aspects of totalitarian government in diffuse situations where the totalitarian effects cannot be easily aggregated back into state apparatuses (Los, 2006, 2010).

There are other aspects of the tension between assembling suspicion, surveillance and democracy but these should suffice to indicate a heightened concern in the literature on surveillance with the way in which diffuse surveillance combined with the deployment of risk techniques impact on democratic principles, processes and institutions. At the heart of many of these analyses is not simply a concern with how security agencies and policies traditionally have always operated in tension with key democratic procedures and principles but also an understanding that the diffuse nature poses particular challenges to democratic processes. Although analyses of the political dimensions often link surveillance to forms of state control, for example by seeing surveillance as part of national security strategy (e.g. Bell, 2006), and retain the formation of authoritarian and totalitarian state apparatuses as the main democratic challenge, Maria Los' intervention indicates that the diffuse nature of the securitising process demands moving away from the spectre of the state and towards taking the nature of the governmental technique itself as the focal point, irrespective of whether it enacts a state-like project or not. Even if the challenges to democracy in the diffusion of insecurity do not clearly coalesce around the formation of authoritarian states and regimes, diffuse securitising is eating away at various components of democratic politics. The difficulty to connect the different components easily to the formation of an authoritarian state make it a necessity to develop a more fractured interpretation of securitising practices and how they enact limits of democracy.

In the remaining sections of the chapter, I use the debates on protection of privacy in surveillance studies to introduce elements of such an interpretation. Privacy is one of the key categorical vehicles of political contestations of surveillance. It has also been the focus of some intense debates in surveillance studies about how to analyse the political effects of expanding and/or diffusing surveillance.

Privacy

Privacy is one of the central stakes in the assembling of suspicion. In particular, surveillance is often contested in name of the protection of privacy. John Wadham, Director of Liberty (from 1995 until 2003) states:[1]

> The information revolution has brought us many benefits, which include the means to more efficient prevention and detection of crime. But this comes with dangers and one is the erosion of our privacy.
>
> (Wadham, 2002)

Possible consequences of police and other state institutions having access to 'private' information go beyond simply data collection. For example, Privacy International raised the importance of privacy protection in the case of the identity registration of refugees by the UNHCR. This information is particularly sensitive. If the governmental powers that the refugee is fleeing from gets hold of this information, it can put at risk the refugee's life and family (Privacy International, 2011).

The question for this and the next section, however, is not how the institutional extraction of information from individuals erodes privacy. The focus is more on the political dimensions: how does assembling of suspicion in surveillance practices enact limits of democracy by challenging privacy? And, what are the limitations of focusing on privacy when trying to understand how surveillance enacts limits of democracy?

'Privacy' refers to the protection from extraction of information on individuals or contexts. The use of 'contexts' recognises that privacy also refers to sites (such as the home) and actions (e.g. walking a street) (Neyland, 2006: 3–4). The key issue is the protection of persons, sites and society as a whole, from arbitrary or unauthorised gathering of information and from authorities overreaching so that privacy is disproportionately challenged in the name of other values.[2] The 'privacy question' is often understood as one of protecting a 'bubble' (Stalder, 2011) that surrounds individuals from intrusion by powerful agencies. The popular imaginary of 'Big Brother' encapsulates both the social and political problematique of privacy. Governing agencies pervade private spheres ranging from private properties over bodies to inner thoughts. In doing so, they hollow out and, in the worst case, destroy the social value of privacy. Both the quotation by Wadham and Privacy International's claim to protect the privacy of refugee identity work within this understanding of privacy. Wadham's is primarily about the social value of privacy, while Privacy International emphasises the safety of the individual from governmental coercion and violence by protecting personal information.

Political intrusions of privacy risks limiting democracy. Protection of the private sphere is often understood to be a necessary condition for the development of social relations between citizens, and for opinion formation that can then be brought to public deliberation and political action. This process needs to be left alone by the democratic state so that a plurality of opinions and actions can be brought to bear on society and politics without being dictated or censored by governmental powers. If citizens are required to actively input into decisions on rights, common goods and values, and policy choices, and if they are an autonomous force of legitimating and holding to account governmental powers, democratic politics requires that citizens can develop relations of trust and autonomy independent of the governing authorities. Privacy is often understood to be a crucial resource here. Haggerty and Samatas summarise this democratic limit as follows:

> Intrusive state surveillance can destroy that distinction [between a public realm of political action and a private realm of personal fulfilment and family intimacy], undermining the private realm and in so doing limiting a person's ability to develop a unique sense of self and of his or her political interests. Such scrutiny can also have more straightforward implications for democracy. Citizens need a space comparatively free of governmental oversight if they are to engage in political action.
>
> (Haggerty and Samatas, 2010b: 4)

A related issue is that surveillance is often relatively unregulated and opaque, and at times secret. If privacy is an important social value then actions that limit or endanger it need to be brought within democratic processes of deliberation and evaluation. 'Privacy enters the discussion because it provides one of the key values available to hold power accountable. Privacy involves a constraint on the use of power—a rationale for setting limitations on its exercise' (Regan, 2011: 498). Privacy is thus not only understood as a condition for democratic political action but also as a value in whose name transparency and political and legal accountability can be made to bear upon often murky and secretive surveillance processes (Bennett, 2011: 491).

Politically the tension between security and privacy is regularly presented as a trade-off between two values. The political question is then what privacy can be traded off for what security, mostly within an understanding that one cannot excessively undermine the other. This trade-off is not only used to set limits to surveillance but also to expand it, however. Richard J. Aldrich, for example, argued that although increased transatlantic intelligence sharing is inhibited by different national privacy legislations, a shared conceptual framework 'within which to tackle the trade-off between security and privacy is essential for closer transatlantic cooperation' (2004: 732). In other words, setting in place a regulative framework for the proportionate protection of privacy can support expansive surveillance. Trade-offs, and arguing for some form of balance between them, are familiar tools for keeping two values in play while structuring the debate around the need for proportionality.

However, such framing often ignores how surveillance is steeped in institutional competitions, embedded in histories of inequality, changes in power relations and reconfigurations of publicness. The 'trade-off' is not simply a matter of societal choice between competing values but a result of private economic interests and their entanglement in political decisions. Moreover, privacy is also socially sorted in the sense that not everyone's privacy is equally intruded upon and the differentiation in the protection of privacy creates and reinforces social differences (Lyon, 2003c). Surveillance often reproduces inequalities in society by targeting more intensely certain categories of people and sites such as single mothers, poorer neighbourhoods, teenagers, particular ethnic groups and unskilled migrants. This argument that surveillance performs a social sorting has led to calls for widening the focus from privacy to broader questions of justice covering a wider range of rights and issues of inequality and freedom (Lyon, 2001: 128).

> [S]urveillance today sorts people into categories, assigning worth or risk, in ways that have real effects on their life-chances. Deep discrimination occurs, thus making surveillance not merely a matter of personal privacy but of social justice.
>
> (Lyon, 2003a: 11)

For these authors, privacy arguments draw attention too much to individual rights and the balancing of two values—security and privacy—consequently ignoring the social conditions and effects of surveillance.

Making social sorting and questions of justice more central to the evaluation of surveillance is thus seen as a correction to privileging privacy as the key issue in political debates on surveillance. In addition, it seeks to draw attention to the diffuse nature in which surveillance produces its effects. Surveillance classifies in various ways, and is often instrumental for private and public service delivery. Discriminatory effects of governmental classifications are well documented; for example, the institutionalising of categories of the 'deserving' and 'non-deserving' in public provisions. Diffuse forms of surveillance are not different. They gather data that socially sort people and spaces; for example, through assigning credit worthiness and levels of insurance premiums. Although diffusing surveillance displaces power from a centralised state bureaucracy to a wide range of agencies, it similarly organises asymmetrical power relations; for example, between global insurance companies and national privacy advocates.

> 'Social sorting' highlights the classifying drive of contemporary surveillance. It also defuses some of the more supposedly sinister aspects of surveillance processes (it's not a conspiracy of evil intentions or a relentless and inexorable process). Surveillance is always ambiguous … .
> At the same time social sorting places the matter firmly in the social and not just the individual realm—which 'privacy' concerns all too often tend to do.
>
> (Lyon, 2003b: 13)

Social sorting of surveillance also questions the idea that the development of technological surveillance makes surveillance more democratic in the sense that everyone becomes equally subjected to it. The assumption is that technology makes prejudices of race, age and looks—for example, during border controls or surveilling shopping malls—irrelevant because technology gathers data from everyone entering its purview, and classifies without interference of subjective judgements of those surveilling. As Garry Marx summarises this assumption with regard to CCTV: 'The video surveillance camera … [does] not differentiate between social classes. Data are gathered democratically from all within their purview' (Marx, 1995: 238). When looking more closely at how surveillance works in practice, however, such democratic effects are an illusion. For example, as Clive Norris shows, research on how surveillance through CCTV works in practice discloses the many discretionary decisions that are made about which information is important, which subjects to focus on, and so on. He concludes that 'rather than promoting a democratic gaze, the reliance on categorical suspicion intensifies the surveillance of those already marginalized and further increases their chance of official stigmatization' (Norris, 2003: 266).

For some in the surveillance literature, the focus on privacy itself—and not just the trade-off and balancing framings—is part of the problem. Privacy emphasises how extraction of information affects individuals and particular spheres of life rather than the wider social and political transformations it sustains and produces. In Regan's words:

> The scale and scope of the problems exist at a systemic level (institutions, social practices, fabric of modern life) not at the level of private space (invading one's house, taking pictures from a distance, overhearing a conversation between two parties).
>
> (Regan, 2011: 497)

Deploying a more systemic angle allows us to introduce more effectively the question of power, as Monahan among others has argued:

> As sociotechnical systems, then, surveillance and security are intimately intertwined with institutions, ideologies, and a long history of social inequality … . From this standpoint, one can begin to ask the kinds of questions worth asking and answering—questions about power.
>
> (Monahan, 2006: 10)

Changing the political question from privacy to power introduces the need to look in greater detail at the distribution of resources for extracting information and the specific use that is made of them. As Phillips states:

> The political (and epistemological) question is not whether individuals are known and typified. We always are. Rather, it is a question of how individuals are known and typified—by whom, to whom, as what, and toward what end we are made visible.
>
> (Phillips, 2005)

In surveillance studies, this criticism of privacy has become widely shared, so much so that Bennett called for saving privacy as an important category for critical engagements with surveillance, while recognising that privacy cannot cover all aspects. He proposed to draw a clearer distinction between privacy analysis and surveillance analysis:

> Privacy applies when personal information is collected on the individual. And, if this is not the central issue then privacy is not the point of

discussion. For example, when focusing on the structuration of power: panoptical surveillance still structures when the cameras are off. That dimension is surveillance analysis, not privacy.

(Bennett, 2011: 492–93)

Privacy remains an important force from which to question surveillance.[3] For example, Richard J. Aldrich, argues that limitations to the international exchange of intelligence are partly due to different privacy legislations in countries. This compartmentalisation prevents large-scale data sharing.

Yet, widening the scope to what Bennett refers to as 'surveillance studies', Regan as 'systemic level analysis', and Monahan as 'questions of power' is particularly important for understanding key elements of the diffusion of surveillance, in the sense of dispersing and non-intensifying monitoring for the purpose of interfering. They bring out various aspects that often get lost in privacy focused analyses. One of these is that contemporary surveillance does not simply function as an externally imposed force—unwanted and illegitimate invasion by state apparatuses of privacy bubbles—but is a constitutive element of the existing social fabric (e.g. Stalder, 2011). Surveillance is an essential part of requesting and delivering services, of market competition, and so on. There is no escape from surveillance that is enacted in fractured ways and driven by different and often not programmatically related functions rather than being centrally organised.

In addition, as more subtle power analyses have shown, surveillance has become widely embedded in many areas of life. Not because people are forced to participate in surveillance practices but because they voluntarily contribute information and largely accept that surveillance is an inherent part of life.

> In our day-to-day lives, privacy is not routinely 'invaded': it is not pried away from a resistant and apoplectic public. Instead, privacy is compromised by measured efforts to position individuals in contexts where they are apt to exchange various bits of personal data for a host of perks, efficiencies, and other benefits. Part of the ongoing politics of surveillance therefore does not involve efforts to 'capture' data, but to establish inducements and enticements at the precise threshold where individuals will willingly surrender their information. Surveillance becomes the cost of engaging in any number of desirable behaviours or participating in the institutions that make modern life possible.

(Bennett, 2011: 488)

In this understanding, seeing surveillance mainly as an invasion by an external authority into a personal sphere is difficult to maintain. Privacy needs rethinking in situations where power operates via inducements and enticements. When surveillance becomes detached from coercive control by a state-like entity, it still remains part of a wide range of everyday practices, including shopping, tourism, buying fertilisers, banking, registering with social media, buying a flat and claiming insurance. To protect oneself from surveillance, retreating into the private is not really an option in these situations (Mubi Brighenti, 2010: 52).[4]

Diffuse surveillance that is technologically driven thus poses some serious challenges to privacy. The political issue, however, is not simply that surveillance challenges privacy but that it challenges the capacity of the democratic categorical mobilisation of privacy to effectively contest developments in surveillance. Why claim rights to privacy when people are volunteering information? Why limit the extraction of data when people are largely indifferent? The democratic grounds for using rights to privacy as a device to question surveillance seems to be under serious pressure in these conditions. Moreover, though privacy is used to define limits to surveillance practice, it can work perversely to appease concerns with the personal and social consequences of increased surveillance. The mere existence of privacy regulation becomes a sign that democracy and privacy are protected, while in fact it may not limit the dispersing of surveillance very much. In that sense, privacy regulation becomes complicit in the dispersing of surveillance by appeasing concerns with the spread of surveillance but also with other consequences such as discriminations and with the reduced ability to bring other societal values to bear upon surveillance agencies and practices, given their diffuse nature.

An increasing demand for and co-opting of people into delivering information not only reduces the value of privacy, however; it also sustains the assembling of suspicion as a mode of relating. Anything or anyone not delivering full transparency, i.e. the data demanded, is to some extent suspicious. Why would one not want to gain points on a loyalty card that can be turned into cash? Why would you try to avoid CCTV cameras when walking the city? Why would you not give full details of personal information when applying for a visa or arriving in the airport? Not volunteering information comes to signify that one has a secret, and what is secret comes to mean 'something suspicious' that needs to be made legible. At this point, surveillance not only challenges privacy but also the political meaning of publicness. As Jodie Dean has argued, a publicity driven technoculture collapses democratic potentials of transparency and public deliberation into a relentless demand for more access to information. Delivering information comes to stand in for transparency and publicness as grounds for political contestation. Information becomes an absolute value in its own right, and not delivering on this value makes one suspicious rather than political. She concludes her critique of the political significance of the public sphere in an era of technologically driven publicity and commodification of data and data gathering with:

> The values articulated together by the notion of the public are important to utopian imaginings of democracy. Unfortunately, they have been co-opted by a communicative capitalism that has turned them into their opposite. For this reason, it may well be necessary to abandon them—if only to realize them.
>
> (Dean, 2002: 172)

For a political analytics of privacy, these observations shift the question from the legitimacy and consequences of intruding upon privacy to how to retain a focus on the extraction of information on individuals while simultaneously introducing the multiple power relations that are enacted in the extraction. How do the techniques of extraction limit the capacity of people to bear upon, call into question and ask for accountability of the practices of surveillance that they are subjected to and participate in? Privacy remains important in this analysis but as one element in the wider democratic questions of participation in the shaping and critique of surveillance and of holding to account governing powers in what is a highly diffused enactment of insecurities (Stalder, 2002). In the next section, I will look at Kirstie Ball's work to introduce in more detail a set of categories that retain the focus on the extraction of information on individuals, and raises further insights in how the assembling of suspicion enacts limits of democracy.

Extraction, bodies, resistance

Kirstie Ball has developed an approach that starts from the intimate presence of surveillance in people's lives and hooks the processes of extraction they experience into wider power relations. The experience of surveillance is the point of departure, rather than privacy rights or reconfigurations of publicness. She proposes an analytics of exposure combined with a political economy of interiority. The extraction of information on individuals remains central but is explicitly placed within power relations that are enacted through surveillance. She does this to unpack the contemporary nature of surveillance and to show how surveillance shapes and limits the possibilities for contestation and resistance.

Drawing on her analysis of surveillance of workers in two call centres, she introduces the concept of 'exposure' to capture that the experience of surveillance is more complex than simply performance monitoring of workers, oppressing subjects, or making bodies docile. For example, the performance monitoring made workers more visible but also created emotional vulnerabilities among the workers. The degree of coping with these vulnerabilities was then monitored and managed in counselling schemes. The experience and exposure of subjects can thus involve more than simply making actions visible.

> They (workers in the call centres) were professionally and personally exposed to both the customer and their employer. Employees often managed that exposure to a great effect, performing to the required standard, and managing their personal inputs accordingly, but where this failed, their underlying anxieties were revealed and they were subject to more intense personal scrutiny. As such, in one sense, subject responses to surveillance concern performativity, but underlying that performativity are vulnerabilities which occasionally break the surface and render the subject much more accountable to whoever is watching.
>
> (Ball, 2009: 642)

As an analytical category 'exposure' thus foregrounds both the experience of the surveilled subject and how that experience exists within a multifaceted relation of monitoring and manipulating exposure. By taking the experience of the surveilled subject as a starting point, an analysis of exposure brings out that surveillance organises insecurity by simultaneously creating and managing vulnerability. The bodies might be docile but they are in the first place vulnerable; exposure creates anxious fragile subjects who then become more accountable, who are surveilled more intensely (e.g. through adding counselling).

Different aspects of the power relation between the manager and worker—or police officer and traveller—are central to this understanding. Starting from experiences of exposure demonstrates the intimate nature of some surveillance practice, both in the sense of extracting information on emotions—anxiety, confidence, troubled or tension—rather than simply actions, and in the sense of how surveillance is integrated in multifaceted and detailed ways in everyday experiences and practice. Rather than the reasoning subjects calculating the costs and benefits of exposing certain aspects of their life, surveillance works upon the body as emotions, and extracts biological information directly from the body; for example through finger prints and bodily behaviour (see also Muller,

2004, 2010). Exposure thus takes place in the interface between technology and the body, rather than between technology and a reasoning subject.

The power relations within which this interface exists and within which exposure operates are not limited to interpersonal relations between managers and workers, police and suspects, or border guards and immigrants. They exist within what Ball refers to as a 'political economy of interiority':

> A process where an aspect of an individual's personal or private world becomes exposed to others, via a process of data representation, interpretation, sharing through intermediaries within a broader surveillance assemblage.
>
> (Ball, 2009: 643)

While the notion of interiority refers to the nature of the exposure, the concept of political economy refers to the interface between technology and bodies being embedded in distributions of commercial and governmental interests, employment relations and markets of extraction technologies. Demand for and supply of surveillance is created in this political economy. The modulations of exposure when crossing borders is tied up with commercial interests in surveillance technology, securing employment for border guards, and the political value of demonstrating effective border control, for example. The experience of exposure is at least partly shaped by the competitions and struggles between these interests resulting in, for example, the introduction of body scanners in airports or the deployment of technological devices reading anxiety from bodily reactions without direct face-to-face contact between border guards and traveller (Muller, 2012).

Although this political economy is not reducible to economics, an economic imperative for firms to expand surveillance technology and data exchange is part of it. This imperative goes beyond selling security technology and has become central to a wide range of economic practices. In particular, targeted advertising and efficiently identifying consumer demand have played an important role in the embedding of surveillance technology in everyday life. This expansion works by bringing consumers and users to volunteering information. They are asked to exchange personal information for benefits (e.g. vouchers when using a loyalty card) or participation (e.g. membership of Facebook). At this point privacy changes from a right to a commodity (Davies, 2001; Campbell and Carlson, 2002). Although this looks like a change that is freely embraced by users of the internet and consumers, there is a serious asymmetry between the power of suppliers and consumers. Not participating in sharing the requested information is often 'punished' with exclusion or a significant extra financial cost (Campbell and Carlson, 2002).

The concept of 'political economy of interiority' foregrounds both the economics of surveillance and the distribution of power between various actors and processes. Power does not reside with a single entity, whether the state watching and controlling society or management manipulating workers. Instead it approaches surveillance and its experience as being shaped and performed in the relations between dispersed private and public interests, multiple moments of competition and decision, managerial fine tuning of processes on a regular basis, and seductive as well as coercive extraction of information.[5]

Understanding surveillance as exposure embedded in a political economy of interiority retains the analytical focus on the extraction of information on persons while embedding the extraction processes strongly into diffuse power relations. Yet the subjects that are exposed remain objects of surveillance rather than subjects engaging, contesting or resisting surveillance practices. It is not clear how people subjected to surveillance and the circulation of suspicion (can) gain a voice to bring their concerns to bear on the management relation, or how they (can) enact themselves into new subjects with the right to hold rights so as to break out of their subjectivisation as anxious subjects in need of therapy and emotional management. In other words, foregrounding the experience of exposure and its relation to the political economy of interiority at the interface between body and technology does not address the question of how surveillance shapes the possibilities of democratic actions. At first sight Ball's interpretation is as dystopian as many security analyses. The political economy of interiority extracts, modulates and circulates data in such a way that subjects have not much chance to significantly bear upon surveillance. In addition, homing in on experiences of exposure reinforces how pervasive extraction is, how exposure is intricately woven into everyday practices and situations and the intimate enactment of one's subjectivity. As a result, contesting surveillance on grounds of a separation between an existing private sphere that remains untouched by surveillance from which political action can spring and spheres of life where surveillance is a legitimate presence is more difficult to maintain.

Moreover, the increased extracting of data directly from the body and at a distance, as well as the creation of virtual 'worlds' and 'subjects' in the circulation of the data, seriously delimits the possibility for reflective engagement with surveillance by those subjected to the extractions. Subjects are not always aware that information is being extracted or how the extracted data are reassembled and used. In this sense, exposure and the political economy of interiority enact limits of democracy not through centralising control and instituting pervasive police apparatus in states but by neutralising the possibility for subjects to reflect on the extraction at the point of it taking place. The possibility for reflection becomes a democratic stake in these processes of diffuse securitising. Democratic actions imply retaining some 'autonomy' of the subjects to bear on the social and political power relations to which they are subjected. This autonomy often assumes a reflective engagement with the conditions and practices of power, i.e. knowing how one is willingly or unwillingly exposed to the political economy of interiority in the extraction of information.

At this point the question arises of what democratic resistance can mean in the absence of explicitly reflective moments and large-scale formal protest and collective mobilisation, and also in situations in which bodies break down in various data flows and are reconstituted in processes of reassembling. To make this question more than a rhetorical expression of political despair, two observations have to be included. The relative lack of awareness and absence of large-scale protest does not necessarily imply universal acceptance of exposure.[6] Nor does it imply that there are no issues, dilemmas, difficulties and possibilities for resistance for the individual. In other words, dissenting sentiments and actions are present within the enactment of exposure and the technique of surveillance, and enactments of suspicion are not a smoothly running machinery with no functional flaws (Marx, 2003; Ball, 2009: 652). In relation to online surveillance, Dupont identifies two trends that allow for autonomous action resisting surveillance (2008). The first, he refers to as 'democratisation of surveillance'. People can buy cheap surveillance technology that allows them to gather information on their family, neighbours, politicians, etc. The diffusion of this technology blurs the distinction between the watched and the watchers, and allows people to appropriate surveillance for various purposes (e.g. Mann, 2005).

This trend complicates the power relations in surveillance. The watchers who are supposed to be in power, because they are controlling visibility and information, can be watched themselves by those they are watching. The latter can expose information that undermines professional integrity or that is personally painful, for example. Although this trend possibly shifts power relations, it does not necessarily resist the diffusion of suspicion. After all, the watched can be practising surveillance too, consequently reinforcing suspicion as an organising principle of social relations. The second trend Dupont describes is the collaborative action of socio-technical networks that resist surveillance by deploying technology to erode, reveal and mock surveillance, such as encrypting, hiding one's identity, and making visible who is surveilling the web. Dupont's main point, however, is that the internet has a distributed rather than strictly hierarchical structure of supervision. Although various power asymmetries exist, including those based on differences in technical skill, they are not organised in clearly vertical lines moving from a centre to a population of users. Surveillance has a variable architecture that also includes variable resistances (Dupont, 2008: 268–69).

Resistance to surveillance and its assembling of suspicion through conscious individual re-appropriation and mobilising collaborative action are thus an integral part of the political economy of surveillance. Yet Ball's point that contemporary surveillance limits reflectiveness and that this demands us to think the relative autonomy of those subjected to the extractions differently is worth exploring a little further.[7] In particular, it brings into sharper focus that interpreting resistance and contestation in terms of mass mobilisation and public protest through invoking rights claims cannot be taken as the default democratic position. They are not irrelevant but they miss something important: the limitations contemporary surveillance sets to the possibility for reflection from which practices contesting, questioning or resisting surveillance can spring.

If the body and distant extraction are central to surveillance, then it makes sense to ask: what does it mean to understand the body rather than the reflective subject as a political actor? The starting point for answering this question is that the body as the point of authority and truth—the provider of authentic data (Muller, 2010)—poses a challenge for surveillance. Surveillance needs to fix information as authentic at the point of extraction, and that authentic quality needs to be retained for later use. Yet bodies are changing and reconstituting themselves all the time. They do things, they make new connections, they change biologically, etc. Bodies are not fixed; they are not the stable biological point in a world in flux but are multiple, continuous becomings (Ball, 2005: 103).[8] They are transient and momentary rather than stable and permanent. As becomings, bodies are made and make themselves through relations, movement and speed, and can thus not be reduced or confined to being something—to their substantive identity, biological trait and character. Bodies are in motion, not in the sense of moving from one place to another or one identity to another, but in the sense of always being in motion not as a whole but in fragments. Change does then not in the first instance refer to changes in maturation, growth and identity but to continuous micro changes in orientations, trajectories and directions that make any identification necessarily inauthentic (Grosz, 1994: 176).

Looked at from a democratic perspective that values autonomy, the friction between changing bodies and security attempting to fix them is a form of resistance. The resistance is not in the first place conscious, like subjects destroying the skin of their finger tips to resist finger printing. It has an ontological quality. Bodies do challenge surveillance and its technology because of what they are. They are a becoming rather than a being, always slightly changing through their interactions, exposures to things and other bodies, biological processes (like ageing), and performances (Hayles, 1999: 194ff; Ball, 2005: 103). This 'resistance' thus takes place all the time; it is inherent in the tension between changing bodies and the security imperative for authentic information that retains its authenticity at least for some time.

Although this understanding of the autonomy of the body clarifies that taking bodies as multiple becomings may be a useful starting point for exploring the challenges to and possibilities of a democratic politics of insecurity, it also leaves a set of issues unresolved. Most obviously, it raises the question why critical analysis of surveillance bothers with the question of resistance and autonomy if bodily performance and being challenge surveillance all the time anyway, irrespective of whether the embodied subject intends it or not, irrespective of how 'good' the surveillance techniques are. When resistance and autonomy take the form of frictions that are immanent to social and political relations, the body-subject as becoming makes democratic capacity ontological. Things happen that escape and disrupt surveillance techniques simply because of what bodies are. Understanding bodies as becoming therefore leaves unresolved the question of how to move from 'friction' to political action. The political issue is about changing 'frictions' into contestations and resistances of power distribution in the political economy of interiority, and its diffusion of security as a set of imperatives that organises subjectivities and relations.[9]

Privacy revisited

The previous section argued that one pathway to rethinking the possibilities for a democratic politics of surveillance starts at the interface between technology and bodies. Understanding that relation as friction between the fixing work of surveillance technology and changing bodies sets technology and bodies in opposition. Yet, bodies and technology are more closely and ambivalently intertwined. Technologies are a central part of the social fabric and of how bodies connect to other bodies and situations. Bodies and technology are working together in producing surveillance; social actions, self-definitions and bodily existence are taking shape in interaction with technology. At the same time, however, bodies have a disjunctive relation to technology; as becoming, they challenge the technological demand for fixity. Bodies are thus simultaneously object and subject of extraction, as well as a friction that disrupts the smooth workings of the technology of surveillance. The bodily challenges can be re-incorporated in surveillance through demands for improved surveillance practice and technology but they also remain disrupting by not fully supplying what is demanded of the body. At the interface with technology, bodies are thus both reproductive and disruptive of the political economy of interiority. They are a source of extraction but also that which remains fluid, changing and therefore challenging. (For a more extensive discussion on technology and politics, see the next chapter.)

The interstitial understanding of the relation between technology and bodies makes it possible to recapture privacy as a political resource. Privacy is one of the devices through which disjunctures in this relation can be politically enacted. However, privacy here does not gain its political significance from instituting protection of bodies from technological governmental intrusion; it is not a matter of mobilising the right to privacy as such. Rather, privacy is a claim or action creating temporary disjunctions in the relations between technology and bodies. Its political meaning rests in momentarily turning ontological frictions into disruptions of the instituted relation of extraction that sustains the political economy of interiority. These actions experiment with privacy so that they raise issues about privacy–public distinctions and about privacy as a bubble where one hides. The issue here is the micro-practices of bodily resistance that challenge not simply particular technologies and extractions but that bear upon the workings of extraction itself rather than the more familiar forms of resistance like encrypting actions on the internet or counter-surveillance by using mobile-phone cameras.

The increasing use of webcams to inflate exposure of one's body rather than shield it from surveillance is an interesting example in which privacy is enacted in creative ways that give rise to such micro-disruptions. This practice turns privacy on its head. Reducing the expectation that things are hidden, overloading surveillance with information, and exposing in great detail without much restraint can disrupt a political economy of surveillance that thrives on demanding increased and increasingly refined extractions. Koskela (2004) draws on this practice, and in particular the example of JenniCAM, to open a set of probing questions about control, power and resistance in relation to self-exposing private life without much regard to what is exposed. JenniCAM was set up by Jennifer Ringley in 1996. She installed a webcam in her dormitory room, streaming uninterrupted images of her daily life. The disruption draws on privacy but not in the usual way. Privacy is not invoked to protect private life from the seeing eye of others. Instead, by inflating exposure far beyond the norm, JenniCAM somehow implodes the boundaries that define the meaning of privacy and its distinction from publicness. Ringley enacts privacy but through indiscriminate exposure, rather than negotiating carefully what is valued as private and what not. In doing so, she somehow dilutes the value of extraction upon which the political economy of interiority relies. The exposure of Ringley's daily doings and her relation to the webcam present a body in becoming. In the most immediate sense, the body is not fixed but exists by continuously doing different things: reading, eating, pondering, sleeping, sitting, standing, being absent, etc. Yet she is also becoming, in the sense of changing, through her intimate relation with the webcam. The exposure has become part of what Ringley is. When asked why she switched the webcam back on after having disconnected it for a while because of harassment, she replied that she felt lonely without the camera.

Clearly, various interpretations of JenniCAM are possible and much has been written about it. I am mainly interested here in Koskela's interpretation, however. Hers is hesitant, not sure whether she is overstating the disruptive and political significance of what Ringley's body and JennyCAM are doing. Yet, she avoids psychoanalytic readings in favour of a socio-political reading of what is happening in the field of vision. Key to her analysis is the bodily enactments of new subjectivities— ones that are not incorporating the self-disciplining required in the public exposure of bodies as mediated by privacy, ones that are ambivalently engaging gendered qualities of the web, and so on. Koskela also shows how various lines of control are disturbed, including the normative work of the public–private distinction, and the distinction between a surveillance camera and a webcam. As already said, at places she is hesitant, expressing uncertainty, expressing the possibility that she is over-interpreting the disruptive qualities of Ringley's exposing. Yet that is what Ringley's act calls for, given that it is full of ambivalences and given that it disrupts categories, limits and boundaries that shape the more established debates and experiences of surveillance. Ringley's act, as read by Koskela, gives us an insight into how the body as becoming in its relation with technology can give rise to different ways of practising privacy and of politicising surveillance in unusual but disruptive modes. As Koskela concludes: 'The question is not about political activism in [the] traditional sense but about *revealing as a political act—intrinsically*' (2004: 210).

While one might agree with the critics of privacy-focused analyses that privacy draws attention to too limited a set of issues in surveillance, replacing it with autonomy (Stalder, 2011) as the key challenge is not straightforward either if we accept that body-subjects are formed in the interstices of technology and bodies. Bodies are not autonomous in the sense of existing outside the interstices with a capacity to disrupt them. Autonomy needs to be rethought in terms of what, if anything, it means to be autonomous with a capacity to rupture the political economy of interiority from within the interstices of bodies and technologies. Following her focus on the experience of surveillance, Ball proposes to look in greater detail at how the relation between bodies and technology is really mediated at the level of the embodied self. This opens indeed a path forward in which key elements of the privacy debate can be revisited from the perspective of the experience of exposure and the rendition of interiority in conditions in which the body-subject cannot be placed—let along, exist—in a bubble outside the 'technologies of power.' It also makes it possible to rethink autonomy in terms of multiple becomings.

The experience of extraction of information on the body-subject, which Ball and the discussions on the need to revisit privacy debates introduce, highlights that surveillance enacts the limits of democracy in ways that make it difficult to uncritically fall back on received understandings of democratic practice. The challenge here is not simply to design new concepts or to reframe existing resources like privacy. It is equally important to avoid 'ontologising' politics by presenting disruptions as simply inevitable frictions generated by body-subjects when they are put under exposure and subjected to the political economy of interiority. Work in surveillance studies like Ball's and others referred to in this section is of crucial importance for political readings of diffuse securitising, not because they formulate a 'new' politics but because they show why, where and how one needs to start rethinking familiar conceptions of democratic politics, like privacy and autonomy, and what is involved in bringing into analysis a diffuse democratic politics of insecurity. In other words, they provide both challenges and building blocks for thinking through what democratic stakes can mean, where they can be located and how they are enacted in a diffuse politics of insecurity. Similar issues arise when looking more closely at another key theme through which risk governance and surveillance are politically interrogated: the technological nature of assembling suspicion, which is the topic of the next chapter.

Conclusion

The chapter developed in more detail how assembling suspicion enacts limits of democracy. The discussion focused on surveillance more generally rather than the rendition of suspicion as such. Yet the issues that arise in relation to surveillance bear directly on assembling suspicion and its unbinding of security, given the key role that surveillance techniques play in the assembling. In a short overview of some of the key democratic issues arising from surveillance, I indicated that diffuse surveillance enacts limits to the available institutional democratic practice because of the dispersed nature of surveillance operations and decisions. This observation is the general background against which the chapter introduced briefly how surveillance more generally bears upon democratic practices, including elections, the capacity for voicing public concerns and bringing surveillance to account. After a brief discussion of the value and limits of using the danger of totalitarian governance and state to understand the effects of assembling suspicion, the analysis homed in on the question of intrusion of privacy as a focal point of how surveillance unbinds democratic limits to security. The starting point was not so much the protection of privacy itself but rather how democratic limits are enacted by intruding on privacy and what are the limits of analysing the effects of surveillance on democracy through the lens of the protection of privacy. Privacy has been in liberal but also republican traditions of politics a condition for democracy: democratic opinion formation and publicly organising political voice in the name of common concerns is often understood to require spheres of life in which political authorities do not interfere. The private sphere is then the condition of possibility to develop opinions that can be brought to bear on public decisions. Although this interpretation of privacy, and in particular the pre-political nature of the private, have been heavily contested, with feminist literature often in the lead, the protection of privacy remains a key resource in contestations of assembling suspicion and surveillance more generally. Studies on surveillance, however, are ambivalent about the importance of privacy as the central category for analysing tensions between democracy and surveillance. Social sorting, reconfigurations of the public sphere, and the shifting of power relations in diffuse and technologically driven surveillance are often foregrounded as at least equally necessary, with privacy being sometimes seen as a liability that distracts the analysis from these more significant effects of surveillance.

The chapter then turned to Kirstie Ball's work where she retains a focus on the extraction of information itself and its intrusion on body-subjects. Her work inflects privacy as the subjective experience of surveillance that is structurally embedded in a political economy of interiority. She argues for starting analyses of surveillance from the experience of the surveilled subject while embedding these experiences in a political economy of accessing private practice, feelings and biological information that distributes and institutes surveillance interests and that shapes subjective experiences. One of the issues she brings out is that current surveillance practice severely limits reflective engagements with the extraction of information, and that the biological body becomes increasingly a main source of extraction. At the juncture between subjects bodies and technological extraction, a serious democratic challenge emerges, given that reflective practice is central to a vast set of democratic practices that emphasise rational deliberation, public voicing and/or mass mobilisation as key politicising strategies. How to reinvent democratic autonomy in a dispersed political economy of interiority that diffuses subjects bodies and reduces reflective capacities, among others by surveilling at a distance, having subjects volunteering information and extracting data directly from bodies?

In reply, Ball introduces the need to rethink autonomy of the subjects, bodies and resistance to surveillance in ways that do not start from reflective engagement. She opens one possible pathway for this rethinking by reading democratic autonomy in terms of bodily becoming. There is an important tension between surveillance's need to fix information for at least a certain period of time and the continuously changing bodies that are surveilled. Bodies are not fixed; they change. There is therefore an autonomy to bodily becoming that creates a gap between the data extracted and the body. However, bodily becoming seems to refer to an ontological state of the body—the body is always becoming. The question then is, why do we need to worry about democratic autonomy if surveillance is always already 'resisted' by the subjects bodies simply because of what they are? I concluded that the democratic political question cannot just stop with such embracing of ontological friction. The democratic challenge is how to develop the ontological notion of bodily becomings into democratic acts with a capacity to disrupt the political economy of interiority. Enacting privacy remains one of several democratic resources through which this ontological friction can be turned into political acts. As illustrated with the example of JenniCAM, this often demands more creative ways of engaging privacy than claiming a right of protection of privacy.

The chapter aimed in the first instance at demonstrating how assembling suspicion and diffuse techniques of securitising enact limits of democracy by challenging the political capacity of democratic categorical practices, such as privacy. Privacy is one of the issues that are often mobilised in attempts to limit the unbinding of security practice, and of surveillance in particular. In doing so I intended to formulate a more challenging point of departure for analyses seeking to both understand how surveillance enacts limits of democracy and explore practices and sites that are reinventing democratic questioning of the assembling of suspicion. The next chapter continues this discussion by looking in more detail at the political implications of technological practice and reasoning in the assembling of suspicion.

Notes

1 Liberty is a UK based non-governmental organisation campaigning for the protection of civil liberties and the promotion of human rights. [www.liberty-human-rights.org.uk/index.php]

2 Although this definition identifies what is often treated as the main aspect of privacy in relation to surveillance, privacy covers a wider range of issues and is a concept with various meanings. For a more elaborate discussion of its meaning in relation to surveillance practice: Neyland, 2006; Waldo *et al.*, 2007; Nissenbaum, 2009.

3 For a more detailed overview of these debates, see Colin Bennett's defence of privacy (2011) and responses to his article in the same issue of *Surveillance and Society*.

4 Andrea Mubi Brighenti (2010) proposes to change the question from intrusion in the private to how the public is reconfigured under conditions of dispersed extensive surveillance. Similarly to social sorting and systemic power, it shifts attention from privacy towards other issues. Each opens a different take on how surveillance enacts the limits of democracy and potentially reconfigures possible modes of democratic practice. Mubi Brighenti's agenda, for example, invites the larger issue of what publicness and public spheres can mean today and whether the received conceptions and practices of deliberative public space are still central to how one can come to critically engage with processes such as surveillance and its institutional configurations.

5 On the role of private economic actors in developing and dispersing of identification technology, in particular in analysis of surveillance after 9/11, see, for example: O'Harrow, 2006; Amoore, 2008.

6 Although the study of resistance is often subjugated to the study of the social and political process of securitising in security studies, there are various analyses of what resistance to surveillance and risk governance can mean. Often they imply mobilisation or reflective moments disrupting what is taken for granted, what is enacted unquestioningly. For example: Marx, 2003; Bibler Coutin, 2008; Raley, 2008; Amoore and Hall, 2010.

7 From a different angle a similar demand for revisiting the conditions of politics in relation to surveillance technology is raised by Amoore and Hall (2009) in their analysis of full-body scanners in airports.

8 Kirstie Ball draws on the work of Elizabeth Grosz here, and in particular her reading of the use of Deleuze and Guattari for feminism (Grosz, 1994: 160–83).

9 For a different take on how surveillance systems are resisted without necessarily mobilising protests but by working the frictions and heterogeneity of surveillance systems and border control, see analyses of the autonomy of migration. Among others: Papadopoulos *et al.*, 2008; Andrijasevic, 2010.

7 Security technology and democratic limits

Data mining, CCTV, satellites, algorithms, digital filing, web servers, credit cards, digital transactions. Making technological solutions to security problems the default option; authority of expert knowledge focusing on the security means rather than societal goals; the expansion of security know-how, training and skills programmes. Technology as both artefact and a method of knowing and authorising (Barry, 2001: 9) plays a key role in diffusing insecurities and unbinding security more generally. Although technology is mobilised to support democratic politics (e.g. organising mass elections, public-opinion polls, designing alternative forms of participation, organising protest), the technological nature of assembling suspicion is one of the key factors through which securitising enacts the limits of democratic politics, as critical interpretations of surveillance and risk governance highlight.

This chapter introduces three modes of technological enactments of democratic limits and the democratic political questions they open up. The first section looks at technology and technical decisions constraining democratic human agency, and the value of non-technical reasoning and legitimacies. The second section explores how surveillance and its unbinding of security breaks down sociality as the condition for human deliberation and association implying a self-feeding generating of insecurities. The third section introduces a less oppositional relation between technology, human agency and sociality to ask how democratic limits are enacted when we take seriously that contemporary life and subjects are so intertwined with technology that human subjectivity and sociality are constituted in relation rather than opposition to technology.

Technological imperative and technocracy

A central aspect of the political critique of assembling suspicion is that it technologically takes democratic politics out of security; in other words, it de-democratises.

The infinity of risk does not ... lead to a democratic politics that debates what is to be done, but to intensified efforts and technological inventions on the part of the risk managers to adjust existing risk technologies or to supplement them. Technologies of intervening upon the future are always failing; their failure, however, is part of governmentality, the very motor of the continuous requirement for new technologies and more knowledge.

(Aradau and van Munster, 2008: 38–39)

For Aradau and van Munster, risk governance imposes a process of technological adjustment that hollows out democratic debate. Similar diagnostics are shared across much of the critical literature on pre-emptive and risk techniques in security studies. They call for debate as a way of bringing democratic politics back into a technological and technocratic process (e.g. de Goede, 2008: 171–72; Mythen and Walklate, 2008).

Instead of deliberating in political institutions about the common good and about what importance to give to governing through risks, technological developments combined with an implicit promise that insecurity problems can be technologically fixed takes over from democratic political decisions. Once at work, this process is partly self-feeding. Since the world changes and technological fixes are not perfect, technology will fail at some point which produces a need for continuously adjusting and developing new technologies. In addition, technological processes subordinate value reasoning to instrumental reasoning. Justifications draw primarily on arguments of increasing effectiveness and efficiency in the delivery of fixed ends, such as reduced rates of violence, burglaries or illegal immigration, rather than contestations of the relative value of delivering security in comparison to delivering other public goods, such as economic urban regeneration, global wealth generation or redistributive aid.[1]

Technological de-democratising links instrumental rationality and technological solutions to insecurity with assertions of a historical necessity to ride the technological security waves. As Gary T. Marx summarises it in a speech by the fictional security professional Richard Bottoms:[2]

The genius of the human species is invention and this is taken to its highest form in Western Civilization, especially in the good ole U.S.A. Human betterment is directly tied to *the inexorable march of information technology*. As surely as day follows night, the new must replace the old.

(Marx, 2007: 89)

In this vision, technological development is not a matter of choice but of progress and necessity. History is driven by technology, and technology is the hallmark of a developed civilisation. Moreover, technology will develop irrespective of whether one thinks it is right or not, good or bad. So there is not much of a choice; unless one wishes to remain behind and endanger human betterment. Deliberating whether it is right to install a new generation of CCTV, databases and profiling technology is then superfluous, at least if one shares an interest in progress. Societies interested in improving security necessarily need to embrace the technological security wave, the argument goes.

Between them Marx and Aradau and van Munster link de-democratisation to what in strategic studies of the arms race became known as the technological imperative (Buzan, 1987: 105–8). This explanation argued that the arms dynamic was fuelled not simply by the external threat of an arming enemy—arming oneself in reaction to the increased armament of a potential enemy—but also by a general process of technological innovation. Qualitative developments of security technology are understood to be embedded in a wider societal drive for new technologies. This process is not simply driven by the arms-production sector but works across various sectors in society and operates often in a global technology market. Military technology is not a self-contained technological sector but one that spills over into civilian technological developments and extracts new developments from the civilian sector. In this interpretation, technological development depends only in a limited way on political decisions and is largely inevitable. If one does not want to remain behind, one better takes part in the technological race. This idea of political decisions having only limited control over technological developments is of course not limited to armament technology. For Gary Marx, the technological imperative—or technological determinism and neutrality,[3] as he calls it—is one of the great fallacies that is extensively used to justify the diffusion of surveillance.

Yet the idea of the technological imperative does not exclude the role of humans; it does not simply refer to technology developing of its own accord and imposing itself onto politics. Aradau and van Munster's quote, for example, identifies a strong input from human agency: risk managers drive the technological adjustments by seeking to improve risk governance. In their policy brief on the Stockholm Programme of the EU, which develops guidelines for common policies on European citizenship and a new security architecture in the area of security, freedom and justice, Bigo and Jeandesboz highlight the significant role of security professionals in a programme that foregrounds technological solutions.

The draft document of the Stockholm programme places considerable emphasis on technology in the context of the EU's security policies. Among its most notable elements is the proposal to establish 'an EU Information Management strategy'. Despite an emphasis on citizens' freedoms and rights, and on the protection of their personal data and privacy, the programme remains overtly oriented towards the reinforcement of the *reliance on technology* within the context of EU security policies, particularly computerised systems of information exchange and data processing. These, in turn, are largely defined in terms of *the priorities and viewpoints of security professionals*. [Emphasis is mine.]

(Bigo and Jeandesboz, 2009: 2)

The argument here is not that enacting a technological imperative excludes humans but rather that it changes decision-making processes in favour of security experts, programmers, engineers and risk managers, who derive their authority from specialised knowledge and skills. Experts gain priority over democratic decision-making processes that are organised to encompass a wider range of groups, people and classes. Despite controversies and disputes between them about the best technology and the most effective approach to security, security experts and professionals embody the idea that expert knowledge is superior, or at least needs to be given priority over lay knowledge, thereby short circuiting other forms of knowledge as well as the authority of people who do not share the security expertise.

In such a situation democracy turns into technocracy, which combines rule by experts with a belief in technological solutions to social and political problems. The politics of insecurity is then a technocratic politics in which authority is vested in knowledge and technical skills rather than open deliberation based on membership in a political community. One way of conceptualising technocratic security policies as a contest and struggle rather than an inevitable process of technologising is to understand technocracy as a form of rule that assembles suspicion as a field effect. Instead of a continuous process of adjustment and improvement of security technology and methods, securitising involves competition within a field of experts over the authority to speak security, and a struggle by experts for the authority to impose their definitions of insecurity and solutions upon other fields, such as the political and media fields. The debates and power struggles between experts and professionals rather than politicians, for example, constitute the heart of the securitising process (Bigo, 1996; Bigo and Tsoukala, 2008: 25). Technocracy is therefore not the same as the technological imperative. It emphasises the authority of security experts and professionals rather than a self-feeding process of technology development. Yet the two are not unrelated in that technocratic authority uses the idea of a technological imperative to justify certain solutions, as Garry Marx showed in Richard Bottom's speech above.

Although technocracy and the technological imperative bring out some key elements of how technologically assembling suspicion enacts limits of democracy, those deploying this interpretation have been criticised for overstating the importance of technological processes and technocratic rationale. In particular, the technological imperative and technocratic reading of securitising are rebuked for overstating the automatic and deterministic nature of technological developments and the power of experts. As a result, securitising is largely understood as a programmatic self-sustaining technological process (Lyon, 2001: 125–54). Garry Marx, for example, listed 38 technological fallacies used in justifications for increased surveillance. They include, among others, the fallacy of political neutrality—technology is merely an instrument that can be used for any political purpose by anyone; the fallacy of quantification—deferring to numbers without asking what is actually being measured, how it is measured and by whom; the fallacy that technological solutions are always preferable; the fallacy that experts always know best; and the fallacy that efficiency should automatically overrule other values such as fairness, freedom and external costs imposed on third parties (Marx, 2007).

Taking the fallacies serious opens towards a more political reading of the technological securitising process. The fallacies draw attention to a more messy and complex process, making it imperative upon critical analyses of risk governance and surveillance to reach beyond unpacking the de-democratising logic of technological processes. One way of using the fallacies critically is to use them to discredit some of the claims that are made to justify technological securitising. The fallacies show that there is a difference between the actual practices (e.g. of value determination under the guise of technological development) and the discursive justifications (e.g. technological neutrality).

However, they can also be taken in a more performative reading. In that case, the fallacies can be understood not as fallacies of representation, i.e. statements that do not match reality, but as enacting as a consensus what actually is a conflict or tension. The claim of technological neutrality is effectively performed in politics but often in tension with counter-claims that foreground value arguments. In other words, the fallacy is not that technological neutrality is wrong per se but rather that one acts as if there is consensus on this point. In practice these arguments do not perform consensus but a conflict or tension between neutrality and value determination that is a defining part of democratic politics. Different fallacies can then be read as expressing tensions that are built into democratic politics and its relation to technology: tensions that are a defining part of democratic politics that frame contestations of technological developments, tensions that technological securitising intensifies. Democratic legitimacy has traditionally included claims of efficient and effective government as well as value claims and instituting particular ways of life. Tensions between rule by experts and rule by politicians, and between the demand to effectively deliver human betterment and popular sovereignty, are an inherent element of politics in democracy. Similarly, democracy has developed hand in hand with processes of industrialisation that have included beliefs that technological progress would considerably improve the human condition and universal participation in wealth as well as serious challenges to these beliefs. These tensions have been captured in various ways in political thought and practice, including contrasting system versus communicative practice, regulative versus popular legitimacy, instrumental versus value judgements, technology versus human interaction, elitist or technocratic versus participatory democracy.

Reading fallacies of technological imperative and technocratic government as expressing tensions that are negotiated and that organise struggles over proper ways of doing politics in modern democracy embeds the technological enactment of democratic limits into a political contestation rather than a de-politicising process. The limits of democracy are then not simply imposed by technological surveillance but are enacted in contestations of the expansion and limiting of technological practice. In other words, assembling security enacts limits of democracy not at the point where democracy gives way to technological and technocratic processes but rather at the point where limits as well as strengths of democratic practice become a matter of dispute and contestation by intensifying tensions related to the political nature of technology and technological reasoning. Such an approach of the technological imperative and technocratic politics would not simply look at how technological securitising takes democratic politics out of security but also at how democracy is enacted in the political contestations of technological processes. Instead of sociologies of depoliticising, we get an analytics of the politics of insecurity, of the contestations and reconfigurations of democratic limits in relation to technological security practice.

Such an analysis of the technological diffusion of insecurity combines an analysis of the security thickness of diffuse securitising and its enactment in risk governance and surveillance with accounts of the disruptive use of technology to counter policing or to support aesthetic, political and other values in the face of the securitising of everyday life. Such an analysis also focuses on the relation between security experts and other professional fields, such as the media, the judiciary, and the political field of parties and parliamentarians who between them negotiate the legitimacy and authority of technocratic governance and the technological imperative. The neutrality of technology, for example, then emerges not simply as a fallacy but as a position in a struggle over the relative place of security practice in society, and the legitimacy of technological methods of providing security.

In this section, I introduced how the technological practice of assembling suspicion enacts limits of democracy by diffusing a form of reasoning (instrumental reasoning combined with a view of a technologically driven history in which technology provides answers to questions about human betterment), legitimising (efficiency and instrumental calculations combined with the necessity to improve technology) and power (vested in technical expertise and specialised knowledge). Technology and technocratic government are placed in tension with democratic forms of reasoning, legitimising and power that are vested in a wider membership of the political community and in combining instrumental reasoning with reasoning in terms of rights and values. Limits of democracy are technologically enacted by skewing instituted tensions between the technological and the popular democratic in favour of the former. Bringing out the fallacies of technocracy and the technological imperative reintroduces the possibility for politics. Technological limiting of democratic politics appears not as an imperative but as a process that sharpens tensions that are built into democracies between technology and technological reasoning on the one hand and democratic decision making on the other. Although a relatively complex set of issues is at play here, they are quite familiar and extensively drawn upon in analyses of the nuclear arms race as well as assembling suspicion.

Breakdown of sociality

So far I have looked at arguments that technocracy and a technological imperative de-democratise surveillance and risk management. Yet, this is not the whole story. Some analysts have argued that surveillance technology and the anxieties they generate undermine human sociality. Sociality refers to processes and practices of exchange and reciprocity between human beings who are purposefully oriented towards one another. Simmel defines sociality as 'the form (realized in innumerably different ways) in which individuals grow together into a unity and within which their interests are realized' (Simmel, 1971: 24). Loss of sociality undermines the capacities and skills of mediating relations and conflicts between individuals and groups; mediation that relies on acting in dialogue and negotiating differences with others. This section briefly looks at these arguments. It starts with explaining how, in undermining sociality, the diffusion of surveillance technology challenges the conditions of possibility of democratic practice as well as diplomacy, which functions, at least formally but also to an extent institutionally, as a pluralist deliberation between like units. In particular, the section introduces how diffuse securitising, and assembling suspicion in particular, bears upon forms of citizenship and institutionalised mediations of estrangement, which are both central areas where democratic politics and its limits are enacted. Citizenship defines the possibilities to become a political subject, both as a subject upon whom authorities act and a subject that is empowered to act upon governmental processes. Mediations of estrangement negotiate the place and limits of democratic politics by negotiating the orientation of strangers towards one another rather than their separation.

Discussing the paradoxes of seeking security, Lucia Zedner (2009: 146–47) explains how warnings that it is dangerous to walk outside in the dark can increase insecurity. If ever more people need the warning and stay at home, everyday social surveillance decreases. When less people are about in streets, neighbourhoods and public parks, social control and policing that takes place through everyday encounters is reduced. As a result a sense of vulnerability is sustained and enhanced in political, educational and media coverage of crime and violence, and in the warnings to be careful.

Yet, this securitising is not simply a matter of a political and media focus on insecurities. The security industry plays a significant role too. They commodify security in the form of technological devices, including car alarms, gating and CCTV, which compensate for a decline in social control. 'Advertising' insecurity is central to sustain the security market. Installing these security technologies also often reinforces a sense of insecurity—gating a neighbourhood expresses an imaginary of an insecure environment. However, security technologies also do something else; they replace the need for engaging with others and negotiating living together with strangers with technologically driven surveillance. One can rely on the police or private security guards watching CCTV footage, and on locking oneself away and using cameras to check if it is safe to open the door or venture outside, for example. Displacing surveillance to security personnel and concierges who access CCTV footage, technology changes the knowledge economy, as McGrail has argued in the context of high-rise housing. Since entrance and exit of buildings is regulated through key fobs and CCTV, tenants have less frequent interaction with each other, which displaces knowledge of tenants and what is going on in the building from tenants to concierge, or to whomever has access to the electronic and video data (McGrail, 1999).

In reducing everyday sociality, technology increases alienation between people and the perception of vulnerability, while decreasing skills to deal with conflicts and transgressions. For these authors, the issue is therefore not simply one of surveillance technology enhancing the perception of insecurity and a sense of anxiety, but also of interaction with and through technology displacing human encounters and exchange. Such a technological reduction in sociality simultaneously reinforces estrangement and reduces relational capacities to deal with conflict and difference. It enhances the assembling of suspicion, not only because suspicion is the operational principle of security technology but also because suspicion functions as an organising principle of 'moving among strangers'—strangers are approached with suspicion until properly security checked.

James Der Derian similarly describes how technology changes the possibilities for mediating estrangement in international politics by diplomatic means (Der Derian, 1992). Estrangement refers to relations in which people are not within a condition of solidarity. Diplomacy is a practice of mediating—'connecting ... for the purpose of reconciling'—relations between estranged entities (Der Derian, 2009: 10). Technological developments supporting global surveillance detach security practice from human interaction, and diplomatic practice in particular. One looks at others through satellite images and data transfers, and enacts increasingly a virtual world produced by technology. Connecting to other entities is not a diplomatic connection with the other persons but a connecting to the data. In security practice satellite surveillance and digital data gathering render in ever more detail the potential dangers of others and the expectation that it is possible to hear and see dangers even better, in more detail, more accurately. This creates potentially a cybernetic system of advanced paranoia (Der Derian, 1992: 31). The technological mediation of relations displaces diplomatic connections aimed at reconciling differences with ever more involved surveilling of the dangerousness of others. The process goes like this: we watch others because we believe them to be dangerous; the closer we look the more potential dangers we see; so we belief even stronger that others are dangerous; we therefore will look even more closely at the dangers; and so on. This relationship is one of distancing from the other. It is not mediated by human interaction seeking reconciliation but by technological renditions of digital worlds of data, blobs on screens and other simulations, and of subjects who are increasingly inward looking and oriented towards their own anxieties. In that sense surveillance technology is anti-diplomatic rather than diplomatic for Der Derian (1987, 1992).[4] It destroys the necessity for human dialogue and other forms of close interaction. Similar to Zedner's analysis, in this reading, engaging the world via technology undermines international sociality through challenging key international institutions that are built to reconcile relations between estranged entities through negotiating and bargaining. Technology here reduces mediatory skills but also the very possibility of mediation in international politics.

For both Zedner and Der Derian the consequences of security technology go beyond empowering technocrats and a self-sustaining process of technological innovation that dilutes democratic deliberation. At issue is a breakdown of sociality, of social exchange and interaction, rather than democratic decision making as such. The combination of diffusing discourses and images of crime, viral infections, wars, economic crises, natural disasters, traffic accidents—to which one sometimes refers as cultures of fear (Furedi, 2002)—and surveillance technology displacing human negotiating, dialogue and bargaining creates subjects who are locked in a world of anxieties and restrained interaction. In this world, anxieties are easily reinforced in a process in which one wants to know in ever more detail and through ever more sophisticated technologies of surveillance and risk calculation (or simulation of such calculations) dangerous aspects of life so as to avoid them. This constitution of anxious subjects with a desire for absolute security that can never be met feeds ever greater insecurity and estrangement.

In this analysis, surveillance technology is a factor in the constitution of what Engin Isin has referred to as the neurotic citizen, 'who governs itself through responses to anxieties and uncertainties' (2004: 223). Since these subjects do not only enact an impossible desire for security but are also continuously promised, by governments, private security industry and international bodies, the possibility of being secure, they turn their anxieties into rights claims: 'the right to security, safety, body, health, wealth, and happiness as well as tranquility, serenity and calm' (Isin, 2004: 232). These rights cannot really be realised since the search for security is inherently tangled in with the identification of insecurities. Discourses of security produce discourses of insecurity, and the diffusion of surveillance technology reinforces ever greater interest in refining the identification of insecurities, as explained above. Striving for the impossible and reproducing the illusion of the entitlement to and possibility of realising the rights of security, of anxiety-free life 'enables [the neurotic citizen] to shift responsibility to objects outside itself with hostility' (Isin, 2004: 233). As a result, the social world of the neurotic citizen is saturated by suspicion and hostility. The neurotic citizens are, in the first instance, focused on themselves, on managing their own anxieties, rather than contesting and sharing in the formation of common goods and rights embedded in a capacity to be oriented towards rather than away from the outside, including the external non-human environment. Their relation to the outside world is, if not hostility, at least unease and suspicion about the potential dangers in relations with strangers, viruses, roads, food, etc.[5] Such renditions of citizenship severely constrain the capacity to move from a collection of private individuals to the summoning of publics that express a collective realisation of interests between strangers (e.g. in transnational protest movements, electronic petitions or neighbourhood committees).[6]

Isin focuses on how neurotic citizens claim security rights that cannot be realised, and enact a mode of governing that is based on rendering affects rather than calculating needs and interests. Zedner's and Der Derian's analyses, on the other hand, bring out more sharply that this form of citizenship is part of processes of securitising that break down sociality and challenge possibilities for mediating difference, conflict and estrangement. These effects are taking place across a wide range of practices—from engaging with neighbours to diplomatic relations between states. Moreover, their analyses show that surveillance technology is a key element in these developments. When taking this reading to its radical conclusion, surveillance technology—and the mode of risk governance linked to it—destroys the fundamental condition for democratic politics in so far as democracy is about enacting realisable rights and common goods and, more generally, conditions of living among and with strangers through mediating conflicts and differences. Such mediation requires a capacity for sociality. Without sociality the social dynamic that supports deliberation, democratic participation, the formulation of realisable rights and the contestation of common goods falls apart.

Post-humanity

Analyses like Zedner's and Der Derian's add significantly to our understanding of how technological processes of assembling suspicion enact democratic limits. Yet in at least one sense they frame the debate on the political implications of the diffusion of surveillance technology and practice in similar terms to the technological imperative. They focus on how technology works upon human interaction and in doing so tend to oppose technology to social and political agency. Like for the critics of the technological imperative, the political challenge remains to break the circle of insecurity or paranoia by reinserting 'real' human interaction that shapes rather than is shaped by technology. The political issue is set up as a conflict between the power of human agency over technology and the loss of human sociality and its interactive capacities and skills in a technological world. Surveillance and risk governance enact limits of democracy by reinforcing the dominance of technology over human agency. A critical politics then takes the form of contesting and resisting the technological limiting of human sociality and political agency.

Yet the question of agency and technology is more complex in the contemporary world of assembling suspicion. Surveillance technology is not an external force or artefact that works upon human relations. Humans and their capacity for action are fundamentally intertwined with technology. For example, mobile phones and computer-mediated chatting has changed the way people interact. This can be read as having destroyed the sociality of face-to-face and bodily exchanges. Yet another way of looking at this is to see mobile phones as a technology that plays an active role in the way relational fabrics and thus sociality is transformed. In the latter interpretation, the mobile phone is a mediator, not in the sense of transporting information from one locale to another but rather as a device that shapes social relations and is itself shaped by them. This same mobile phone transmits data that can hook the persons calling into a database registering the place and time of the phone call, which can be mined by the police as well as market agencies interested in connecting transactional patterns to particular bodies through the mediation of files or algorithms. The mobile phone, the file, the algorithm, the database are not just things used by humans or things constraining human agency, they are active in the sense that they mould social interaction and are moulded by it (for example, in the sense that they shape conversations into transactional information that operates within surveillance practices).

Concepts like 'post-human' and 'cyborgs' (Haraway, 1991) have been introduced in the social sciences to capture how bodies and nature are actively constituted through technological modification and, more generally, to question the dichotomy between passive technology and active humans. The central issue here is not the debate of the industrial revolution about whether technology improves or harms human conditions—is progressive or regressive—but rather a discussion of what it means to be human if one can no longer understand humanity in terms of a clear distinction between technology and nature. As Nicholas Gane states in his succinct dictionary introduction to the concept of 'post-human':

> The posthuman ... is not about 'progress' per se, but is rather a new
> culture of transversalism in which the 'purity' of human nature gives
> way to new forms of creative evolution that refuse to keep different
> species, or even machines and humans, apart. The posthuman, then,

is a condition of uncertainty … in which the essence of things is far from clear.

(Gane, 2006: 432)

The post-human, in this reading, focuses on the uncertainties surrounding the adequateness of distinguishing between bodies as machine and bodies as nature. This plays out in the many debates about the difference between human and artificial intelligence; a discussion in which artificial intelligence becomes to some extent the measure of defining what counts as being human.

The enactment of bodies as data doubles in surveillance and policing practices raises similar issues. Mostly the data doubles are not generated as purely virtual imaginations; they are based on extractions of data from concrete subjects bodies, their movements and their transactions. They are also re-inscribed upon concrete subjects bodies when the data double becomes the measure of suspicion at border controls or insurance claims. The distinction between bodies existing in technology and bodies as human beings of 'flesh and blood' blurs; the technological bodies (data doubles) are in multiple ways intertwined with the natural bodies, making it difficult to clearly point to the difference. For example, when crossing borders technologically links subjects bodies and identities with modes of mobility. Identities of safe passengers are inscribed upon subjects bodies through advanced registering combined with electronic border checks. The interaction with technology creates a particular mode of being mobile (e.g. in an airport moving faster through border control when registered with iris recognition, or queuing in an e-passport line or not). Identities, movement and technology are interconnected in various ways to the surveillance system, producing different identities and channelling bodies differently—slower, through severe data checks, more suspiciously for some, faster, more limited data checks, and less suspiciously for others. People exist as different data-doubles, move along different paths in the airport, traverse borders that simply are different (Van Der Ploeg, 2006; Muller, 2010b). This close co-existence of technology, bodies and identities is a more general phenomenon in contemporary societies, going well beyond assembling suspicion. People are extensively 'tied into' multiple and continuous data-gathering exercises and risk-management practices when consuming, walking cities, claiming services, and so on.

Although the focus in post-human, as introduced above, is on the subject body, a similar analysis of the intertwining of technology and the human can be applied to the understanding of agency and sociality. Instead of sociality being the interaction between discrete individuals, groups or entities, the sociality in a technological world is better understood as 'agencements'. As Ruppert explains: '[C]onceiving of practices as agencements … bring[s] to the fore how agency and action are contingent upon and constituted by the sociotechnical arrangements that make them up' (Ruppert, 2011c: 225). Such a conception of sociality places technologies and agency differently. Technologies are not facilitators or inhibitors of human interaction but are inherent to the forms of acting in a technological world; they define the substance of what it means to act. 'Agencement brings to the fore the mutually constitutive relations between logics, humans, and technologies … . Data are not simply "collected," but are the result of multiple sociotechnical arrangements of technological and human actors that configure agency and action' (Ruppert, 2011c: 225). Sociality in this understanding is inherently technological sociality. The interstices between the technological and social is key to understanding surveillance as well as agency, and so is the banality of these interstices. The political challenge cannot be reduced to surveillance technology constraining agency and sociality when technology is routinely as well as creatively engaged in all aspects of life—when technology is part of how life is enacted, how people engage, how sociality is created today (Lyon, 2010: 335).

The starting point of this reading of agency and the enactment of sociality is to conceptualise technology itself as acting. Technology, just like a human being, is something that acts in the sense of modifying 'a state of affairs by making a difference' (Latour, 2005: 71). To express this de-anthropomorphised understanding of action, Latour (2005: 54–55) introduces the concept of an actant. He borrows this from linguistic theory (Greimas and Courtés, 1993). Stories are not so preoccupied with limiting capacity for action to human actors. Boulders, magic, animals, lightning, machines can make something happen, can move the story forward. Yet taking technology as an actant is in itself not that dissimilar from how technology is interpreted in the technological imperative in which technology actively drives history or in Zedner's and Der Derian's analysis of technologies destroying sociality. Technology is an active and not a passive component in these analyses.[7] Although ascribing agency to artefacts is an important step, the notion of agencements implies something more important: agency emerges in the intertwining—the mutual constitution—of humans, technology (as an artefact) and knowledge. What we need to get at is an understanding of how technologies are actants 'netting' people, objects and issues together, and being netted themselves, which implies embedding agency in relations rather than agents or actants. By intertwining rather than dichotomising technological and human agency, the agential capacity is constituted in the moments of connecting and is not the property of either humans or technology. Such a conception of the relation between technologies and humans dilutes the stark opposition between them that informs the analyses about technological de-democratising that I referred to in the previous sections of this chapter.

The concept of the post-human, however, does not only draw attention to a close relation between technology and humanity but also introduces a distinct ontology, a non-anthropocentric way of being in contemporary worlds.[8] Questioning the sharp distinction between objects and subjects, between artefacts and humans, between technological and human agency invites a different understanding of what agency and sociality mean, one that does not take the human wilful subject as its starting point.[9]

> [T]he posthuman does not really mean the end of humanity. It signals instead the end of a certain conception of the human, a conception that may have applied, at best, to that fraction of humanity who had the wealth, power, and leisure to conceptualize themselves as autonomous beings exercising their will through individual agency and choice.
>
> (Hayles, 1999: 287)

This ontology brings into perspective that a political reading of assembling suspicion needs to pay attention to how the technological sociality that it enacts hollows out the anthropocentric focus of democracy as deliberation between humans and as the expression of human will. At stake is not simply the relative dominance of technology over human value choices and freedom but rather the very possibility of enacting humanity as a ground of political subjectivity that separates politics from machines and nature in the contemporary world.

Fukuyama's attempt to define human essence in his evaluation of the consequences of development in the biosciences, illustrates the political stakes that are involved. His work is an example of a counter-move to post-human processes for the purpose of protecting (liberal) democratic politics. For Fukuyama, the biosciences and other dilutions of the distinction between human nature and technology are challenging the very possibility of democratic politics by hollowing out a concept of human essence—that which makes humans distinctly human. In discussing Huxley's *Brave New World*, Fukuyama introduces the key political question as follows:

> [N]ature itself, and in particular human nature, has a special role in defining for us what is right and wrong, just and unjust, important

and unimportant. So our final judgment on 'what's wrong' with Huxley's brave new world stands or falls with our view of how important human nature is as a source of values.

The aim of this book is to argue that Huxley was right, that the most significant threat posed by contemporary biotechnology is the possibility that it will alter human nature and thereby move us into a 'posthuman' stage of history. ... Human nature shapes and constrains the possible kinds of political regimes, so a technology powerful enough to reshape what we are will have possibly malign consequences for liberal democracy and the nature of politics itself (p.7).

The ultimate political question raised by biotechnology is, what will happen to political rights once we are able to, in effect, breed some people with saddles on their backs, and others with boots and spurs? (pp. 9–10).

(Fukuyama, 2002)

For others, post-humanity is not endangering democracy as a form of politics. Rather it implies a need to change the terms in which politics, and in particular core concepts of democratic politics, can be imagined and enacted. Donna Harraway's *Cyborg Manifesto* (1991: 149–81) is among the most famous of how the blurring of divisions between machine and organism—and between fiction and non-fiction—creates possibilities for renewing feminist politics by challenging humanist universalism and totalities. She is not the only one, however. For example, for Katherine Hayles, the political stakes in debates about post-human are not whether human rights and deliberation over common values as such are still relevant but rather that they need to be engaged differently, given that the terrain in which they are currently enacted and shaped has changed.

[T]he prospect of humans working in partnership with intelligent machines is not so much a usurpation of human right and responsibility as it is a further development in the construction of distributed cognition environments, a construction that has been ongoing for thousands of years (pp. 289–90).

What it means to be human finally is not so much about intelligent machines as it is about how to create just societies in a transnational global world that may include in its purview both carbon and silicon citizens (p. 148).

(Hayles, 2005)

There is no need to go into detail here. The main point is that understanding agency as agencements and the relationship between technology and humanity as post-human brings into focus how technological practices of assembling suspicion can enact a political terrain in which the challenges to democratic practice emerge not simply because of technologies seriously constraining human political agency and sociality, as set out in the previous two sections. Instead, the political stake is also whether—and how—democratic politics and citizenship is possible when the intertwining of technology and humanity questions the autonomy of the human will and conceptions of rights linked to individual agency and choices. For understanding how technology enacts the limits of democracy and what kind of politics is actually taking place and is possible in the worlds of technological surveillance and its diffuse securitising, it is therefore important to start from thinking through the changing forms of political sociality that emerge in processes of 'agencements'.

To illustrate how this political question plays out in relation to surveillance—rather than biosciences and biotechnology more generally—let us return to the decentring of the subject in digital surveillance practice. (Although I decided to focus on technology and surveillance in this section, certain modes of governing of and through risk and uncertainty also play a significant role in shifting securitising processes and, in particular, the conception of history they enact to a post-human terrain, as I explain in the short appendix to this chapter on Mick Dillon's work.) In Chapter 5, I showed how surveillance technology disembodies individuals by producing data doubles that exist in digital communications and data flows. Individual bodies as persons, who are an anchoring point—or a point of unification—for various biographical traces, decentre into a multiplicity of virtual subjects that are assembled and reassembled in the data and knowledge flows. Relations and transactions are disembodied and maintained in databanks and networked computer systems rather than in human memory (Lyon, 2001: 16). This 'abstracting' process destroys relations as interactions between 'whole' persons characterised by a will to act, a capacity to deliberate and take responsibility, and an orientation towards exchanging with others and engaging politically through rights claims. Instead, individuals fragment into multiple virtual subjects circulating in information flows. As a result, modes of social integration have also changed: '[T]oday's modes of social integration are more and more electronically enabled, abstract and disembodied' (Lyon, 2001: 145). Looked at from this angle, the assembling of suspicion through surveillance technology dislocates 'real' embodied political and social life of persons to virtual worlds where persons become subjects who exist as digital data in circulation.

Yet the embodied subject remains an active part of the technological worlds of data gathering and processing (Ball, 2006). Bodies are not just treated as passive data sources from which technologies construct virtual body-doubles, they are acting as subjects bodies whose practices are both affected by, and work themselves into, the virtual data worlds (Lyon, 2001: 124–25). Subjects bodies need to be on the move so as to leave traces of credit card use, border crossings, consumption patterns and so on. Lyon takes this 're-embodying' of persons as a starting point for a critical politics of surveillance: 'the way in which surveillance systems work should be influenced by the conviction that we are embodied persons, as should the social theories within which we try to explain such things' (Lyon, 2001: 151). Politically this is a call for reinserting citizens as embodied rights holders who can take positions on how to introduce technology into society and challenge the powers driving the diffusion of surveillance. The embodied persons gain their political significance from being distinct from the body-double and the technology they interact with. They can bear upon surveillance from outside the technological worlds as rights holding and deliberative subjects bodies—rather than virtual body doubles—with capacities to define and contest issues of common concern.[10]

There are at least two limits to this re-insertion of the citizen in the virtual worlds of surveillance, however. A simple call for reinstating the embodied rights holder and the interaction between whole persons as grounds for a democratic politics contesting surveillance technology, skirts a little around the key issues that the discussion of the post-human condition identified: technology is always embodied and hence the challenging issue is to understand the transformation of citizenship as humans have become closely intertwined with surveillance technology. As Kirstie Ball argues in relation to Haggerty and Ericsons's understanding of how surveillance technology breaks bodies down into data flows where they are reconstituted into various data-doubles: 'Haggerty and Ericson do not venture far enough: the degree of tension and in-betweenness characterizing the hybrid or cyborgian subject is underemphasized' (Ball, 2005: 95). It invites analyses to drop the opposition between 'real' and 'virtual' bodies and the idea that virtuality is a loss of humanity. Understanding the possibilities of a democratic politics of insecurity demands instead to explore how the embodiment of political agency exists precisely in the relations that are established between technology and subjects bodies (Hayles, 1999: 290). This is a complex agenda that strays into discussions on genetic modification, use of technology in political protest, bioethics, artificial intelligence, and so on.[11]

There is a second limit to endorsing the embodied citizen as the basis for democratic politics in the technological assembling of suspicion.

Emphasising that embodied subjects are still active in the technological world of surveillance does not necessarily reinstate the capacity of citizens to bear significantly on the process. Activity is not the same as power. Subjects do a lot, they are very active consuming, swiping credit cards, walking streets, phoning. These activities and transactions are an immediate interaction with and through technology. The interaction creates data that are used to govern subjects and their activities. Streets are reconstructed, supermarket offers are changed, subjects are searched in the airport. As Amoore and de Goede state in their exploration of the increasing importance of transactions for security practice and its political implications:

> [T]ransactions people make are, quite literally, taken to be traces of daily life, they are conceived as a way of mapping, visualising and recognising bodies in movement.
>
> (Amoore and de Goede, 2008: 176)

Ruppert and Savage speak of transactional governance (2011). While traditional data sources engage subjects as identities or fixed populations, transactional governance derives information directly from the interactions and transactions. 'Subjectivity or identity is less an issue and instead associations and correlations in conduct are deemed more empirical and descriptive than subjective and meaningful' (Ruppert, 2011c: 228). Transactional governance decentres subjects into transactions; what matters is not subjects with opinions or identities but transactions that take place. It is a mode of governing that seeks to quickly adapt delivery of services, control and coercion to changing behaviours by deriving and processing information directly from the everyday 'doings' of people. Transactional surveillance is increasingly important in security practice, as de Goede and Amoore observe:

> [T]he transaction is becoming central to security practice because it is assumed to provide a complete picture of a person, an 'electronic footprint' that makes it possible to identify a suspicious body in movement and, most importantly, to verify or deny access *in advance* (p. 173).
>
> In what has become the calculative and ever-vigilant face of the war on terror, the transaction has become the primary means of reconciling the mobility and security of public space (p. 175).
>
> (Amoore and de Goede, 2008)

Although highly active, the acting subjects engage the technology of governance without having—and often to a large extent without being able—to make decisions about or challenge issues of legitimacy and wider societal consequences. By just continuing their everyday activities they are always already part of the governance that is taking place. Moreover, governmental technology is so integrated into life that it is almost impossible not to engage with it. People are thus compelled to engage with technology in ways that make it more difficult to resist the surveillance it generates.

Although people's actions are heavily intertwined with the technology, the embedding of surveillance into everyday life has limited the capacity of people to enact themselves as subjects of a particular collective, a particular population, with certain rights. Their identities, needs and interests are constructed for them. Instead of imposing these from above (e.g. in line with a particular ideological position of the government), transactional governance defines needs, interests and identities through the people's own actions. No need for social movements, charities or other civil society actors to mediate interest formation. The technology allows to extract it directly from people's practices.

Ruppert names this form of action that does not translate into political capacity 'interpassive':[12]

> Interpassivization refers to a 'kind of detachment', or loss of capacities or powers, where the subject is not passive but engaged in much doing: registering, applying, travelling, filing returns, and so on. But, through all of this doing, subjects are less able to challenge, avoid or mediate their data-double and the enactment of population objects.
> (Ruppert, 2011c: 227)

Transactional surveillance is thus not about creating passive subjects bodies or fixing subjects in identities but rather capturing the activities of highly active subjects bodies and their many transactions as the basis for governing. The technologies used are so embedded into the activities themselves that life without the technology becomes difficult to perform. They are part of how people action their everyday lives. At the same time, the technology transfigures the many activities into multiple data doubles, populations and activity patterns that take actions and subjects bodies out of their context to structure governance of various issues, ranging from insurance over supply of consumer goods to public services and risk profiling. As an interpassive world, the world of assembling suspicion is a highly active world but one in which the link between action and political power has been broken.

The democratic political question that follows from this analysis of interpassivity in transactional governing and the decentring of the subject for Ruppert is:

> If people no longer account or attest for themselves in the enact-
> ment of population what then are the implications for subjects and
> their capacity to constitute themselves as citizens who not only bear
> rights but also have the right to claim rights?
>
> (Ruppert, 2011c: 228)

In her work, Ruppert drew the distinction between identity and transactions and its implications for political action from comparing how
populations are governed and protest in the case of the traditional census
with transactional population metrics. In the traditional census people
will make political statements by inventing answers, refusing to answer
or coordinating particular ways of answering certain questions. In doing
so, they can express certain common concerns by creating a new category of people (e.g. inventing the ethnic category of 'Canadian' in
protest to a census seeking to classify people according to various ethnic
categories) (Ruppert, 2011a, 2011b). They cannot resist transactional
population metrics in the same way because these derive from complex
and continuous extractions from their everyday practices.

In so far as diffuse securitising governs transactionally—creating
governable populations and sites by connecting transactions—it thus does
not only decentre the subject but also limits the capacity for popular
challenges and disruptions. Somehow governance is folded into the
social, which does indeed raise the double question of what is left of
citizenship as the enactment of rights and the right to have rights,
and of popular agency as a key political force participating in deciding
what knowledge about themselves can be legitimately created and what
populations should be objects of governance in democracies. As Ruppert
states:

> If population knowledge is indispensable to governing and the
> allocation of rights then what are the means and mechanisms for
> citizens to engage in the making of knowledge about themselves
> and the enactment of population?
>
> (Ruppert, 2011c: 229)

Charlotte Epstein comes to a similar conclusion in her analysis of the US
VISIT programme. In extracting risk data from bodily movement and
transactions that are then re-inscribed through risk profiles onto subjects
bodies, border controls delete the 'voice' of the embodied subject. When
control is not negotiated through narratives but directly imposed onto
the body through technological authentication of a match between body
and data that were extracted directly from daily activities, claiming rights

and enacting oneself as a subject with rights becomes challenging (Epstein, 2008: 183–86; also Muller, 2010a).

In worlds of transactional governance, a simple call for reinstating the embodied rights holder and the interaction between whole persons as grounds for a democratic politics contesting surveillance technology, skirts around the key issues that agencements and the post-human identify: (a) technology is always embodied and hence the challenging issue is to understand the transformation of citizenship as humans have become closely intertwined with surveillance technology; and (b) what it means to be active in ways that can bear upon processes of surveillance has changed, given that actions are often interpassive. Such an approach requires letting go of opposing 'real' and 'virtual' subjects bodies—which reproduces the idea that virtuality is loss of humanity—and explore how the embodiment of agency exists precisely in the relations that are established between technology and subjects bodies (Hayles, 1999: 290).

Moreover, rethinking what democratic politics can mean in modes of assembling suspicion that dilute distinctions between technology and human agency is complicated by the fact that conceptual cornerstones for recapturing democratic sociality, especially the concept of a volitional subject (and an anthropocentric conception of time—see the appendix), are challenged in the technological practice of surveillance and risk management. Some modes of assembling suspicion, such as transactional surveillance, thus do not simply enact limits of democratic practice (e.g. democratic deliberation) but challenge the ontological categories upon which democratic action rests (see also the appendix for further elaboration in relation to risk governance). At stake is then not simply de-democratising effects of technology and technological reason but the viability and reconfiguration of conceptions of democratic political subjectivity, practice and sociality themselves. As Ruppert asked: how can people constitute themselves as citizens with rights and the right to have rights when governmental power works not through narrating but through extracting information from and applying policy directly upon transactions and bodies? Does democratic political subjectivity and sociality have to be conceived differently to understand the possibilities for democratic politics in transactional modes of assembling surveillance?

To conclude, the main purpose of this section was to introduce a higher complexity in how technological diffuse securitising enacts limits of democratic practice. Rather than asking how technology destroys sociality, the question was how the processes of intertwining of human action and contemporary technology—of blurring the strict distinction between humanity and technology—reform conceptions of sociality, political being and what it means to be active. The question of how technologies of surveillance enact the limits of democracy is then not one of the limitation of democratic political being by technology but the continuous modulations and re-modulations of political subjectivity, sociality and rights at the interstices between technology and humanity. Judgements can be made about the good or bad of certain workings and certain renewed articulations of political subjectivity and rights. Yet whatever the normative judgements, the enactment of democratic limits in assembling suspicion raises the question of how to conceive of democratic practice in post-human worlds in which human essence is challenged and in which agential capacity is connected to technology and disconnected from volitional action as such.

Conclusion

Technology plays a major role in assembling suspicion, and in diffusing insecurities more generally. In this chapter, I unpacked how the technological practices of surveillance and risk governance enact democratic limits. The starting point of many security analyses is to oppose technology to democratic politics—and, politics more generally. When technological solutions dominate the governing of political and social problems, democratic politics is expected to come under severe strains, mainly for two reasons. First, technological development is understood to be a process that works according to its own logic and that cannot be democratically controlled. If certain developments are stopped in one place, other companies and organisations will take it up elsewhere; institutional processes sustain technological solutions to problems. Secondly, experts and professionals with specialised technical knowledge are understood to overshadow democratically elected politicians and popular expressions of values and interests in decision-making processes. Technocratic organisation of political power is opposed to or in competition with wider popular power that favours value reasoning and deliberative processes of deciding rights, obligations and common goods.

Yet others argue that surveillance technology and risk governance also work the limits of democracy by challenging its social basis. Increasingly, using technological surveillance combined with the discursive iterations and material technological inscriptions of suspicion impacts negatively on human sociality, on the capacity to be together with strangers and to negotiate conflicts of interest, insecurities, and value differences. Hooking technological practice into transformations of sociality delivers a more complex picture of how technology enacts limits of democracy. In particular it shows how the diffusion of security technology pervades social relations in banal but consequential ways that contribute to the formation of neurotic citizens who enact a mode of political being that is challenging for democratic processes. The deliberative aspect of democracy, the negotiating of common goods and interests is displaced by a focus on managing one's fears. In addition, the technological mediation of relations through CCTV, gated communities and satellite imaging enhances estrangement and undercuts interpersonal skills and habits of negotiating differences, conflicts and insecurities.

These interpretations present technology largely as an external force that constrains and hollows out the conditions of democracy and democratic conceptions of power and empowerment. Implicitly they oppose two worlds: a world of democratic politics and a world of technology and technocracy, with the latter having seriously limiting effects on the former. The diffuse politics of insecurity is then very much one of seeking to recover the possibilities of human political agency against technology.

Yet contemporary life is extremely intertwined with technology, which does raise some questions about taking the opposition between technology and political humans as a core device for interrogating the political effects of technological practices of diffuse securitising. Human beings do not relate simply to technology by being acted upon by technology. They exist in diffuse networks in which technologies and people both act upon one another and in which the actantial capacities— or agency—of both humans and technology are constituted by being netted into one another. Technologies are then not an artefact blocking human sociality but are an acting and constituting, yet not determining, part of diffuse socialities in which technologies and humans are closely intertwined.

In the final section, I explored how taking such an approach to technology shifts our understanding of how assembling suspicion enacts limits to democratic practice. In particular, the intertwining of technology and subjects bodies challenges notions of human nature and the autonomy of the human will. It raises the perspective of post-human worlds in which democratic notions of citizenship and rights that are grounded in a conception of free will and/or human distinctness are questioned. The critical issues involved in technology taking democratic politics out of security are then not limited to the technological imperative, technocracy and how surveillance technology breaks down sociality. Although these are important, the political effects of assembling suspicion also require an understanding of how agency and political subjects are deconstructed in technological relations. In that sense, it is not simply technology that frames politics but also the reconfigurations of political subjectivity that can be enacted in modes of diffuse securitising in which technologies, humans, and objects share relational agency. Key questions that emerge are not simply about re-politicising technology and technocracy but also what sociality can mean in a technological world, how citizenship can be reinvented in relation to transactional governance and, more generally, what it can mean to be democratically political in a post-human history.

This is a challenging proposition that indicates that gaining democratic leverage on some modes of assembling suspicion may imply reconfiguring some of the key concepts through which democratic politics has been enacted in modernity. This is a major difference with exceptionalist securitising, which largely enacts a politics of insecurity that works through and on the basis of central tensions that have been constitutive of modern politics (such as legal versus political legitimacy and fundamental rights versus security) and, in particular, the conception of sovereignty. What at first appeared as a rather straightforward replaying of the old politics of the relation between technology and politics, the technological processes of diffuse securitising seem to enact a far more complex and challenging set of limits to democratic politics. At stake in the politics of assembling suspicion is the diffusion of democratic politics itself; 'diffusing' in the sense of the unravelling of the parameters defining what it means to be democratically political (e.g. one of these parameters is the tension between technological efficiency and effectivity versus deliberating over common values). Core categories through which democratic politics have been enacted are put under pressure. Seriously engaging this question would take us into another project, which is beyond the limits of what I intended to do in this book. Yet the question itself makes the important point that a political analysis of assembling suspicion and its unbinding of security needs to move beyond the comfort zone of familiar ways of thinking about the democratic implications of security technology largely in terms of technocracy and technological imperatives.

Appendix: post-human history, risk, contingency

In his understanding of risk as biopolitical security, Mick Dillon gives us another insight into how processes I have sought to capture in assembling suspicion, and diffuse securitising more generally, challenge the conceptions of democratic politics not only by decentring the human subject and questioning the relation between action and power in transactional governance but also by shifting the conception of political history. In particular, he argues that governing through risk foregrounds 'evental contingency' as its generative principle, which challenges anthropocentric conceptions of history that have been central to security studies.

Political histories of security are generally understood as being created by wilful subjects. Security history is mostly understood to be made by strategic, calculating and/or emotionally driven subjects that act upon their environment. Al Qaeda making history by carrying out terrorist violence on US territory in 2001; Rwanda invading Eastern Congo to secure the country against attacks from Hutu extremists in 1996; NATO supporting the Libyan uprising in 2011; Germany seeking to expand its 'Lebensraum' and asserting superiority of the Arian race in the 1930s and 40s; humanitarian organisations working against human deprivation; the EU deploying development aid to limit and manage migration flows are a few examples of how the history of security foregrounds purposeful, calculative, emotional, but in each case, wilful human subjectivity is its driver. It is an anthropocentric history in the sense that human will rather than viruses, genetic changes, molecular changes, shifts in air quality or any other event make life what it is.

For Dillon, risk governance moves security techniques from this anthropocentric focus on 'will'—the enemy as aggressor, for example—to a focus on 'events'.

> Rule through risk … secures individuals and populations locally and globally by locating them in a general economy of the contingent in which the 'event' rather than 'the will' reigns supreme.
>
> (Dillon, 2008: 327)

To understand what is implied in this quote, we need to take a step back and very briefly introduce Dillon's biopolitical conception of security (2003, 2007, 2008). In biopolitical government, security of the subject, whether individual or collective (e.g. state), is replaced by security of the species, and more accurately, life.

Life is not calculative like the subject and neither is it an entity. It is contingent and transactional. Life is formed and changed in a multiplicity of transactions between human as well as non-human (e.g. viruses) organisms, and, ultimately, between molecules. The transactions are contingent in the sense of not being connected in a predetermined or teleological way.

> No divine providence or historical teleology explains the account of human existence as biological existence. It has no necessary cause external to it and follows no predetermined course. It underwrites itself and appears as the continually emergent sum total of its transactional encounters with the contingent conjunctures that are said to characterize the life of living things.
>
> (Dillon, 2008: 312)

Life happens and consists of conjunctures of transactions, called events, such as global warming, spread of Mexican flu, infections of chestnut trees and the dying out of bees. Human transactions are immanent to these events but they do not make or control them. They can seek to steer certain transactions and change patterns but they are not the makers of life, the agencies with capacity to secure life. Technology, viruses, humans, animals, rocks can interfere in life but they do not control it.

> There is no motor to the event, only conjunctures. Patterns can be detected through distribution and probability analysis, for example. But, the patterns are mobile and mutable ... .
>
> (Dillon, 2008: 328)

Risk is a technique of making this contingent transactionality a domain of rule and calculability by patterning in terms of probabilities and distributions. Yet, the patterns are not stable, they change because life as a transaction continues to change, and thus the conjunctures from which patterns are built change too. Therefore, rule and calculability cannot aspire to control transactional life and its contingency. Instead, it aims at regulating exposure to contingency (Dillon, 2008: 320) in terms of probabilities. For example, one can try to regulate the chances of catching the flu by taking a cocktail of anti-flu injections. Taking the jab does not guarantee one will not get the flu since viruses mutate. Yet it will reduce the probability of getting the flu by reducing one's vulnerability to certain kinds of flu. That is what is meant by saying that rule by risk is a technique of securing life by managing its exposure to events (like a virus, death, flood). This management can take the form of compensations (e.g. life insurance) and of choices of action in terms of acceptable exposure to harm or loss (high-risk or low-risk taking by taking or not taking the anti-flu jab).

The choice element does not reintroduce the anthropocentric conception of history, however. Life goes about its business in the many transactions that make life what it is. The wilful subjects remain just an element in transactions and thus remain exposed to—rather than in control of—the events of life. For Dillon, the subject of risk governance is thrown into a contingent world ruled by events. Freedom is not a property of individuals but is transactional contingency; the creativity of transactions and the continuous emergence of events is freedom, rather than subjects seeking freedom from 'natural' and 'social' constraints to bend history in a desired direction. Thus, when Dillon says that rule through risk locates humans into a general economy of the contingent in which the event rather than will reigns supreme, he means that biopolitical securitising takes sovereign will out of history and replaces it with transactional conjunctures and contingencies that are not limited to transactions between humans but consists of multiple connections that include molecular reactions, non-human organic life, things and humans. This biopolitical securitising enacts limits of democratic rule by changing the conception of human action. As in Ruppert's analysis, the idea is not that human beings have become passive. They are hyperactive but the activity does not translate into power as control over the forces they act upon. Instead, they always act within a multiplicity of transactions in which human practice is tied up with various non-human life forms, molecules, genes, things transacting with one another. This form of securitising diffuses human will in transactional patterns that neither humans nor the security practices control. We can therefore say that this securitising enacts 'post-human' worlds—worlds in which humanity does no longer have a privileged place in history. The best security practice can do is regulating exposure to it. This de-anthropomorphising of history as events and contingency radically challenges modern conceptions of democratic politics. It asks what deliberation, popular sovereignty, citizenship, and authority can mean in a history in which 'the figure of man recedes' (Dillon, 2007: 17).

Several interpretations of surveillance and insecurity that were introduced in this chapter show how diffuse securitising that operates through surveillance technology, transactional metrics and/or risk management work the limits of democratic politics by challenging the volitional reasoning subject. Lyon sees this taking place in the decentring of the embodied subject in multiple data-doubles that are generated within the surveillance practices and technologies. Ruppert does it by showing how transaction metrics break the link between action and power (the conception of interpassivity). Dillon does it by showing how governing through risk substitutes a contingent life that exists as events for a history made and controlled by humans.

Notes

1 Implicitly the argument of historical necessity and instrumental reasoning often draws on an understanding that security is the first good or right without which other rights and public goods are meaningless. This makes it possible to play the security card as the one that trumps others.

2 Drawing on years of research on surveillance, Gary T. Marx (2007) wrote a fictional speech of a security professional for the journal *International Political Sociology* in which he brings together nearly 40 techno-fallacies regularly used in justifications and presentations of surveillance.

3 'Fallacies of technological determinism and neutrality. These involve the failure to see the role played by humans in developing and applying technology and

they reduce issues of cultural and political dispute into matters to be resolved by the application of technology' (Marx, 2007: 97).

4 For an introduction to Der Derian's work on anti-diplomacy: Huysmans, 1997.

5 Jodi Dean argues similarly, in her analysis of the relation between secrecy and publicity in democracy, that '[a] fundamental compulsion to know generates suspicions that displace that element of belief in the belief of the other which is necessary to sustain social institutions' (Dean, 2002: 11). Publicity, for Dean, refers to a system that generates the public as a symbolic entity and practice (Dean, 2002: 11).

6 'Summoning publics' refers to struggles about the remaking of relations between public, private and personal in times of increasing questioning of the value of publicness. Newman and Clarke focus on neo-liberal injections of the private market in all spheres of life, and how new publics are emerging that challenge the delegitimisation of publicness. Rather than an emerging public sphere, they are interested in the more fractured practices in which various publics come into being and in which services realise socialities rather than socialities being taken as the condition for providing public services (Newman and Clarke, 2009). Such publics are of course not necessarily critical of securitising. They can come into being as exclusionary publics that connect people through hostility towards others. This opens towards a more complex reading of how assembling of suspicion does not simply 'atomise' individuals but also can hook them together into a sociality that unites around interests to protect against insecurities, including through surveillance technology and risk governance. However, such publics are summoned through processes of estrangement and, as inherently insecure, are vulnerable in their search for security to the rendition of suspicions that break down socialities, as I described in this section.

7 There is an increasing literature on what some have called 'the material turn' in international and security studies (Aradau, 2010). This literature is a good starting point for further developing some of the insights introduced in this section. It places the actantial dimensions—or agency—of materials within a broader analysis of how social and political relations are shaped in the interstices of nature, humanity and technology rather than human interaction as such (e.g. Barry, 2001; Walters, 2002; Coward, 2008; Weizman, 2010; Voelkner, 2011; Coward, 2012).

8 As Latour states it colourfully: 'it is important to notice that this has nothing to do with a "reconciliation" of the famous object–subject dichotomy. To distinguish a priori 'material' and 'social' ties before linking them together again makes about as much sense as to account for the dynamics of a battle by imagining a group of soldiers and officers stark naked with a huge heap of paraphernalia—tanks, rifles, paperwork, uniforms—and then claim that "of course there exist some (dialectical) relation between the two". One should retort adamantly "No". There exists no relation whatsoever between "the material" and "the social world", because it is this very division which is a complete artefact. To reject such a divide is not to "relate" the heap of naked soldiers "with" the heap of material stuff: it is to redistribute the whole assemblage from top to bottom and beginning to end. There is no empirical case where the existence of *two* coherent and homogeneous aggregates, for instance technology "and" society could make any sense' (Latour, 2005: 75–76).

9 In security studies this opens various interesting questions, including of course implications for conceptions and political mobilisations of human security. Nadine Voelkner's (2011) work, for example, takes the interconnection between

human and artefacts as central to understanding how human security works. Although she focuses on the governmentalising effects of technology, her analysis can be used as a springboard to challenge the notion of 'humanity' in human security from a post-human perspective. What would be the implications of understanding human security and its politics as post-human?

10 On Lyon's notion of citizenship and on related conceptions of reconceptualising citizenship as cyber citizenship in digital technological worlds, see David Lyon's *Identifying Citizens* (2009), James Hughes' *Citizen Cyborg* (2004), and Chris Hables Gray's *Cyborg Citizen* (2001).

11 Among others, debates in feminism on cyborg politics and how to understand an also productive rather than simply constraining relation between bodies and technology, humans and machines offer a source of insights from which to develop such research (Haraway, 1991; Munster, 1999), as does work in surveillance studies on bodies as a political site and being (see Chapter 6).

12 On the concept of interpassivity, see also: Van Oenen, 2006; Zizek, 2006.

8   Insecurity, democracy, political

Security studies has boomed since Al Qaeda flew planes into the Twin Towers and the Pentagon on 11 September 2001. Global counter-terrorist policies went hand in hand with an academic flood of texts on the changing nature of global and national insecurity. It was not the first time that a spectacular event led to revisiting security priorities and the nature of insecurity. The detonation of the first nuclear weapon and, in particular, the time two superpowers obtained nuclear capabilities were two other such moments. Prior to '9/11', the end of the Cold War arguably held a similar significance for security studies (Buzan and Lene, 2009). To some extent the very discipline of international studies arose from the watershed moment of the First World War.

In some sense these events were global moments. They resonated in significant ways beyond the confines of a few countries or regions. State and non-state actors acted upon both events in ways that took the world as a whole as their area of operation. Yet spotlighting security developments tied in with these events implies choices in terms of whose insecurities, what kind of insecurities and which modes of practices are taken as priorities. Enough has been written in security studies on the question of whose security and the performativity of security knowledge in the last two decades for this political selectiveness and its implications to be known (e.g. Wæver, 1995; Walker, 1997; McSweeney, 1999; Bigo, 2006; Huysmans, 2006). In response, there has been an increase in calls—beyond feminist international studies which has been driving such an agenda for decades now (Wibben, 2011)—for writing on insecurities from other positions and security concerns than the usual security priorities of European and North American states and the regional and international security organisations they dominate (e.g. Bubandt, 2005; Stern, 2005; Barkawi and Laffey; 2006, Bilgin, 2010; Tickner and Blaney, 2012). This book, however, is more conservative; it works largely within the confines of these European and North American biases. I neither developed a critical analysis of epistemological and political limits nor wrote systematically from a set of alternative positions and insecurities. Instead, I picked up a difference between debates following the end of the Cold War and those generated by 9/11 in this largely North American and European-driven security studies to introduce a political reading of securitising.

In both debates, academic literature mirrored the political understanding that something fundamental had changed in the security landscape. Previous evaluations of insecurities were considered to be either no longer relevant or in need of adaptation in light of new insecurities. Key debates following the end of the Cold War focused on the widening of insecurities beyond military inter-state relations. They raised questions about the political and social consequences of mobilising security discourses and institutions in areas such as migration, the environment and aid policy. 9/11 triggered similar revisiting but this time focusing on the question of networks as security actors, the diffusion of counter-terrorism measures into society, and changes from threat to risk and pre-emption.

One important difference between these two moments in security studies, however, was that democracy became 'at stake' in security post 9/11. Democracy was not a major contentious issue in analyses of security after the end of the Cold War. The main focus was on the legitimacy of extending security governance to new and multiple policy areas, known as the widening of security, and on how democratising sustained peace and security. With democracy being 'at stake', I mean that security policies were approached as potentially threatening democratic institutions and practice that they claim to protect (e.g. rights to political dissent and the rule of law). As a result, political critique—the analysis of the conception of politics contained in security practice—pervaded security studies in a more immediately visible way than before. The critique focused in particular on how exceptional security measures risked to hollow out or reduce protection of fundamental rights, institutional checks and balances, and international normative principles of non-intervention, sovereignty and human rights. In addition, the rise of governance through risk, pre-emption and surveillance led to an increased interest in the depoliticising effects of highly technocratic and managerial security processes. Key political concepts like citizenship, resistance, empire and sovereignty were revisited in attempts to bring out the political dimensions of these developments. They were interrogated and reconfigured in relation to changes in and challenges posed by security practice. Recent work in citizenship studies on resistance of irregular migrants, acts of citizenship and the governing of citizenship through securitising, for example, has created interstices between security and citizenship studies where the category of citizenship in various guises is used for the purpose of critical political analysis of security (e.g. Isin and Nielsen, 2008; Rygiel, 2008; Nyers, 2009; Guillaume and Huysmans, 2013). Similarly, the category of sovereignty has been intensively revisited to develop a political critique of security practice, and security practices have been drawn on to revisit the current significance of sovereignty (e.g. Butler, 2004; Epstein, 2008; Brown, 2010; Walker, 2010).

Interest in the political nature of security did not just emerge post 9/11. In the first chapter, I used Neumann's work to introduce a longer historical line but there are other more recent examples. In 1990 Rob Walker proposed similarly to examine the conceptions of politics—and, in particular, conceptions of political community—that are a constitutive element of securitising practice and that make prevailing accounts of security practice seem plausible; as did Michael Dillon a few years later (Walker, 1990; Dillon, 1996).[1] This book, however, is located quite explicitly at the juncture in which the exceptionalist nature of security practice has been given prominence for the purpose of questioning the inherent dangers that security measures are posing for democratic politics since 2001.

Besides this juncture and the questions it highlights in security studies, the book has also picked up longer term concerns with the rise of digital surveillance technology and preventive policing, the commodification of security, the dispersal of risk governance, and the formation of cultures of fear in European and North American societies. These developments have led to various questions about the resilience of democratic practice and institutions. Among the key concerns are effects on the public accountability of security policies in light of the profusion of security markets, the depletion of rights to privacy by the spread of surveillance technology, the hollowing out of fundamental principles of criminal justice in the wake of preventive policing, and the impact of pervasive discourses and images of insecurities on political opposition and active citizenship more generally (Garland, 2001; Furedi, 2002; Bauman and Lyon, 2013). International security studies have picked up on these in analyses of intelligence and managing radically uncertain futures in the wake of 9/11, the growth of private security markets, and the securitisation of migration and borders, among others.

Against this background, I proposed a political reading of security practice that defined security as a practice of enacting limits of democracy. When security enters politics it generates concerns with transgressions of democratic procedures, limitations of democratic citizenship and depletions of democratic rights. From being the given mode of conducting politics, democracy transforms into a political stake. Understanding the democratic stake in this context requires analyses of the specificity of securitising practices and their effects on democratic institutions and practice. I introduced a difference between exceptionalist securitising and diffuse assembling of suspicion as a tool for capturing key issues and challenges that the current conjuncture poses for democratic practice and for our understanding of the nature of the securitisations that are taking place. One of the claims of the book is that the profusion of insecurity discourses and security technologies into intimate and ordinary sites of life, the widespread application of risk and pre-emptive governance, and the transversal proliferation of security institutions and techniques challenges to democratic practice are not limited to the familiar authoritarian transgressions into democracy. In particular, falling back on analysing how security practice challenges liberty–security balances, the threat of a coup d'état, or the hollowing out of fundamental rights—although all important—will not get us to some of the ways in which the assembling of suspicion puts democratic practice under pressure, such as surveillance at a distance limiting possibilities for reflective engagement and collective mobilisation.

The book draws a rather pronounced difference between exceptionalist and diffuse techniques of securitising. I have done this to bring out more sharply that there are different modes of rendering and governing insecurities. Not all techniques of securitising work in the same way and it is particularly important at the moment to not reduce diffuse processes of assembling suspicion to exceptionalist renditions of national security. In counter-terrorist policies and its critique, both techniques are brought into contact in a particularly intense way. Surveillance technology, managing risk and uncertainty, and a pre-emptive orientation to insecurities are seen as part of changing national security strategies. The profusion of security practice is explicitly connected here to claiming existential emergencies to the state. 9/11 and counter-terrorism have become a focal point from which interests in surveillance enter international security studies. As a result, analyses of diffuse processes often remain framed within an exceptionalist security politics. While security practice is diffusing, its political significance continues to be analysed extensively around contestations of the legitimacy of extraordinary policies that transgress the limits of democratic politics in the name of existential threats to the state. Diffuse assembling of suspicion, however, operates in other areas than counterterrorism; areas where the connection with exceptionalist securitising is less pronounced, if present at all. Yet techniques of diffuse securitising equally, and in some ways more profusely, challenge democracy. Moreover, their mode of operation, and especially their decentring of power make a political analysis in exceptionalist terms inadequate, if not redundant in some cases. The specific nature and impact of diffuse securitising techniques make it a

serious matter of concern for critical analyses of securitising and demand
that the assembling of suspicion is analysed in its own terms without
immediately making it part of a largely exceptionalist securitising.

The lead theme of the book is a particular stake that defines the politics
of insecurity across both techniques of securitising: the unbinding of
security. Security unbound refers to security changing from a practice
that works largely within a relatively narrow set of institutional and
habitual limits that define what are matters of security and legitimate
modes of security practice to a forceful practice that significantly dilutes
these limits. Security unbound does not necessarily imply that security
becomes completely unrestricted, infinite or total, making all politics a
matter of security. Yet whatever its modulation—national security, exceptionalist global security or assembling suspicions—the unbinding of
security implies that security practice becomes profuse and generates
political, legal and social struggles over its limits and boundaries. Rights
to privacy, for example, set such limits to surveillance and remain a stake
around which the legitimacy of surveillance is negotiated and contested.
International laws of war and crimes against humanity that define limits
to the international legitimate use of violence are another example.
Although I developed the theme of security unbound extensively in the
chapters on diffusing insecurities and assembling suspicion, it is also a
leading stake in contemporary developments in exceptionalist securitising.
I illustrated this in particular in the discussion of national security turning
into a practice that takes society as a whole, whether national or global,
as its plane of operation (Chapter 3).

Security unbound is a main political stake that the book draws attention
to and that defines its programme for a critical analysis of the politics of
security. The unbinding of security does not only refer to moments and sites
in which security limits are challenged but also to the profusion of security
practice in social and political life challenging the possibility for, and on
occasions even the very legitimacy of, democratic practice. This connection between a concern with the pervasion of insecurities in social
and political relations and security enacting the limits of democracy is a
variation of the insight taken from Franz Neumann. He extensively
drew attention to the destructive implications for democratic politics of
instituting fear of the enemy as the organising principle of a political
system and to the role that intensified profusions of insecurities play in
making it possible for fear of the enemy to become the central principle
of political organisation (see Chapter 1). The main purpose of this book
has been to take this critical sensitivity to the proliferation of insecurities
and its negative consequences for democratic politics and develop it into
a political analysis of contemporary security practices.

At this point it is worth saying that this book is, in the first instance, an intervention in security studies. It is not a call for changing focus from security to analyses of democracy as such. Much can be gained from dipping into democracy literature, and analyses of democratic practice and its crises. Yet this book interpreted the limits of democracy from within the securitising processes. That is the reason why the book does not contain a particular definition of democracy, give an overview of various interpretations of democracy or engage literature on crises of democracy. The analysis is driven first of all by a concern with how contemporary securitising brings the limits of democracy into social and political play rather than with crises of democracy arising from changes in political practice and institutions, such as the rise of political apathy, the changing nature of political parties, regional integration and forms of populist politics.

In the remaining sections, I return to the distinction between exceptional and diffuse techniques of securitising. In particular, I highlight two related issues for which the distinction is instrumental. First, the distinction helps to introduce more sharply a key difference in the method of evaluating the impact of security practice on democracy. The political contestation of exceptionalist securitising tends to mobilise the danger of authoritarianism and, in particular, a concern with the displacement of a democratic by an authoritarian state. Diffuse securitising and, in particular, the assembling of suspicion invites a less statist and more fractured evaluation of how securitising challenges democratic practice. The latter results in a more fractional picture of multiple, situated challenges that are not aggregated back into a fear of an authoritarian state project. Secondly, taking diffuse assembling of suspicion in its distinctness brings out that the contemporary problematique of the unbinding of security cannot be fully understood within the conceptual comfort zone of international security studies. Although exceptionalist securitising also dissolves limits to security, it hooks a political evaluation back into familiar issues of statecraft and a traditional distinction between authoritarian and democratic government. Diffuse securitising sharply brings out that one of the key challenges today is that not only security limits dissolve but also the power relations through which insecurities are governed. This raises questions about how to move political analyses of securitising beyond statist methods that unify fractional processes by making them expressions of a state, a system or another totality.

Exceptionalising politics

How does security practice enact limits of democracy? The immediate answer in international security conjunctures at the start of the 21st

184 Insecurity, democracy, political

century was 'by exceptionalising politics'. The term 'exceptionalising politics' does not refer to politics becoming something rare, something that does not happen often. Instead it refers to conditions in which the scope of and limits to transgressions of instituted democratic practices and principles in the name of exceptionally destabilising or dangerous developments define contests over what is politically possible and acceptable and what not. Security's capacity to exceptionalise politics has been very visible in public debate, at least in North American and European political institutions, civil society and the news media. Instituting extraordinary spaces to hold people, including detention centres and off-shore prisons, extraordinary renditions, and transgressions of privacy and the right to political organisation, among others, have generated intense debates about the consequences of transgressing democratic political practice and the normative and practical limits of such transgressions. The revival of interest in exceptionalism, both in political and academic debates, was often linked to counter-terrorism and the securitising of migration. Yet it expressed a more general concern with how security practice challenged democracy as a form of government, in particular in those countries that at the same time were seeking to export democracy across the world.

Exceptionalist securitising is a particular technique of enacting insecurities. It combines existentialising challenges as matters of survival, with intensifying the implementation and contest of exceptionalist political practice that transgresses instituted and habitual democratic modes of politics. Politically it often questions the capacity of democratic policy formulation and implementation to be sufficiently effective and speedy so as to protect democracies from the dangers they face. In these cases exceptionalist securitising challenges democratic practice on the grounds of an inherent limitation to democratic polities—its inherent weakness to deal with extraordinary, existential situations. The point here is not simply that security comes into play when democracies reach these operational limits that prevent them from taking the necessary and speedy actions but rather that exceptionalist modes of securitising enact this conception of democracy into being. This technique of securitising takes on political significance by making the limits of democratic institutions and practices to effectively deal with existential insecurities a matter of concern.

In this book, I looked in particular at two modalities of how exceptionalist securitising enacts democratic limits. The first is a constitutional mode of rendering limits of democracy. It organises political contestation around tensions between legal and generalised normative constraints to the arbitrary exercise of political power and political demands for transgressing these constraints in the name of security. Contests over balancing security and liberty and the legitimacy of transgressing fundamental rights, procedures of due process and parliamentary scrutiny are familiar manifestations of this modality. The second mode concerns expanding the political role of the military. Securitising here challenges democratic limits to the political power of the military and, more generally, politicises tensions between civilian politics and its militarisation. Among the most radical manifestations of this second mode of exceptionalist securitising is a military coup in the name of national security. Although both modulations at first sight seem to draw a sharp distinction between the security concerns of the state and the everyday life of people by emphasising top-down governmental practices that are required to secure the state and its population, they often pervade the everyday and intimate lives of people. The latter therefore can become sites from which political contest of securitising can be organised. As I developed towards the end of the chapter on exceptionalist securitising, the political contestation of exceptionality is thus not limited to struggles between political, judicial and military elite over the legitimate mode of politics but includes multifaceted mobilisations challenging the transgressions of democratic principles and the violence of securitising as they play out in the lives people live on a daily basis.

A rise of authoritarian politics is a defining political concern in moments of exceptionalist securitising. This does not have to be an immediate danger of institutionalising an authoritarian state. It can also be a concern with authoritarian instances of government and their increased legitimacy within democracy. For example, contestations of offshore prison camps, like in Guantanamo Bay, and detention centres, like those in the Maghreb countries aimed at controlling migration flows into Europe, do not necessarily claim that the US, Italy, Spain, the UK or Germany have changed from democratic into authoritarian states. Yet the threat of authoritarian modes of government informs the concern with transgressions of values and rights that are considered to be defining parts of the institutional fabric of democracies.

Although nowadays observers may express more confidence in the robustness of democratic forms of government than writers in interwar and immediate post-war Europe and the US like Franz Neumann, the political analyses of the dangers of security policy and its profusion I looked at in Chapter 3 work within a similar line of thought to Neumann's. The various processes Neumann analysed in his work on 'anxiety and politics' and 'the political concept of freedom' come together in an understanding that when fear of the enemy becomes the energetic principle of politics, the democratic state is fundamentally undermined and transforming into an authoritarian state. Current debates on violations of fundamental rights or on the power of border guards retain elements of this concern with authoritarian government seeping into the democratic fabric. Judith Butler's coining of the term 'petty sovereigns' to characterise how coercive state power has been excessively exercised by and dispersed between individual border guards is one such an example (Butler, 2004: 56). The criticisms of counter-terrorism on grounds of disproportionately skewing the tension between liberty and security in the direction of the latter or of enacting a matrix of war that takes a global societal plane as the legitimate site of security action reminiscent of totalising national security practices in dictatorships in the 1960s and 70s are two other examples. A spectre of authoritarianism very often remains the basis for understanding what makes exceptionalist security policies politically problematic.

Diffusing politics

When many of the securitising processes are transversal and to some extent global, I am not sure that we gain as much as in the 1930s or 50s from foregrounding the spectre of the authoritarian state in political analyses of the effects of security practices. Although the coercive and violent capacity of state institutions remains a central concern, the security challenges to democracy are much more varied and do not as clearly as in Neumann's time coalesce around the formation of authoritarian states and regimes. Exceptionalist securitising works by aggregating and intensifying issues through renditions of existential threats. However, many of the social and political processes that circulate, distribute and commodify insecurities today are diffusing, in the sense of being both dispersed and non-intense.

Compared to exceptionalist securitising these processes decentre insecurities in a double sense. First, they disperse security decisions and management over many points of decision that are not connected to or rendered as expressions of a single hierarchically organised political unit. I borrowed the terminology of 'assembling' and 'rhizome' to distinguish this diffuse organisation of securitising from modes of security practice that remain primarily organised in terms of states or other aggregated political units—in particular, national security. Secondly, diffusing processes decentre not only the state as the decisional security unit but also the organisation of dangers in relation to an overarching threat. In this book, I drew in particular on surveillance and the renditions of risks and uncertainty in dispersed information flows to explain how diffuse securitising connects issues, while retaining them spread out rather than subsume them under a national, regional or global security threat.

Besides its decentring qualities, diffuse techniques of securitising also de-intensify insecurities. They assemble suspicion in routinised, often low-key, unspectacular practices rather than mobilise existential threats and emergencies.

Locating political aspects of securitising primarily in the modern, bureaucratic state and its transformations privileges hierarchical moments of control and authority in a social process in which power relations have become highly devolved. Such privileging of state power makes analyses highly vulnerable to misrecognising where the actions of control and autonomy take place, as well as what their modes of operation are. The growing interest in surveillance studies, and networks and assemblages in the security literature, ranging from counter-terrorism analyses, over-policing networks, and global assemblages of private security companies and intelligence agencies, is indicative of a general sense that security practices are indeed operating in diffuse modes and are reconfiguring and challenging securitising capacities of the bureaucratic modern states. If that reading is correct, then understanding the limits of democracy exclusively in light of an overriding concern with transformations from democratic to authoritarian state forms or modes of governance will offer only limited insights into how diffusing techniques of securitising are challenging democratic practice. As I drew out, for example in relation to the protection of privacy, surveillance does not simply endanger democracy through enhancing the traditional bureaucratic and coercive capacities of a state but through challenging reflective autonomy of actors in the minutiae of their everyday, ordinary relations with other people. Diffusing techniques of securitising like assembling suspicion, which has been the main diffusing security technique this book engaged, ask for a more creative understanding of what it means to enact the limits of democracy than the standard forms of analysis that are often endorsing instituted statist traditions of protecting democracy against the effects of security practice and that locate the political challenges in the exception-alising modalities of security practice rather than in its de-intensifying and decentring work.[2]

To analyse this diffuse enactment of the limits of democracy I worked as follows. I took familiar categories for accounting how surveillance and risk governance break limits to the dispersal of security practices in democracy. In particular, I looked at how assembling suspicion challenges the limits that privacy and citizenship, or, more generally, the democratic capacity to enact oneself as an autonomous political subject, set to expanding securitising. Instead of hooking privacy into a political evalua-tion of tendencies to authoritarian government, I treated it as a categorical democratic practice. A categorical practice is the enactment of a category, privacy in this case, through which democratic modalities are brought to bear upon security practice. In other words, these categories have become historically defined as an a priori given vehicle for inscribing democratic politics into social relations. These categories are taken as fractions of democratic practice that have political analytical value in themselves. Their significance does not derive from showing how hollowing out these categorical practices contributes to authoritarian government. Such an approach keeps democratic practice, and challenges to it, fractional.

In the first instance I evaluated how diffuse techniques of securitising enact these categorical practices, such as surveillance undermining but also negotiating privacy rights, and what the political consequences are of doing so. But the analysis also probed at places whether diffuse techniques of securitising are more radically challenging the very relevance of the categorical practices as vehicles for a political critique of diffuse securitising. In other words, at places I also asked if securitising operates in such a way that it fundamentally undermines the political adequacy of existing democratic resources, like privacy or citizenship. To do this the analysis probed securitising processes in greater detail to identify new analytical anchor points through which less immediately familiar but challenging effects on central democratic categories and practice become visible. For example, probing the limits of 'privacy' for understanding how surveillance enacts democratic limits led to the observation that assembling suspicion does not only challenge privacy rights but considerably limits the possibility for people to organise a political voice that can challenge the diffuse power structures through which surveillance operates. Surveillance technology increasingly works at a distance and extracts information directly from the body. This reduces the opportunities for direct reflexive engagement with the processes of extraction and control. By engaging people individually rather than as populations, it reinforces the isolation of individuals: it is me and the technology, not us as a population sharing certain characteristics. These modes of surveillance keep people more strongly within a private relation with themselves. It inhibits the categorical democratic practice of a private subject with opinions enacting public subjectivity through collective claims and actions. The assembling of suspicion through surveillance thus poses challenges to the formation of a public life of deliberation, negotiating and bargaining in which people come together as a public to contest and partly settle a matter of common concern. At this point in the analysis, an agenda opened up for probing the democratic question of organising political 'voice' from a different angle: the friction that bodies which are continuously changing and simultaneously placed in multiple relations insert into the smooth working of surveillance. To what extent can this friction be understood as a mode of enacting autonomy and power within a diffuse technique of surveilling? Can the categorical democratic practice of privacy and gaining autonomous voice be reinterpreted as a practice of bodily becoming?

In the chapter on technology, I probed similarly the particular ways in which assembling suspicion enacts limits of democratic citizenship through intensifying the technological nature of 'interaction' and 'governing'. Such developments limit the political relevance of enacting oneself as democratic subject by claiming rights and the right to have rights. This observation then led to the question of what conception of democratic citizenship, if any, can be developed when technology and human agency intensely intertwine; a conception that makes visible the possibilities of disrupting these limits that diffuse securitising imposes on democratic citizenship.

If securitising exists in much more decentred, unbound relations, the democratic stakes in relation to security are changing. It is not fully clear what counts as democratic practice that can effectively define limits to diffusing security governance; what democratic politics can mean if governmental powers cannot be straightforwardly organised in terms of 'the state', intensity and aggregated structures of decision making. The value of familiar categorical democratic practices that are mobilised to gain political purchase on a diffuse process of securitising, such as privacy, citizenship, democratic deliberation and constitutional constraints on political power cannot be taken for granted.

Times and sites of diffuse securitising thus invite research that explores practices and events that allow us to see if and how democratic practices (can) exist in diffuse modalities and if and how they bear upon diffuse power relations within which they need to operate. They thus call not only for a diffuse understanding of securitisation, such as assembling suspicion and its difference with exceptionalist securitising, but also for a diffuse conception of democratic politics. The latter invites a political reading of securitising that prioritises more diffuse interpretations of democratic practice and takes experimental democratic practices that challenge diffuse governing powers as an object of analysis in security studies.

The political stake of security unbound is then not simply democratically reinstating limits to security practice but also reinventing what a democratic politics can be that can bear upon highly dispersed and low-intensity security practice. Here I have reached the limits of the book, however. Such a political reading requires another study that looks more intensely and systematically at experimental practices that diffuse politics in attempts to constrain, hold to account and/or disrupt the unbinding of security. At places in this book, I indicated ways of developing such a reading (e.g. understanding political agency in terms of 'becoming bodies' in Chapter 6). Yet overall I prioritised a focus on the internal workings of security practice, on how securitising techniques unbind security and enact limits of democracy.

Conclusion

To conclude, let me put the reading of securitising that this book developed and the political stake that informs this reading in a nutshell. I took the tension between democracy and security as a starting point to develop a political critique of security. Security was defined as the enactment of limits of democracy. Different ways of how security practice brings limits to democracy into political play were then unpacked in relation to two techniques of securitising: exceptionalist securitising and the diffuse securitising technique of assembling suspicion. Of specific interest was that these techniques of securitising do not only challenge democratic practice but at moments also unbind security, in the sense of both dispersing insecurities and diluting institutional and customary limits to security practice. Running through the book is a claim that when security becomes unbound the democratic political stake is to prevent insecurity from becoming the organising principle of politics and other areas of life. As Neumann warned us, more than half a century ago, democratic practice is incompatible with a political and social system that governs through insecurities, that has insecurity as its organising device. I took Neumann's insight and made it the basis for a political analysis of contemporary securitising. This book thus developed a research agenda for critical security studies based on a contemporary variation of an old concern that security can never be simply treated as a method of protecting democracy because it inherently also undermines democratic practice.

Notes

1 Since then there has been a growing literature in critical approaches to security that has foregrounded the question of the conceptions of the political that are implied in securitising knowledge and practice. To mention a few of these: Lene Hansen argued that defining securitisation as speech excludes from analysis those for whom speaking their insecurity is too dangerous (Hansen, 2000); Claudia Aradau developed a critique of security as depoliticising leading to an argument for a politics out of security, as did Mark Neocleous (Aradau, 2004, 2008; Neocleous, 2008); Andreas Behnke's Schmittean readings of the politics of insecurity, in his

analyses of 9/11 and NATO are another example (Behnke, 2004, 2005, 2011); as is Annick Wibben's feminist work (Wibben, 2011) and my earlier work on the politics of insecurity (Huysmans, 1998, 2006).

2 Some analyses reintroduce the exceptionalising of politics as a main vehicle for a political critique of diffuse securitising (Van Munster, 2004; Amoore and de Goede, 2008; Salter, 2008). The understanding of exceptionality, however, differs from traditional engagements with the exception. The key political challenge does not seem to be a revival of exceptionalist transgressions nibbling at constitutional limits but the fact that 'the exception has become the rule'. Referring to Agamben's work on exception, the diagnosis is that we are now no longer in a time in which the tense relation between exceptional politics and normal politics are bound by a set of institutions and laws. For Agamben, the distinction norm/exception is no longer a defining device of politics, which means the bankruptcy of exceptionalist readings of politics. The latter are organised around contestations of how the relation between exceptional rule and normal rule can be legitimately organised. They require retaining a distinction between norm and exception that is linked to a constitutional order that institutes a rule of law. The 'exception being the rule' means, for Agamben, that the constitutional normative order is no longer constraining political practice. Law has given way to a myriad of administrative regulations and functionally fragmented quasi-laws. Political power acts directly upon people without being mediated through legal constraints. Paradoxically, rather than being a continuation of the exceptionalising politics of securitising, this interpretation actually de-exceptionalises politics. It asks for a different understanding of how power is and can be exercised and constrained. I have no space to go into the particular answers Agamben and others give to this question. However, as I have argued elsewhere, diagnosing contemporary issues in terms of exceptionalist interpretations of politics is not very conducive to understanding how democratic practices are and can work within what are diffuse power relations (Huysmans, 2008, 2011).

Bibliography

Abrahamsen, Rita and Williams, Michael C. (2010). *Security beyond the state: Private security in international politics*, Cambridge: Cambridge University Press.

Adam, Barbara, Beck, Ulrich and Van Loon, Joost (eds) (2000). *The risk society and beyond: Critical issues in social theory*, London: Sage.

Adler, Emanuel and Barnett, Michael (eds) (1998). *Security communities*, Cambridge: Cambridge University Press.

Agamben, Giorgio. (2002). L'état d'exception. *Le Monde*, 12 December.

Aldrich, Richard J. (2004). Transatlantic intelligence and security cooperation. *International Affairs*, 80(4): 731–53.

Amicelle, Anthony (2011). Towards a 'new' political anatomy of financial surveillance. *Security Dialogue*, 42(2): 161–78.

Amoore, Louise (2008). Governing by identity. *In*: Bennett, Colin J. and Lyon, David (eds) *Playing the identity card: Surveillance, security and identification in global perspective*, London: Routledge, pp. 42–56.

Amoore, Louise and De Goede, Marieke (2008). Transactions after 9/11: The banal face of the preemptive strike. *Transactions of the Institute of British Geographers*, 33(2): 173–85.

—— (2008a). Introduction: Governing by risk in the War on Terror. *In*: Amoore, Louise and De Goede, Marieke (eds) *Risk and the War on Terror*, London: Routledge, pp. 5–19.

Amoore, Louise and de Goede, Marieke (eds) (2008b). *Risk and the War on Terror*, London: Routledge.

Amoore, Louise and Hall, Alexandra (2009). Taking people apart: Digitised dissection and the body at the border. *Environment and Planning D: Society and Space*, 27 (3): 444–64.

—— (2010). Border theatre: On the arts of security and resistance. *Cultural Geographies*, 17(3): 299–319.

Andrijasevic, Rutvica (2010a). From exception to excess: Detention and deportations across the Mediterranean space. *In*: De Genova, Nicholas and Peutz, Nathalie (eds) *The deportation regime: Sovereignty, space and the freedom of movement*, Durham, NC: Duke University Press, pp. 147–65.

—— (2010b). *Migration, agency and citizenship in sex trafficking*, Basingstoke: Palgrave Macmillan.

Annan, Kofi (2003). UN must confront threats and challenges. *UN Secretary General Kofi Annan's address to the General Assembly*, 23 September.

Aradau, Claudia (2004). Security and the democratic scene: Desecuritization and emancipation. *Journal of International Relations and Development*, 7(4): 388–413.

—— (2008). *Rethinking trafficking in women. Politics out of security*, Basingstoke: Palgrave Macmillan.

—— (2010). Security that matters: Critical infrastructure and objects of protection. *Security Dialogue*, 41(5): 491–514.

Aradau, Claudia, Lobo-Guerrero, Luis and van Munster, Rens (2008a). Security, technology of risk, and the political. *Security Dialogue*, 39(2–3): 147–54.

—— (2008b). Special issue on security, technologies of risk, and the political. *Security Dialogue*, 39(2–3): 147–357.

Aradau, Claudia and van Munster, Rens (2007). Governing terrorism through risk: Taking precautions, (un)knowing the future. *European Journal of International Relations*, 13(1): 89–115.

—— (2008a). Insuring terrorism, assuring subjects, ensuring normality: The politics of risk after 9/11. *Alternatives*, 33(2): 191–210.

—— (2008b). Taming the future: The *dispositif* of risk in the war on terror. *In:* Amoore, Louise and De Goede, Marieke (eds) *Risk and the war on terror*, London: Routledge, pp. 23–40.

—— (2011). *Politics of catastrophe: Genealogies of the unknown*, Abingdon: Routledge.

Ash, Timothy Garton (2002). In the terror trap. *The Guardian*, 17 October. Available: www.theguardian.com/world/2002/oct/17/september11.uk [Accessed 31 August 2013].

Ashley, Richard (1987). The geopolitics of geopolitical space. Toward a critical social theory of international politics. *Alternatives*, 12(4): 403–34.

—— (1988). Untying the sovereign state: A double reading of the anarchy problematique. *Millennium: Journal of International Studies*, 17(2): 227–61.

Balibar, Etienne (1976). *Sur la dictature du prolétariat*, Paris: François Maspero.

—— (2002). *Droit de cité*, Paris: Quadrige/puf.

—— (2003). *L'Europe, l'Amérique, la guerre: Réflexions sur la médiation Européenne*, Paris: Editions La Découverte.

Ball, Kirstie (2005). Organization, surveillance and the body: Towards a politics of resistance. *Organization*, 12(1): 89–108.

—— (2006). Organization, surveillance and the body: Towards a politics of resistance. *In:* Lyon, David (ed.) *Theorizing surveillance*, Cullompton: Willan Publishing, pp. 296–317.

—— (2009). Exposure. *Information, Communications & Society*, 12(5): 639–57.

Ball, Kirstie, Daniel, Elizabeth, Dibb, Sally and Meadows, Maureen (2010). Democracy, surveillance and 'knowing what's good for you': The private sector origins of profiling and the birth of 'citizens relationship management'. *In:* Haggerty, Kevin D. and Barkawi, Tarak & Laffey, Mark (2006). The postcolonial moment in security studies. *Review of International Studies*, 32(2): 329–52.

Barry, Andrew (2001). *Political machine: Governing a technological society*, London: The Atlone Press.

Bartelson, Jens (1997). Making exceptions: Some remarks on the concept of coup d'etat and its history. *Political Theory*, 25(3): 323–246.

Bauman, Zygmunt (2000). *Liquid modernity*, Cambridge: Polity Press.

Bauman, Zygmunt and Lyon, David (2005). 9/11 und die Grenzen des Politischen. *Zeitschrift für Internationale Beziehungen*, 12(1): 117–40.

—— (2011). *NATO's security discourse after the Cold War: Representing the West*, Abingdon: Routledge.

—— (2013). *Liquid surveillance*, Cambridge: Polity Press.

Beck, Ulrich (1992). *Risk society: Towards a new modernity*, London, Sage.

Behnke, Andreas (2004). Terrorising the political: 9/11 within the context of the globalisation of violence. *Millennium. Journal of International Studies*, 33(2): 279–312.

—— (2011). *NATO's security discourse after the Cold War: Representing the West*, Abingdon: Routledge.

Bell, Colleen (2006). Surveillance strategies and populations at risk: Biopolitical governance in Canada's national security policy. *Security Dialogue*, 37(2): 147–65.

Bennett, Colin J. (2011). In defence of privacy: The concept and the regime. *Surveillance & Society*, 8(4): 485–96.

Bibler Coutin, Susan (2008). Subverting discourses of risk in the war on terror. *In*: Amoore, Louise and De Goede, Marieke (eds) *Risk and the war on terror*, Abingdon: Routledge, pp. 218–32.

Bigo, Didier (1995). Grands débats dans un petit monde. *Cultures & Conflits*, (19–20): 7–41.

—— (1996). *Polices en réseaux: L'expérience européenne*, Paris: Presses de Sciences Po.

—— (2000). When two become one: Internal and external securitisations in europe. *In*: Kelstrup, Morten & Williams, Michael C. (eds) *International relations theory and the politics of European integration: Power, security and community*, London: Routledge, pp. 171–204.

—— (2002). Security and immigration: Toward a critique of the governmentality of unease. *Alternatives*, 27(Special Issue): 63–92.

—— (2006). Security, exception, ban and surveillance. *In*: Lyon, David (ed.) *Theorizing surveillance*, Cullompton: Willan Publishing, pp. 46–68.

—— (2008). Globalized (in)security: The field and the ban-opticon. *In*: Bigo, Didier and Tsoukala, Anastassia (eds) *Terror, insecurity and liberty*, Abingdon: Routledge, pp. 10–48.

Bigo, Didier & Guittet, Emmanuel-Pierre (eds) (2004). *Militaires et sécurité intérieure. L'Irlande du Nord comme métaphore*. Special issue of *Cultures et Conflits*, no. 56, pp. 5–182.

Bigo, Didier & Jeandesboz, Julien (2009). Border security, technology and the Stockholm Programme. *IN:EX – Converging and conflicting ethical values in the internal/external security continuum in Europe* (European Commission 7th Framework). Brussels: Centre for European Policy Studies (CEPS).

Bigo, Didier & Tsoukala, Anastassia (eds) (2008a). *Terror, insecurity and liberty: Illiberal practices of liberal regimes after 9/11*, Abingdon: Routledge.

Bigo, Didier & Tsoukala, Anastassia (2008b). Understanding (in)security. *In*: Bigo, Didier & Tsoukala, Anastassia (eds) *Terror, insecurity and liberty*, Abingdon: Routledge, pp. 1–9.

Bigo, Didier, Bonelli, Laurent and Deltombe, Thomas (eds) *Au nom du 11 septembre... Les démocraties à l'épreuve de l'antiterrorisme*, Paris: La Découverte, pp. 36–48.

Bigo, Didier, Carrera, Sergio, Guild, Elspeth & Walker, R.B.J. (eds) (2010). *Europe's 21st century challenge: Delivering liberty*, Aldershot: Ashgate.

Bilgin, Pinar (2010). The 'Western-centrism' of security studies: 'Blind spot' or constitutive practice? *Security Dialogue*, 41(6): 615–22.

Blair, Tony (2001). *Speech to the Labour Party conference.* Available: http://politics.guardian.co.uk/labour2001/story/0,1414,562006,00.html [Part 1]; http://politics.guardian.co.uk/labourconference2001/story/0,1220,561988,00.html [Part 2] [Accessed 31 August 2013].

Blair, Tony (2003). *Speech opening debate on Iraq crisis in the House of Commons, as released by 10 Downing Street*, 18 March. Available: www.theguardian.com/politics/2003/mar/18/foreignpolicy.iraq1 [Accessed 2 October 2013].

Bonditti, Philippe (2004). From territorial space to networks: A Foucaultian approach to the implementation of biopolitics. *Alternatives*, 29(4): 465–82.

—— (2007). Biometrics and surveillance. *In*: Bigo, Didier (ed.) *The field of the EU internal security agencies*, Paris: L'Hamattan, pp. 97–114.

—— (2008). *L'antiterrorisme aux Etats-Unis (1946–2007): Une analyse Foucaldienne de la transformation de l'exercise de la sourveraineté et de l'art de gouverner*. Doctoral thesis, Institut d'Etudes Politiques de Paris.

Booth, Ken (1991). Security and emancipation. *Review of International Relations*, 17(4): 313–26.

Boundary News (2011). *Frontex begins Operation Hermes in Lampedusa following request from Italy*. Durham: International Boundaries Research Unit, Durham University. Available: www.dur.ac.uk/ibru/news/boundary_news/?itemno=11608&rehref=%2Fibru%2F&resubj=Boundary+news%20Headlines [Accessed 7 October 2013].

Boyle, Philip and Haggerty, Kevin D. (2009). Spectacular security: Mega-events and the security complex. *International Political Sociology*, 3(3): 257–74.

Braverman, Irus (2008). Checkpoint gazes. *In*: Isin, Engin F. and Nielsen, Greg M. (eds) *Acts of citizenship*, London: Zed Books, pp. 211–14.

Brouwer, Evelien (2009). *The EU passenger name record system and human rights: Transferring passenger data or passenger freedom?* CEPS Working Document No. 320/September 2009, 1–30.

Brown, Wendy (2010). *Walled states, waning sovereignty*, New York: Zone Books.

Bruneau, Thomas C. and Matei, Florina Cristiana (2008). Towards a new conceptualization of democratization and civil-military relations. *Democratization*, 15(5): 909–29.

Bubandt, Nils (2005). Vernacular security: The politics of feeling safe in global, national and local worlds. *Security Dialogue*, 36(3): 275–96.

Bush, George W. (2003). *Statement by His Excellency Mr. George W. Bush, President of the United States of America address to the United Nations General Assembly*, September 23. Available: www.un.int/usa/03_146.htm [Accessed 24 April 2009].

Butler, Judith (2004). *Precarious life: The powers of mourning and violence*, London: Verso.

Buzan, Barry (1983). *People, states and fear: The national security problem in international relations*, Brighton: Harvester.

—— (1987). *An introduction to strategic studies: Military technology and international relations*, London: Macmillan.

—— (1991). *People, states & fear: An agenda for international security studies in the post-Cold War era*, London: Harvester Wheatsheaf.

Buzan, Barry and Lene, Hansen. (2009). *The evolution of international security*, Cambridge: Cambridge University Press.

Buzan, Barry, Wæver, Ole and De Wilde, Jaap (1998). *Security: A new framework for analysis*, Boulder, CO: Lynne Rienner Publishers.

Campbell, Bruce B. (2000). Death squads: Definitions, problems, and historical context. *In*: Campbell, Bruce B. and Brenner, Arthur D. (eds) *Death squads in global perspective: Murder with deniability*, New York: St. Martin's Press, pp. 1–26.

Campbell, David (1992). *Writing security: United States foreign policy and the politics of identity*, Minneapolis, MN: University of Minnesota Press.

—— (1998). *Writing security: United States foreign policy and the politics of identity*, Manchester: Manchester University Press.

—— (2002). Time is broken: The return of the past in the response to September 11. *Theory and Event*, 5(4): 1–16. Available www.david-campbell.org/wp-content/documents/Time_is_broken.pdf [Accessed 14 October 2013].

Campbell, John Edward and Carlson, Matt (2002). Panopticon.Com: Online surveillance and the commodification of privacy. *Journal of Broadcasting and Electronic Media*, 46(4): 586–606.

Campbell, Nancy D. (2006). Everyday insecurities: The microbehavioral politics of intrusive surveillance. *In*: Monahan, Torin (ed.) *Surveillance and security: Technological politics and power in everyday life*, London: Routledge, pp. 57–75.

Carothers, Thomas (2003). Promoting democracy and fighting terror. *Foreign Affairs*, 82(1): 84–97.

Carter Hallward, Maia (2008). Negotiating boundaries, narrating checkpoints: The case of Machsom Watch. *Middle East Critique*, 17(1): 21–40.

Cassils, J. Anthony (2004). Overpopulation, sustainable development, and security: Developing an integrated strategy. *Population and Environment*, 25(3): 171–94.

Cawthra, Gavin & Luckham, Robin (eds) (2003). *Governing insecurity: Democratic control of military and security establishments in transitional democracies*, London: Zed Books.

Center for Constitutional Rights (2002). *The state of civil liberties: One year later. Erosion of civil liberties in the post 9/11 era*. Available: http://ccrjustice.org/v2/reports/docs/Civil_Liberities.pdf [Accessed 31 August 2013].

Chan, Janet (2008). The new lateral surveillance and a culture of suspicion. *Sociology of Crime, Law and Deviance*, 10223–39.

Chandler, David (2009). War without end(s): Grounding the discourse of 'global war'. *Security Dialogue*, 40(3): 243–62.

Cohen, Stanley (1985). *Visions of social control: Crime, punishment and classification*, Oxford: Polity Press.

—— (2002 [1972]). *Folk devils and moral panics* (3rd edn), London: Routledge.

Coker, Christopher (2002). *Globalization and insecurity in the twenty-first century: NATO and the management of risk*, London: International Institute of Security Studies.

Collier, Stephen J. (2006). Global assemblages. *Theory, Culture & Society*, 23(2–3): 399–401.

Connolly, William E. (1995). *The ethos of pluralization*, Minneapolis, MN: University of Minnesota Press.

Constantinou, Costas M. (2008). On the Cypriot states of exception. *International Political Sociology*, 2(2): 145–64.

Council of the European Union (2004). *Council regulation (EC) no. 2007/2004 of 26 October 2004 establishing a European Agency for the Management of Operational Coop- eration at the External Borders of the Member States of the European Union*. Brussels: Official Journal of the European Union, L 349. Available: http://eur-lex.europa. eu/LexUriServ/LexUriServ.do?uri=OJ:L:2004:349:0001:0011:EN:PDF [Accessed 7 October 2013].

Coward, Martin (2008). *Urbicide: The politics of urban destruction*, London: Routledge.

—— (2012). Between us in the city: Materiality, subjectivity, and community in the era of global urbanization. *Environment and Planning D: Society and Space*, 30(3): 468–81.

Crozier, Michel, Huntington, Samuel P. and Watanuki, Joji (1975). *The crisis of democracy: Report on the governability of democracies to the Trilateral Commission*, New York: New York University Press.

Daase, Christopher and Kessler, Oliver (2007). Knowns and unknowns in the 'war on terror': Uncertainty and the political construction of danger. *Security Dialogue*, 38(4): 411–34.

Dal Lago, Alessandro and Palidda, Salvatore (eds) (2010a). *Conflict, security and the reshaping of society. The civilization of war*, Abingdon: Routledge.

Dal Lago, Alessandro and Palidda, Salvatore (2010b). Introduction. *In*: Dal Lago, Alessandro and Palidda, Salvatore (eds) *Conflict, security and the reshaping of society: The civilization of war*, Abingdon: Routledge, pp. 1–18.

Dal Lago, Alessandro (2004). Police globale. *Cultures et Conflits*, 56: 157–69.

—— (2008). La Police globale, état de conflit permanent du capitalisme globalisé. *In*: Dalby, Simon (2009). *Security and environmental change*, Cambridge: Polity Press.

Dandeker, Christopher (1990). *Surveillance, power and modernity*, Cambridge: Polity Press.

—— (1994). National security and democracy: The United Kingdom experience. *Armed Forces & Society*, 20(3): 353–74.

Davidshofer, Stephan. (2009). *La gestion de crise Européenne ou quand l'Europe rencontre la sécurité. Modalité pratiques et symboliques d'une autonomisation*. Doctoral thesis, Institut d'Etudes Politiques de Paris.

Davies, Simon G. (2001). Re-engineering the right to privacy: How privacy has been transformed from a right to a commodity. *In*: Agre, Philip E. and Rotenberg, Marc (eds) *Technology and privacy: The new landscape*, Cambridge, MA: MIT Press, pp. 332.

de Goede, Marieke (2008a). Beyond risk: Premediation and the post-9/11 security imagination. *Security Dialogue*, 39(2–3): 155–76.

—— (2008b). Risk, preemption and exception in the war on terrorist financing. *In*: Amoore, Louise and De Goede, Marieke (eds) *Risk and the War on Terror*, Abingdon: Routledge, pp. 97–111.

—— (2012). *Speculative security: The politics of pursuing terrorist monies*, Minneapolis, MN: University of Minnesota Press.

de Goede, Marieke and de Graaf, Beatrice (2013). Sentencing risk: Temporality and precaution in terrorism trials. *International Political Sociology*, 7(3): 313–31.

Dean, Jodi (2002). *Publicity's secret: How technoculture capitalizes on democracy*, Ithaca, NY: Cornell University Press.

Deflem, Mathieu (2002). *Policing world society: Historical foundations of international police cooperation*, Oxford: Oxford University Press.

Deleuze, Gilles and Guattari, Félix (2004 [1980]). *A thousand plateaus: Capitalism and schizophrenia*, London: Continuum.

Demirel, Tanel (2005). Lessons of military regimes and democracy: The Turkish case in a comparative perspective. *Armed Forces & Society*, 31(2): 245–71.

Der Derian, James (1987). *On diplomacy: A genealogy of Western estrangement*, Oxford: Basil Blackwell.

—— (1992). *Antidiplomacy: Spies, terror, speed and war*, Cambridge, MA: Blackwell.

—— (1993). The value of security: Hobbes, Marx, Nietzsche and Baudrillard. *In*: Campbell, David and Dillon, Michael (eds,) *The political subject of violence*, Manchester: Manchester University Press, pp. 94–113.

—— (2009). *Critical practices in international theory. Selected essays*, London: Routledge.

Derrida, Jacques (1997). *Politics of friendship*, London: Verso.

—— (2003). *Voyous*, Paris: Galilée.

Dick, Philip K. (2002 [1956]). *Minority report*, London: Gollancz.

Dillon, Michael (1996). *Politics of security*, London: Routledge.

—— (2003). Virtual security: A life science of (dis)order. *Millennium – Journal of International Studies*, 32(3): 531–58.

—— (2007). Governing terror: The state of emergency of biopolitical emergence. *International Political Sociology*, 1(1): 7–28.

—— (2008). Underwriting security. *Security Dialogue*, 39(2–3): 309–32.

Dillon, Michael and Reid, Julian (2009). *The liberal way of war: Killing to make life live*, Abingdon: Routledge.

DOD (2009). *DOD dictionary of military terms. US Department of Defense*. Available: www.dtic.mil/doctrine/jel/doddict/index.html [Accessed 1 July 2009].

Dominguez, Jorge I. (2007). *International security and democracy: Latin America and the Caribbean in the post-Cold War era*, Pittsburgh, PA: University of Pittsburgh.

Doyle, Michael (1997). *Ways of war and peace*, New York: W.W.Norton.

Dryzek, John S. (1999). Transnational democracy. *Journal of Political Philosophy*, 7(1): 30–51.

—— (2006). Transnational democracy in an insecure world. *International Political Science Review/Revue internationale de science pol*, 27(2): 101–19.

Duffield, Mark (2007). *Development, security and unending war: Governing the world of peoples*, Cambridge: Polity Press.

Dupont, Benoît (2008). Hacking the panopticon: Distributed online surveillance and resistance. *Sociology of Crime, Law and Deviance*, 10: 259–80.

Dupont, Benoît and Wood, Jennifer (2006). Conclusion: The future of democracy. *In*: Wood, Jennifer and Dupont, Benoît (eds) *Democracy, society and the governance of security*, New York: Cambridge University Press, pp. 241–48.

Dyzenhaus, David (1997). *Legality and legitimacy. Carl Schmitt, Hans Kelsen and Herman Heller in Weimar*, Oxford: Oxford University Press.

Edkins, Jenny (2003). *Trauma and the memory of politics*, Cambridge: Cambridge University Press.

Enloe, Cynthia (1989). *Bananas, beaches and bases: Making feminist sense of international relations*, London: Pandora.

—— (2010). *Nimo's war, Emma's war. Making feminist sense of the Iraq war*, Berkeley, CA: University of California Press.

Epstein, Charlotte (2008). Embodying risk: Using biometrics to protect the borders. *In*: Amoore, Louise and De Goede, Marieke (eds) *Risk and the war on terror*, Abingdon: Routledge, pp. 178–93.

Ericson, Richard V. and Haggerty, Kevin D. (1997). *Policing the risk society*, Oxford: Oxford University Press.

Etzioni, Amitai (2007). *Security first: For a muscular, moral foreign policy*, New Haven, CT: Yale University Press.

European Commission (2009). *Towards a more secure society and increased industrial competitiveness*. Security research projects under the 7th Framework Programme for Research. Brussels: European Commission. Available: ftp://ftp.cordis.europa.eu/pub/fp7/security/docs/towards-a-more-secure_en.pdf [Accessed 8 June 2011].

Favarel-Garrigues, Gilles, Godefroy, Thierry and Lascoumes, Pierre (2009). *Les sentinelles de l'argent sale: Les banques aux prises avec l'antiblanchiment*, Paris: La Découverte.

Fierke, Karin (1998). *Changing games, changing strategies: Critical investigations in security*, Manchester: Manchester University Press.

—— (2007). *Critical approaches to international security*, Cambridge: Polity Press.

Foucault, Michel (1984). What is enlightenment? *In*: Rabinow, Paul (ed.) *The Foucault reader*, New York: Pantheon Books, pp. 32–50.

Frazier, Lessie Jo (1999). 'Subverted memories': Countermourning as political action in Chile. *In*: Bal, Mieke, Crewe, Jonathan and Spitzer, Leo (eds) *Acts of memory: Cultural recall in the present*, Hanover, NH: University Press of New England, pp. 105–19.

Fukuyama, Francis (2002). *Our posthuman future: Consequences of the biotechnology revolution*, New York: Farrar, Straus and Giroux.

Furedi, Frank (2002). *Culture of fear: Risk-taking and the morality of low expectation*, London: Continuum.

Gane, Nicholas (2006). Posthuman. *Theory, Culture & Society*, 23(2–3): 431–34.

Garcia Castro, Antonia (1996–1997). La mémoire des survivants et la révolte des ombres: Les disparus dans la société Chilienne (1973–1995). *Cultures et Conflits*, (24–25): 257–71.

Garland, David (2001). *The culture of control*, Oxford: Oxford University Press.

Gearty, Conor (2013). *Liberty and security*, Cambridge: Polity Press.

Geyer, Florian (2008). *Taking stock: Databases and systems of information exchange in the area of freedom, security and justice.* CHALLENGE research paper no. 9, Brussels: CEPS.

Giddens, Anthony (1985). *A Contemporary Critique of Historical Materialism: The nation-state and violence.* Volume Two of a Contemporary Critique of Historical Materialism, Cambridge: Polity Press.

Gray, Chris Hables (2001). *Cyborg citizen. Politics in the posthuman age,* London: Routledge.

Greenwood, Christopher (2002). International law and the 'war against terrorism'. *International Affairs,* 78(2): 301–17.

Greimas, Algirdas and Courtés, Joseph (1993). *Sémiotique: Dictionnaire raisonné de la théorie du langage,* Paris: Hachette.

Grosz, Elizabeth (1994). *Volatile bodies: Towards a corporeal feminism,* Bloomington, IN: Indiana University Press.

Guillaume, Xavier and Huysmans, Jef (eds) (2013). *Citizenship and security: The constitution of political being,* Abingdon: Routledge.

Guiraudon, Virginie (2000). European integration and migration policy: Vertical policy-making and venue shopping. *Journal of Common Market Studies,* 38(2): 251–71.

—— (2003). The constitution of a European immigration policy doma. *In:* A political sociology approach. *Journal of European Public Policy,* 10(2): 263–82.

Guittet, Emmanuel-Pierre (2006). *La genèse de la coopération antiterroriste en Europe et l'implication de l'Espagne dans la (re)définition de l'identité Européenne. De la raison d'état à la raison de la gouvernementalité européenne?* Doctoral thesis, Université Paris X-Nanterre.

Haftendorn, Helga (1991). The security puzzle: Theory-building and discipline-building in international security. *International Studies Quarterly,* 35(1): 3–17.

Haggerty, Kevin D. and Ericson, Richard V. (2000). The surveillant assemblage. *British Journal of Sociology,* 51(4): 605–22.

Haggerty, Kevin D. and Samatas, Minas (eds) (2010a). *Surveillance and democracy,* Abingdon: Routledge.

Haggerty, Kevin D. and Samatas, Minas (2010b). Surveillance and democracy: An unsettled relation. *In:* Haggerty, Kevin D. & Samatas, Minas (eds) *Surveillance and democracy,* Abingdon: Routledge, pp. 1–16.

Hall, Stuart, Critcher, Chas, Jefferson, Tony, Clarke, John and Roberts, Brian (1978). *Policing the crisis: Mugging, the state, and law and order,* London: Macmillan.

Halperin, Irit (2007). Between the lines: The story of Machsom Watch. *Journal of Humanistic Psychology,* 47(3): 333–39.

Hansen, Lene (2000). The Little Mermaid's silent security dilemma and the absence of gender from the Copenhagen School. *Millennium: Journal of International Studies,* 29(2): 285–306.

Haraway, Donna J. (1991). *Simians, cyborgs, and women: The reinvention of nature,* New York: Routledge.

Hayles, N. Katherine (1999). *How we became posthuman: Virtual bodies in cybernetics, literature, and informatics,* Chicago, IL: University of Chicago Press.

—— (2005). Computing the human. *Theory, Culture & Society,* 22(1): 131–51.

Held, David (1995). *Democracy and the global order. From the modern state to cosmopolitan governance,* Cambridge: Polity Press.

Hibou, Béatrice (2012). *La bureaucratisation du monde à l'ère néolibérale*, Paris: La Découverte.

Hindess, Barry (2001). The liberal government of unfreedom. *Alternatives*, 26(2): 93–108.

Homer-Dixon, Thomas (2002). The rise of complex terrorism. *Foreign Policy*, (128): 52–62.

Hönke, Jana (2013). *Transnational companies and security governance*, Abingdon: Routledge.

Huggins, Martha K. (1998). *Political policing: The United States and Latin America*, Durham, NC: Duke University Press.

Hughes, Beverly (2003). *Debate in House of Commons 5 November*. Hansard, col. 315WH.

Hughes, James (2004). *Citizen cyborg: Why democratic societies need to respond to the redesigned human of the future*, Cambridge, MA: Westview Press.

Huysmans, Jef (1997). James Der Derian: The unbearable lightness of theory. *In:* Neumann, Iver B. and Wæver, Ole (eds) *The future of international relations*, London: Routledge, pp. 337–58.

—— (1998a). Security! What do you mean? From concept to thick signifier. *European Journal of International Relations*, 4(2): 226–55.

—— (1998b). The question of the limit: Desecuritisation and the aesthetics of horror in political realism. *Millennium: Journal of International Studies*, 27(3): 569–89.

—— (2004). Minding exceptions: Politics of insecurity and liberal democracy. *Contemporary Political Theory*, 3(3): 321–41.

—— (2006a). International politics of insecurity: Normativity, inwardness and the exception. *Security Dialogue*, 37(1): 11–29.

—— (2006b). *The politics of insecurity: Fear, migration and asylum in the EU*, London: Routledge.

—— (2008). The jargon of exception – on Schmitt, Agamben and the absence of political society. *International Political Sociology*, 2(2): 165–83.

—— (2009). Conclusion: Insecurity and the everyday. *In:* Noxolo, Patricia and Huysmans, Jef (eds) *Community, citizenship and the 'war on terror': Security and insecurity*, Basingstoke: Palgrave Macmillan, pp. 198–207.

—— (2011). What is in an act? On security speech acts and little security nothings. *Security Dialogue*, 42(4–5): 371–83.

Huysmans, Jef and Angel Eye Media (2010). OpenLearn podcast. *The insecurity of security: Track 2*. Available: www.open.edu/openlearn/society/politicspolicy-people/politics/the-insecurity-security?track=9d5783306f [Accessed 2 May 2013].

Huysmans, Jef and Buonfino, Allessandra (2008). Politics of exception and unease: Immigration, asylum and terrorism in parliamentary debates in the UK. *Political Studies*, 56(4): 766–88.

Huysmans, Jef and Ragazzi, Francesco (eds) (2009). *Liberty & security. Multi-media teaching and training module:* Challenge. Available: www.libertysecurity.org/module [Accessed 18 October 2013].

Huysmans, Jef, Dobson, Andrew and Prokhovnik, Raia (eds) (2006). *The politics of protection: Sites of insecurity and political agency*, London: Routledge.

Ikenberry, G. John (2002). American grand strategy in the age of terror. *Survival*, 43(4): 19–34.

Isin, Engin F. (2002). *Being political. Genealogies of citizenship*, Minneapolis, MN: University of Minnesota Press.

Isin, Engin F. and Nielsen, Greg M. (eds) (2008). *Acts of citizenship*, London: Zed Books.

Jabri, Vivienne (2007). *War and the transformation of global politics*, Basingstoke: Palgrave Macmillan.

Jeandesboz, Julien (2011). *Les Usages du voisin. Genèse, enjeux et modalité de voisinage de l'Union Européenne.* Doctoral thesis, Institut d'Etudes Politiques de Paris.

Johnston, Les and Shearing, Clifford (2003). Governing security: Explorations in policing and justice. *London: Routledge. Journal of International Law*, 84(4): 859–66.

Kagan, Robert (2002). Power and weakness. *Policy Review*, (113): 3–28.

—— (2003). *Of paradise and power: America and Europe in the new world order*, New York: Alfred Knopf.

Kaiser, Karl (1969). Transnationale Politik. Zu einer Theorie der multinationalen Politik. *In*: Czempiel, Ernst-Otto (ed.) *Die anachronistische Souveränität*, Köln: Westdeutscher Verlag, pp. 80–109.

Kaiser, Karl (1971). Transnational relations as a threat to the democratic process. *In*: Keohane, Robert O. and Nye, Joseph S. Jr. (eds) *Transnational relations and world politics*, Cambridge, MA: Harvard University Press, pp. 356–70.

Kelsen, Hans (1967). *Pure theory of law*, Berkeley, CA: University of California Press.

Kessler, Oliver and Werner, Wouter (2008). Extrajudicial killing as risk management. *Security Dialogue*, 39(2–3): 289–308.

Kirchheimer, Otto (1996 [1932]). Legality and legitimacy. *In*: Scheuerman, William E. (ed.) *The rule of law under siege: Selected essays of Franz L. Neumann and Otto Kirchheimer*, Berkeley, CA: University of California Press, pp. 44–63.

—— (1996 [1940]). Criminal law in national socialist Germany. *In*: Scheuerman, William E. (ed.) *The rule of law under siege: Selected essays of Franz L. Neumann and Otto Kirchheimer*, Berkeley, CA: University of California Press, pp. 172–91.

Koskela, Hille (2004). Webcams, TV shows and mobile phones: Empowering exhibitionism. *Surveillance & Society*, 2(2/3): 199–215.

Krause, Keith and Williams, Michael C. (eds) (1997). *Critical security studies*, London: UCL Press.

Latour, Bruno (2005). *Reassembling the social: An introduction to actor-network-theory*, Oxford: Oxford University Press.

Law, John (1999). After ANT: Complexity, naming and topology. *In*: Law, John and Hassard, John (eds) *Actor network theory and after*, Oxford: Blackwell Publishers, pp. 1–14.

Leander, Anna (2005). The power to construct international security. On the significance of private military companies. *Millennium: Journal of International Studies*, 33(3): 803–25.

—— (2010). The paradoxical impunity of private military companies: Authority and the limits of legal accountability. *Security Dialogue*, 41(5): 467–90.

Leander, Anna (ed.) (2013). *The commercialization of security in Europe. Consequences for peace and reconciliation*, New York: Routledge.

Lenin, Vladymir I. (1946 [1917]). *L'état et la révolution*, Paris: Editions sociales.

Levy, Yagil and Mizrahi, Shlomo (2008). Alternative politics and the transformation of society military relations: The Israeli experience. *Administration & Society*, 40(1): 25–53.

Liese, Andrea (2009). Exceptional necessity: How liberal democracies contest the prohibition of torture and ill-treatment when countering terrorism. *Journal of International Law and International Relations*, 5(1): 17–47.

Loader, Ian (2000). Plural policing and democratic governance. *Social & Legal Studies*, 9(3): 323–45.

Loader, Ian and Walker, Neil (2007). *Civilizing security*, Cambridge: Cambridge University Press.

Los, Maria (2006). Looking into the future: Surveillance, globalization and the totalitarian potential. *In*: Lyon, David (ed.) *Theorizing surveillance*, Cullompton: Willan Publishing, pp. 69–94.

—— (2010). A trans-systemic surveillance: The legacy of communist surveillance in the digital age. *In*: Haggerty, Kevin D. and Samatas, Minas (eds) *Surveillance and democracy*, Abingdon: Routledge, pp. 173–94.

Luhmann, Niklas (2008 [1991]). *Risk: A sociological theory*, Piscataway, NJ: Transaction Publishers.

Lund Petersen, Karen (2012). Risk analysis – A field within security studies? *European Journal of International Relations*, 18(4): 693–717.

Lyon, David (2001). *Surveillance society: Monitoring everyday life*, Maidenhead: Open University Press.

—— (2003a). Introduction. *In*: Lyon, David (ed.) *Surveillance as social sorting: Privacy, risk, and digital discrimination*, London: Routledge, pp. 1–9.

—— (2003b). Surveillance as social sorting: Computer codes and mobile bodies. *In*: Lyon, David (ed.) *Surveillance as social sorting. Privacy, risk, and digital discrimination*, London: Routledge, pp. 13–30.

—— (2009). *Identifying citizens: ID cards as surveillance*, Cambridge: Polity Press.

—— (2010). Liquid surveillance: The contribution of Zygmunt Bauman to surveillance studies. *International Political Sociology*, 4(4): 325–38.

Lyon, David (ed.) (2003c). *Surveillance as social sorting: Privacy, risk, and digital discrimination*, London: Routledge.

Mann, Steve (2005). Sousveillance and cyborglogs: A 30-year empirical voyage through ethical, legal and policy issues. *Presence*, 14(6): 625–46.

Manning, Peter K. (2000). Policing new social spaces. *In*: Sheptycki, James (ed.) *Issues in transnational policing*, London: Routledge, pp. 177–200.

Mansfield, Edward D. and Snyder, Jack (1995). Democratization and the danger of war. *International Security*, 20(1): 5–38.

Marcus, George E. and Saka, Erkan (2006). Assemblage. *Theory, Culture & Society*, 23(2–3): 101–9.

Marx, Garry T. (1995). The engineering of social control: The search for the silver bullet. *In*: Hagan, John & Peterson, Ruth D. (eds) *Crime and inequality*, Stanford, CA: Stanford University Press, pp. 225–46.

—— (2003). A tack in the shoe: Neutralizing and resisting the new surveillance. *Journal of Social Issues*, 59(2): 369–90.

—— (2007). Rocky bottoms: Techno-fallacies of an age of information. *International Political Sociology*, 1(1): 83–110.

Mattelart, Armand (1979). Notes on the ideology of the military state. *In*: Mattelart, Armand and Siegelaub, Seth (eds) *Communication and class struggle. 1. Capitalism, imperialism*, New York: International General, pp. 402–27.

—— (2007). *La globalisation de la surveillance. Aux origines de l'ordre sécuritaire*, Paris: La Découverte.

Mayerfeld, James (2007). Playing by our own rules: How U.S. marginalization of international human rights law led to torture. *Harvard Human Rights Journal*, (20): 89–140.

McCahill, Michael (2008). Plural policing and CCTV surveillance. *In*: Deflem, Mathieu & Ulmer, Jeffrey T. (eds) *Surveillance and governance: Crime control and beyond*, Sociology of Crime Law and Deviance, Volume 10, Emerald Group Publishing Limited, pp. 199–219.

Mcclintock, Michael (1992). *Instruments of statecraft: U.S. guerilla warfare, counterinsurgency, counterterrorism 1940–1990*, New York: Pantheon Books.

Mcgrail, Brian (1999). Communication technology and local knowledges: The case of 'peripheralized' high-rise housing. *Urban Geography*, 20(4): 303–33.

Mcsherry, J. Patrice (2002). Tracking the origins of a state terror network: Operation Condor. *Latin American Perspectives*, 29(1): 38–60.

—— (2007). Death squads as parallel forces: Uruguay, Operation Condor, and the United States. *Journal of Third World Studies*, 24(1): 13–52.

Mcsweeney, Bill (1999). *Security, identity and interests: A sociology of international relations*, Cambridge: Cambridge University Press.

Mearsheimer, John (1990). Back to the future. Instability in Europe after the Cold War. *International Security*, 15(1): 5–56.

Mills, C. Wright (1956). *The power elite*, New York: Oxford University Press.

Monahan, Torin (2006). Questioning surveillance and security. *In*: Monahan, Torin (ed.) *Surveillance and security: Technological politics and power in everyday life*, London: Routledge, pp. 1–23.

Morgenthau, Hans J. (1933). *La Notion du 'politique' et la théorie des différends internationaux*, Paris: Librairie du Recueil Sirey.

Mubi Brighenti, Andrea (2010). Democracy and visibility. *In*: Haggerty, Kevin D. and Samatas, Minas (eds) *Surveillance and democracy*, Abingdon: Routledge, pp. 51–68.

Muller, Benjamin (2004). (Dis)qualified bodies: Securitization, citizenship and 'identity management'. *Citizenship Studies*, 8(3): 279–94.

Muller, Benjamin J. (2010a). *Security, risk and the biometric state*, Abingdon: Routledge.

—— (2010b). Unsafe at any speed? Borders, mobility and 'safe citizenship'. *Citizenship studies*, 14(1): 75–88.

—— (2012). *Borderworld: Biometrics, avatar and global criminalization*. Paper presented at the Annual Convention of the International Studies Association, 1–4 April. San Diego.

Munster, Anna (1999). Is there postlife after postfeminism? Tropes of technics and life in cyberfeminism. *Australian Feminist Studies*, 14(29): 119–29.

Mythen, Gabe and Walklate, Sandra (2008). Terrorism, risk and international security: The perils of asking 'what if?'. *Security Dialogue*, 39(2–3): 221–42.

Naaman, Dorit (2006). The silenced outcry: A feminist perspective from the Israeli checkpoints in Palestine. *NWSA Journal*, 18(3): 168–80.

Naim, Moisés (2002). Al Qaeda, the NGO. *Foreign Policy*, (129): 99–100.

Nathanson, Charles (1988). The social construction of Soviet threat: A study in the politics of representation. *Alternatives*, 13(4): 443–83.

NATO (1949). *The north atlantic treaty.* Washington D.C. – 4 april. Available: www. nato.int/docu/basictxt/treaty.htm [Accessed 5 January 2009].

——— (1991). *The Alliance's new strategic concept agreed by the heads of state and government participating in the meeting of the North Atlantic Council.* Brussels: NATO. Available: www.nato.int/cps/en/natolive/official_texts_23847.htm [Accessed 28 October 2009].

——— (1999). *The Alliance's strategic concept approved by the heads of state and government participating in the meeting of the North Atlantic Council.* Brussels: NATO. Available: www.nato.int/cps/en/natolive/official_texts_27433.htm [Accessed 28 October 2009].

——— (2005). *Democracy best answer to terror says NATO secretary general.* Available: www. nato.int/docu/update/2005/03-march/e0310a.htm [Accessed 5 January 2009].

Neal, Andrew (2009). Securitization and risk at the EU border: The origins of Frontex. *Journal of Common Market Studies*, 47(2): 333–56.

——— (2010). *Exceptionalism and the politics of counter-terrorism: Liberty, security and the war on terror*, Abingdon: Routledge.

——— (2012). Normalization and legislative exceptionalism: Counterterrorist law-making and the changing times of security emergencies. *International Political Sociology*, 6(3): 260–76.

Nelson, Daniel N. (2002). Armies, security, and democracy in Southeastern Europe. *Armed Forces & Society*, 28(3): 427–54.

Neocleous, Mark (2008). *Critique of security*, Edinburgh: Edinburgh University Press.

Neumann, Franz L. (1954). *Angst und Politik*, Tübingen: Verlag J.C.B. Mohr.

——— (1967 [1944]). *Behemoth. The structure and practice of National Socialism 1933–1944*, London: Frank Cass and Co.

——— (1996 [1953]). The concept of political freedom. *In*: Scheuerman, William E. (ed.) *The rule of law under siege. Selected essays of Franz L. Neumann and Otto Kirchheimer*, Berkeley, CA: University of California Press, pp. 195–230.

Newman, Janet and Clarke, John (2009). *Publics, politics and power: Remaking the public in public services*, London: Sage.

Neyland, Daniel (2006). *Privacy, surveillance and public trust*, Basingstoke: Palgrave Macmillan.

Nissenbaum, Helen (2009). *Privacy in context. Technology, policy, and the integrity of social life*, Redwood City, CA: Stanford University Press.

Norris, Clive (2003). From personal to digital. CCTV, the panopticon, and the technological mediation of suspicion and social control. *In*: Lyon, David (ed.) *Surveillance as social sorting: Privacy, risk, and digital discrimination*, London: Routledge, pp. 249–81.

Nyers, Peter (ed.) (2009). *Securitizations of citizenship*, Abingdon: Routledge.

O'Harrow, Robert (2006). *No place to hide*, New York: Free Press.

Ochs, Juliana (2011). *Security and suspicion: An ethnography of everyday life in Israel. The ethnography of violence*, Philadelphia, PA: University of Pennsylvania Press.

Olsson, Christian (ed.) (2003). Les entreprises para-privées de coercition: De nouveaux mercenaires? *Special issue of Cultures et Conflits*, 52: 1–184.

Ottaway, Marina. (2003). Thinking big: Democratizing the Middle East. *Boston Globe*, 5 January. Available: http://carnegieendowment.org/publications/index. cfm?fa=view&id=1151&prog=zgp&proj=zdrl [Accessed 5 January 2009].

Owen, John M. (1994). How liberalism produces democratic peace. *International Security*, 19(2): 87–125.

—— (1997). *Liberal peace, liberal war: American politics in international security*, New York: Cornell University Press.

—— (2005). Iraq and the democratic peace. *Foreign Affairs*, (November/December): 122–27.

Papadopoulos, Dimitris, Stephenson, Niamh and Tsianos, Vassilis (2008). *Escape routes: Control and subversion in the 21st century*, London: Pluto Press.

Phillips, David J. (2005). From privacy to visibility: Context, identity and power in ubiquitous computing environments. *Social text*, 23(2): 95–108.

Phillips, Joost (2006). Agencement/assemblage. *Theory, Culture & Society*, 23(2–3): 108–9.

Pineu, Daniel. (2009). *The pedagogy of security: Police assistance and liberal governmentality in American foreign policy*. Doctoral thesis, University of Wales Aberystwyth.

Pion-Berlin, David and Lopez, George A. (1991). Of victims and executioners: Argentine state terror 1975–79. *International Studies Quarterly*, 35(1): 63–86.

Poster, Mark (1997). *The second media age*, Cambridge: Polity Press.

Pram Gad, Ulrik and Lund Petersen, Karen (2011). Concepts of politics in securitization studies. *Security Dialogue*, 42(4–5): 315–28.

Privacy International (2011). *Why we work on refugee privacy?* Available: www.privacy international.org/blog/why-we-work-on-refugee-privacy [Accessed 9 October 2013].

Pye, Lucian W. (1962). Armies in the process of political modernization. *In*: Johnson, J.J. (ed.) *The role of the military in underdeveloped countries*, Princeton, NJ: Princeton University Press, pp. 85–122.

Raley, Rita (2008). Border hacks: The risks of tactical media. *In*: Amoore, Louise and De Goede, Marieke (eds) *Risk and the war on terror*, Abingdon: Routledge, pp. 197–217.

Rasmussen, Mikkel Vedby (2006). *The risk society at war. Terror, technology and strategy in the twenty-first century*, Cambridge: Cambridge University Press.

Regan, Priscilla M. (2011). Response to bennett: Also in defence of privacy. *Surveillance & Society*, 8(4): 497–99.

Reid, Julian (2006). *The biopolitics of the War on Terror: Life struggles, liberal modernity and the defence of logistical societies*, Manchester: Manchester University Press.

Reisman, Michael W. (1990). International law after the Cold War. *The American*.

—— (1999). Kosovo's antinomies. *The American Journal of International Law*, 93(4): 860–62.

Rimington, Stella (1994). *Security and democracy – Is there a conflict?* Transcript of the Richard Dimbleby lecture by the Director General of the Security Service, Dame Stella Rimington, 12 June. Available: www.mi5.gov.uk/output/direct or-generals-richard-dimbleby-lecture-1994.html [Accessed 28 November 2008].

Robin, Corey (2004). *Fear: The history of a political idea*, Oxford: Oxford University Press.

Ronald D. (ed.) *Western responses to terrorism* London: Frank Cass Publishers, pp. 14–25.

Rudolph, Christopher (2006). *National security and immigration*, Redwood City, CA: Stanford University Press.

Ruppert, Evelyn (2011a). Population objects: Interpassive subjects. *Sociology*, 45(2): 218–33.

—— (2011b). *The census: More than just a snapshot*. The Open University (UK). Available: www.open.ac.uk/openlearn/society/politics-policy-people/the-census-more-just-snapshot [Accessed 21 February 2012].

—— (2011c). Is there still sense in running a census? *The Independent*, 28 February.

—— (2012). The governmental topologies of database devices. *Theory, Culture and Society*, 29(4–5): 116–36.

Ruppert, Evelyn and Savage, Mike (2011). Transactional politics. *Sociological Review*, 59(s2): 73–92.

Russett, Bruce (1994). *Grasping the democratic peace*, Princeton, NJ: Princeton University Press.

Rygiel, Kim (2008). The securitized citizen. *In*: Isin, Engin F. (ed.) *Recasting the social in citizenship*, Toronto: University of Toronto Press, pp. 210–38.

Salter, Mark (2006). The global visa regime and the political technologies of the international self: Borders, bodies, biopolitics. *Alternatives*, 31(2): 167–89.

—— (2008). When the exception becomes the rule: Borders, sovereignty, citizenship. *Citizenship studies*, 12(4): 365–80.

Samatas, Minas (ed.) *Surveillance and democracy*, Abingdon: Routledge, pp. 111–26.

Sandler, Todd (1995). On the relation between democracy and terrorism. *Terrorism and Political Violence*, 7(4): 1–9.

Saward, Michael (1998). *The terms of democracy*, Cambridge: Polity Press.

Scheper-Hughes, Nancy (1992). *Death without weeping: The violence of everyday life in Brazil*, Berkeley, CA: University of California Press.

Scheuerman, William E. (2006). Survey article: Emergency powers and the rule of law after 9/11. *Journal of Political Philosophy*, 14(1): 61–84.

Schmid, Alex P. (1993). Terrorism and democracy. *In*: Schmid, Alex P. and Crelinsten,

Schmitt, Carl (1985 [1922]). *Political theology: Four chapters on the concept of sovereignty*, London: MIT Press.

Segal, David R. (1994). National security and democracy in the United States. *Armed Forces & Society*, 20(3): 375–93.

Seri, Guillermina S. (2010). Vicious legacies? State violence(s) in Argentina. *In*: Esparza, Marcia, Huttenbach, Henry and Feierstein, Daniel (eds) *State violence and genocide in Latin America: The Cold War years*, New York: Routledge, pp. 182–95.

Shadgett, P. (1990). *An observation study of police patrol work*. Master's thesis, University of Toronto.

Shalom, Piki Ish (2008). Render unto Caesar that which is Caesar's: On the joint pursuit of morality and security. *American Behavioral Scientist*, 51(9): 1285–1302.

Shaw, Martin (1991). *Post-military society*, Cambridge: Polity Press.

Sheehan, Michael (2005). *International security: An analytical survey*, Boulder, CO: Lynne Rienner Publishers.

Sheptycki, James (2000a). Introduction. *In*: Sheptycki, James (ed.) *Issues in transnational policing*, London: Routledge, pp. 1–20.

—— (2000b). Policing the virtual launderette: Money laundering and global governance. *In*: Sheptycki, James (ed.) *Issues in transnational policing*, New York: Routledge, pp. 135–76.

Sheptycki, James W.E. (ed.) (2000). *Issues in transnational policing*, London: Routledge.

Shklar, Judith (1989). The liberalism of fear. *In*: Rosenblum, Nancy L. (ed.) *Liberalism and the moral life*, Cambridge, MA: Havard University Press.

Simmel, Georg (1971). The problem of sociology. *In*: Levine, Donald N. (ed.) *Georg Simmel on individuality and social forms*, Chicago, IL: University of Chicago Press, pp. 23–35.

Stalder, Felix (2002). Opinion. Privacy is not the antidote to surveillance. *Surveillance & Society*, 1(1): 120–24.

—— (2011). Autonomy beyond privacy: A rejoinder to bennett. *Surveillance & Society*, 8(4): 508–12.

Stern, Maria (2005). *Naming security – constructing identity: 'Mayan-women' in Guatemala on the eve of 'peace'*, Manchester: Manchester University Press.

Sylvester, Christine (2002). *Feminist international relations: An unfinished journey*, Cambridge: Cambridge University Press.

The Schengen Acquis (2000). Convention implementing the Schengen agreement of 14 June 1985 between the governments of the states of the Benelux Economic Union, the Federal Republic of Germany and the French Republic on the gradual abolition of checks at their common borders. *Official Journal L 239 22/09/2000 P. 0019–0062*, European Union.

Thompson, Edward P. (1980). Notes on extremism, the last stage of civilization. *New Left Review*, (121): 3–31.

Thony, J.-F. (1996). Processing financial information in money laundering matters: Financial intelligence units. *European Journal of Crime, Criminal Law and Criminal Justice*, 4(3): 257–82.

Tickner, Arlene B. and Blaney, David L. (eds) (2012). *Thinking international relations differently*, Abingdon: Routledge.

Tsoukala, Anastassia (2004a). Democracy against security: The debates about counterterrorism in the European parliament, September 2001 – June 2003. *Alternatives*, 29(4): 417–39.

—— (2004b). Les Nouvelles politiques de contrôle du hooliganisme en Europe: De la fusion sécuritaire au multipositionnement de la menace. *Cultures & Conflits*, (51): 83–96.

—— (2006). Democracy in the light of security: British and French political discourse on domestic counter-terrorism policies. *Political Studies*, 54(4): 607–27.

—— (2008). Boundary-creating processes and the social construction of threat. *Alternatives*, 33(2): 137–52.

—— (2009). *Football hooliganism in Europe: Security and civil liberties in the balance*, Basingstoke: Palgrave Macmillan.

van Der Ploeg, Irma (2006). Borderline identities: The enrollment of bodies in the technological reconstruction of borders. *In*: Monahan, Torin (ed.) *Surveillance and security: Technological politics and power in everyday life*, London: Routledge, pp. 177–93.

van Loon, Joost (2006). Network. *Theory, Culture & Society*, 23(2–3): 307–22.

van Munster, Rens (2004). The war on terrorism: When the exception becomes the rule. *International Journal of Semiotics of Law*, 17141–53.

van Oenen, Gijs (2006). A machine that would go of itself: Interpassivity and its impact on political life. *Theory & Event*, 9(2).

Vanni, Michel (2004). *Démocratie à venir? Colloque l'exclusion démocratique*. Strasbourg. Available: www.jacquesderrida.com.ar/comentarios/democratie_a_venir.htm [Accessed 10 December 2008].

Venn, Couze (2006). A note on assemblage. *Theory, Culture & Society*, 23(2–3): 107–8.

Virilio, Paul (1977). *Vitesse et politique: Essai de dromologie*, Paris: Editions Galilée.

Voelkner, Nadine (2011). Managing pathogenic circulation: Human security and the migrant health assemblage in Thailand. *Security Dialogue*, 42(3): 239–59.

Wadham, John (2002). Private lives. *The Guardian*, 14 September. Available: www.guardian.co.uk/uk/2002/sep/14/privacy.freedomofinformation1 [Accessed 20 April 2012].

Wæver, Ole (1995). Securitization and desecuritization. *In*: Lipschutz, Ronnie (ed.) *On security*, New York: Columbia University Press, pp. 46–86.

Wæver, Ole, Buzan, Barry, Kelstrup, Morten and Lemaitre, Pierre (1993). *Identity, migration and the new security agenda in Europe*, London: Pinter.

Waldo, James, Lin, Herbert S. and Millett, Lynette I. (eds) (2007). *Engaging privacy and information technology in a digital age*, Washington, DC: The National Academy Press.

Waldron, Jeremy (2003). Security and liberty: The image of balance. *Journal of Political Philosophy*, 11(2): 191–210.

Walker, R.B.J. (1988). *One world, many worlds: Struggles for a just world peace*, Boulder, CO: Lynne Rienner Publishers.

—— (1990). Security, sovereignty, and the challenge of world politics. *Alternatives*, 15(1): 3–27.

—— (1997). The subject of security. *In*: Williams, Michael C. and Krause, Keith (eds) *Critical security studies: Concepts and cases*, London: UCL Press, pp. 61–81.

—— (2010). *After the globe, before the world*, Abingdon: Routledge.

Walt, Stephen (1991). The renaissance of security studies. *International Studies Quarterly*, 35(2): 211–39.

Walters, William (2002). The power of inscription: Beyond social construction and deconstruction in European integration studies. *Millennium*, 31(1): 83–108.

—— (2011). Rezoning the global: Technological zones, technological work, and the (un)making of biometric borders. *In*: Squire, Vicki (ed.) *The contested politics of mobility: Borderzones and irregularity*, London: Routledge, pp. 51–73.

Waltz, Kenneth N. (1954). *Man, the state and war. A theoretical analysis*, New York: Columbia University Press.

—— (1979). *Theory of international politics*, New York: McGraw-Hill.

Weber, Max (1978). *Economy and society*, Berkeley, CA: University of California Press.

Weiss Fagen, Patricia (1992). Repression and state security. *In*: Corradi, Juan E., Weiss Fagen, Patricia and Garretón, Manuel Antonio (eds.) *Fear at the edge. State terror and resistance in Latin America*, Berkeley, CA: University of California Press, pp. 39–70.

Weizman, Eyal (2010). Forensic architecture: Only the criminal can solve the crime. *Radical Philosophy*, (164): 9–24.

Weldes, Jutta, Laffey, Mark, Gusterson, Hugh and Duvall, Raymond (eds) (1999). *Cultures of insecurity: States, communities, and the production of danger*, Minneapolis, MN: University of Minnesota Press.

Whitaker, Beth Elise (2007). Exporting the Patriot Act? Democracy and the 'war on terror' in the third world. *Third World Quarterly*, 28(5): 1017–32.

Wibben, Annick T.R. (2011). *Feminist security studies. A narrative approach*, Abingdon: Routledge.

Wight, Martin (1966). Why is there no international theory? *In*: Butterfield, H. and Wight, M. (eds) *Diplomatic investigations: Essays in the theory of international politics*, London: Allan & Unwin, pp. 17–34.

Williams, Michael C. (2007). *Culture and security: Symbolic power and the politics of international security*, Abingdon: Routledge.

Wilson, David (1963). Nation-building and revolutionary wars. *In*: Deutsch, Karl W. and Foltz, W.J. (eds) *Nation-building*, New York: Atherton Press.

Wolfers, Arnold (1952). National security as an ambiguous symbol. *Political Science Quarterly*, 67(4): 481–502.

—— (1962). *Discord and collaboration*, Baltimore, MD: John Hopkins University Press.

Wood, Jennifer and Dupont, Benoît (eds) (2006). *Democracy, society and the governance of security*, New York: Cambridge University Press.

Wood, Jennifer and Shearing, Clifford (2007). *Imagining security*, Cullompton: Willan Publishing.

Wyn Jones, Richard (1999). *Security, strategy, and critical theory*, Boulder, CO: Lynne Rienner Publishers.

Yaniv, Avner (ed.) (1993). *National security and democracy in Israel*, Boulder, CO: Lynne Rienner Publishers.

Zakaria, Fareed (2004). No security, no democracy, US edn. *Newsweek*. Available: www.fareedzakaria.com/articles/newsweek/052404.html [Accessed 5 January 2009].

Zedner, Lucia (2009). *Security*, Abingdon: Routledge.

Zizek, Slavoj (2003). *The Iraq War: Where is the true danger?* Available: www.lacan.com/iraq.htm [Accessed 21 October 2013].

—— (2006). *How to read Lacan*, London: Granta.

Index

Taylor & Francis

eBooks

FOR LIBRARIES

ORDER YOUR
FREE 30 DAY
INSTITUTIONAL
TRIAL TODAY!

Over 23,000 eBook titles in the Humanities,
Social Sciences, STM and Law from some of the
world's leading imprints.

Choose from a range of subject packages or create your own!

Benefits for
you

▶ Free MARC records
▶ COUNTER-compliant usage statistics
▶ Flexible purchase and pricing options

Benefits
for your
user

▶ Off-site, anytime access via Athens or referring URL
▶ Print or copy pages or chapters
▶ Full content search
▶ Bookmark, highlight and annotate text
▶ Access to thousands of pages of quality research
   at the click of a button

For more information, pricing enquiries or to order
a free trial, contact your local online sales team.

UK and Rest of World: **online.sales@tandf.co.uk**

US, Canada and Latin America:
e-reference@taylorandfrancis.com

www.ebooksubscriptions.com

ALPSP Award for
BEST eBOOK
PUBLISHER
2009 Finalist

Taylor & Francis **eBooks**
Taylor & Francis Group

A flexible and dynamic resource for teaching, learning and research.

Lightning Source UK Ltd.
Milton Keynes UK
UKOW06f0728101115

262401UK00016B/214/P